**SAGE** was founded in 1965 by Sara Miller McCune to support the dissemination of usable knowledge by publishing innovative and high-quality research and teaching content. Today, we publish over 900 journals, including those of more than 400 learned societies, more than 800 new books per year, and a growing range of library products including archives, data, case studies, reports, and video. SAGE remains majority-owned by our founder, and after Sara's lifetime will become owned by a charitable trust that secures our continued independence.

Los Angeles | London | New Delhi | Singapore | Washington DC | Melbourne

# POLITICAL ECONOMY
## of CASTE IN INDIA

Thank you for choosing a SAGE product!
If you have any comment, observation or feedback,
I would like to personally hear from you.

*Please write to me at* **contactceo@sagepub.in**

**Vivek Mehra,** Managing Director and CEO, SAGE India.

**Bulk Sales**
SAGE India offers special discounts
for purchase of books in bulk.
We also make available special imprints
and excerpts from our books on demand.

*For orders and enquiries, write to us at*

Marketing Department
SAGE Publications India Pvt Ltd
B1/I-1, Mohan Cooperative Industrial Area
Mathura Road, Post Bag 7
New Delhi 110044, India

*E-mail us at* **marketing@sagepub.in**

**Subscribe to our mailing list**
Write to **marketing@sagepub.in**

This book is also available as an e-book.

# POLITICAL ECONOMY of CASTE IN INDIA

## K. S. CHALAM

Los Angeles | London | New Delhi
Singapore | Washington DC | Melbourne

Copyright © K. S. Chalam, 2020

All rights reserved. No part of this book may be reproduced or utilized in any form or by any means, electronic or mechanical, including photocopying, recording or by any information storage or retrieval system, without permission in writing from the publisher.

First published in 2020 by

**SAGE Publications India Pvt Ltd**
B1/I-1 Mohan Cooperative Industrial Area
Mathura Road, New Delhi 110 044, India
www.sagepub.in

**SAGE Publications Inc**
2455 Teller Road
Thousand Oaks, California 91320, USA

**SAGE Publications Ltd**
1 Oliver's Yard, 55 City Road
London EC1Y 1SP, United Kingdom

**SAGE Publications Asia-Pacific Pte Ltd**
18 Cross Street #10-10/11/12
China Square Central
Singapore 048423

Published by Vivek Mehra for SAGE Publications India Pvt Ltd. Typeset in 10/12.5 pt ITC Stone Serif by Zaza Eunice, Hosur, Tamil Nadu, India.

**Library of Congress Control Number: 2020939491**

**ISBN:** 978-93-5388-407-9 (HB)

**SAGE Team:** Rajesh Dey, Satvinder Kaur and Rajinder Kaur

# Contents

List of Tables............................................ vii
Preface.................................................. ix

Chapter 1. Caste Mode of Production:
Concept and Content..................................... 1

Chapter 2. Colonial Approach to Hindutva and
Marxist Writing .......................................... 33

Chapter 3. Caste and Economic Power in India ............... 49

Chapter 4. Inequity in the Development of
Human Capital in India.................................... 59

Chapter 5. Economic Deprivation and Social Exclusion
of Marginalized Castes ................................... 79

Chapter 6. New Economic Policy: The *Dvija* Project .......... 107

Chapter 7. Caste and the Advent of Crony Capitalism
in India.................................................. 123

Chapter 8. Judiciary and Deprivation of Social Justice .........139

Chapter 9. Social Barriers as Impediments of
Information Flow .........................................162

Chapter 10. Physical Alienation: Offences and
Atrocities against Scheduled Castes .......................173

Chapter 11. The Fragmented Assertion:
Divide and Rule..........................................194

Chapter 12. Globalization and the Future of Dalits
and Adivasis .............................................209

Chapter 13. Democracy, Dalit Rights and
the Paradigm Shift .......................................234

Select Bibliography .......................................254
About the Author .........................................265
Index ....................................................266

# List of Tables

| | | |
|---|---|---|
| 6.1 | Macroeconomics Indicators | 117 |
| 6.2 | Top 10 Companies in India (₹ in Crores) | 119 |
| 9.1 | Respondents' Knowledge about the Incentives (in Percentage) | 165 |
| 9.2 | Communication Channels | 167 |
| 9.3 | Role Perception of Respondents about VEC (in Percentage) | 169 |
| 9.4 | Decision-Makers in the Family (in Percentage) | 171 |
| 10.1 | Main Offences Committed against Scheduled Castes in India during 1979–2016 | 179 |
| 10.2 | Offences and Atrocities Committed against Scheduled Castes in Andhra Pradesh during 1982–2016 | 180 |
| 10.3 | Number of Villages Represented in the Commission in Andhra Pradesh | 182 |
| 10.4 | Discrimination against Scheduled Castes in Andhra Pradesh (PCR), 2000–2001 | 184 |
| 10.5 | Composite Index of Caste Discrimination | 187 |

| | | |
|---|---|---|
| 10.6 | Incidence of Cognizable Crimes (IPC) against Scheduled Castes in Andhra Pradesh during 2000 | 190 |
| 11.1 | Total Number of Existing Castes and Their Percentage to Total Population in India 1991 | 197 |
| 11.2 | Numerically Large Caste Groups, 2011 | 200 |
| 11.3 | Post-matric Scholarship for SCs during 1993–1994 (Provisional) | 202 |

# Preface

The concept of mode of production (MOP) in political economy is an important academic topic for study and discussion. Though it is considered as a Marxist approach in social sciences, non-Marxists have also been using it salubriously in different contexts. One of the most contested themes under MOP is the Asiatic MOP, particularly in India. I have been following the debates as a student of economics for more than four decades. I have seen scholars, mostly historians, debating on the futility of the concept in the Indian context. The engagement of economists in this debate is reduced to that of discussing relations of production in the agriculture sector and some debating about the transition from feudalism to capitalism. Curiously, very few of the contenders have used it to understand the vexed question of caste and the overwhelming influence of fundamentalism in using the caste structure vigorously in the era of globalization. I have written on the question of caste not only as an important economic category in the socio-economic formation but also as a dominant factor in excluding marginalized groups to benefit from the so-called economic opportunities under globalization and the resultant focus of social or political disruptions. I thought why not I reflect on the situation using the concept of caste MOP. My approach here is only experimental (of course not randomized controlled trial) to provoke debate with a hope that the issue might take centre stage in the intellectual traditions of India. I am always willing to learn and amend my argument; after all, it is a process of argument. I thank several friends and activists who have encouraged me to publish it in English when I made the presentation in groups in Telugu. My personal assistant, Mr P. Meghanadh, has done an excellent job of bringing all my papers together. I appreciate the forbearance of my wife and the comforts she has extended in the preparation of the manuscript at home. Mr Rajesh Dey of SAGE Publications was quick in responding to my requests. I thank him and SAGE Publications for encouraging me to publish with them.

# 1

# Caste Mode of Production
## Concept and Content

The study of political economy generally starts with a discussion on the mode of production (MOP). The concept of MOP is one of the brilliant contributions of Karl Marx to social sciences. It is this approach that has carried integration among all social sciences and facilitated the disciplines to move away from metaphysical speculations. Kuhn's[1] work has further strengthened the science of socio-economic discourse with his concepts of pre-paradigmatic stage in research to that of a paradigm shift, making countenance for social sciences episteme go beyond verifiability and falsifiability. In this context, Marxism and the concepts such as MOP, including Asiatic mode of production (AMP), are open to scrutiny beyond a section of the so-called vulgar Marxists. And now Marxism itself has become a reference point along with J. S. Mill to resolve three disputes in social science to bring unity among the disciplines. Martin Hollis has identified the three disputes as ontological, methodological and epistemological.[2] In the ontological dispute, Marx contended that action is determined by structure, and Mill insisted that all phenomena of society arise from the actions and passions of human beings. In the methodological dispute, the key issues identified are necessity or regularity or laws of nature to the particular or specific mechanisms. In the epistemological dispute, Mill upheld empiricist view that knowledge is a matter of experience, while Marx held the view of essentiality of theory which allows knowledge of an underlying reality. In fact, social sciences have gone beyond these disputes, resolving some and accumulating few others, to provide a cosmic ground for social science discourse to continue as an endless process. The contributions of Gramsci,[3] Foucault[4] and others in the tradition of hermeneutics have further revolutionized the scope and method of social sciences in the 21st century. The disciplines of history and historiography are also equipped with the science of the methodology of the subject. We are mentioning here the discipline of history as an important aspect to grit MOP, particularly, AMP and feudalism that are being extensively used in Marxist methodology. In fact, the Indian Marxist historians from the time of Dange,[5] Kosambi,[6] Sharma,[7] Prabhat Patnaik,[8] Murzbaban Jal[9] and others have continued the debate. The MOP debate is an unending option that has entered into discourses of left political parties. *Economic and Political Weekly* has been publishing papers and issuing special numbers on this issue since 1965, and a volume in 1990 was published based[10] on these papers.

Interestingly, very few of the historians and the first-generation scholars in India, unlike the Soviet,[11] Frankfurt school,[12] ever raised the issue of the so-called queer concept of AMP used by Marx himself. Except scholars, such as Harbans Mukhia,[13] Shakti Padhi[14] and Murzban Jal, nobody ever candidly raised the relevance of AMP to India. In fact, it was blasphemy to refer to or speak about it and even Kosambi called names for the Congress Socialist Party (CSP) Group that edited Marx's writings on India.[15] Kosambi was perhaps the earliest Marxist historian to debunk AMP by introducing the concept of feudalism 'from above and feudalism from below'. Though

Kosambi did not question the original formulation of Marx, he used the above terms to beguile the concept of Asiatic Mode of Production. The entire materialist historian group has sincerely trolled Kosambi. In fact, Dange was more concerned about the specificity of Marxian formulation to India in his third preface to the ostracized book.[16] We do not know much about the political bickering of the left parties up to the 1990s until the collapse of the Soviet Union. The findings of these historians, however, did not enhance our understanding of India by denying the Marxian concept of AMP. The allegation that Marx never defined AMP and it was only aberration was later contested by scholars.[17] Anne M. Bailey noted that the AMP concept was in the process of development over a period of 30 years starting from the newspaper articles of Marx in the 1850s (critiqued by Kosambi) and down to his analysis of the same in *Capital* Vol I. Scholars generally refer to the preface of 'A Contribution to the Critique of Political Economy' of Marx for the basic structure of the concept of MOP.[18] Maurice Dobb, in his introduction to 'the little book', noted that, 'Marx's theory of value was something more than a theory of value as generally conceived: it had the function not only of explaining exchange value or prices in a quantitative sense, but exhibiting the historico-social basis in the labour—process of an exchange of commodity—society with labor-power itself become a commodity'.[19] It is here (little book) Marx once again referred to AMP and the famous reference to 'material productive forces of society come into conflict with the existing relations of production or this merely expresses the same thing in legal terms with the property relations within the framework of which they have operated hitherto'. Though the book started with commodity in general, half of it is devoted to money. Marx, however, found time to refer to patriarchy here. He said that,

> under the rural patriarchal system of production, when spinner and weaver lived under the same roof—the women of the family spinning and the men weaving say for the requirement of the family—yarn and linen were social products,

and spinning and weaving social labour with in the frame work of the family.[20]

Again in the same-page footnote, Marx referred to 'a careful study of Asiatic, particularly *Indian* [emphasis added] forms of communal property would indicate that the disintegration of different forms of primitive communal ownership gives rise to diverse forms of property'. Thus, Krader[21] noted that Marx brought out AMP in several stages. In his youth, Marx made a fleeting reference to oriental despotism. In the second stage, he addressed himself to oriental society as a whole, paying attention to the political and social characterization of the society in his articles to *New-York Daily Tribune*. In the next stage, he formulated the theory of the AMP in legal and political forms in their economic relations. This was further developed in *Capital* with specific reference to India and the unchanging nature of Asiatic (caste) MOP.[22]

In order to understand AMP with reference to India, one needs to understand the category of 'caste'. Caste is considered by social scientists as a unit of social stratification that places its units and subunits in an order of high and low rank by birth (more details are given later). Class, on the other hand, is a Western notion being developed as a method of economic stratification of society. Marxists have extended the concept further with reference to labour value and creation of surplus value. We discuss next caste mode of production (CMOP) as a part of AMP that the Indian Marxists of a particular collective seem to have considered the category as an outcaste. It appears that the 'Brahminical over lordship has strangely also seeped the established left through the form of ignorance of the caste question'. It is strange to find that the narrative of Brahminical over lordship model of Adishankara counter-revolution that Murzban Jal[23] narrated in his paper is not different from Marxist scholars who not only did not agree with the perception of AMP, but also complimented the Indian soul, race memory, the victory of ideals and the innate glory of the four-caste system.[24] Yet, they used the Vedic and Hindu Epic sources to construct a materialist base of history without referring to the *dharmashastras* to eulogize that there was no slavery in India. Kosambi has noted that 'Brahmin priesthood have more humane observances' as ideological superstructure in his footnotes. This kind of materialist interpretation of history did not enhance our understanding of the 'unchangeable' nature of CMOP by which *Dvijas* kept on earning their rents, and it also made the class analysis a mockery of the everyday reality of life for generations of leftists to come. In fact, the spirit of AMP as far as India is concerned was *varna* in the Vedic period and later developed as a caste system with untouchable castes and service castes who were forced to supply free labour. Chalam[25] raised the issue of AMP and the role of caste in India with a critical review of literature on the subject in 1988. It was noted that there were already nine theories of caste, and class analysis had three streams along with Marxian classes based on ownership of means of production. The Weberian class with three categories based on power distribution and functional theory built around core values of qualities, performances and possessions are in use in social sciences. But neither the Marxist nor the ordinary theories of class analysis made by Indian scholars, who have experienced the tyranny of caste in their everyday life, ever took it as a challenge to enlighten the cadres who were fighting for economic justice in the streets and in jungles about the 'caste question'. Now the whole system of left and democratic movement crumbled and we are witnessing today in the streets how Dalits and sections of minorities (who migrated from these castes) are lynched to shove that they are supposed to provide symbolically free labour and not to go in for secular jobs. However, Marx was not to be found fault for this lapse, as it was abundantly made clear by him in his *Capital* Vol I under section 'Division of Labour in Manufacture and Division of Labour in Society' about the vagaries of Indian caste. Unfortunately, the Indian critiques of AMP did not understand the economic significance of this formulation.

## What Is Mode of Production?

The discussion on the role of caste in economic transformation of India through globalization made us to assume that a caste like MOP has been in operation in India. The MOP debate in social sciences as noted above is a serious academic exercise undertaken by scholars to understand the successive stages of development of particular societies. There are several competent Indian scholars of international repute who have participated in this debate and enhanced the capacity of the scientific world to understand the unexplored. In this context, the debate on the Indian version of development is explained here with the introduction of a new MOP as an illuminating exercise. The economic structure of the Indian society during the colonial period and the stagnant nature of this structure were explained by Jairus Banaji and others[26] in terms of a 'colonial MOP'. According to him, it is a residual category, a sort of 'non-Europe', which Marx believed that the ruling class was subsumed in State. The construct was found to be essential as the existing analytical tools of feudalism or state MOP were found to be inadequate to explain the Indian situation. In fact, the debate itself has opened new vistas in the area of political economy of agriculture in India. Though Ashok Rudra, Alavi, Gail Omvedt and others discussed the issue of class formation in capitalist agriculture within the broad framework of MOP in the same place, they were, however, unsuccessful to go deep into the agrarian relations in the rural economy that was based on caste divisions and *jajamani*. The edited volume by Utsa Patnaik[27] has contained papers that debated some of the issues relating to third-world economies, including India, but could not come out with an agreeable model to study India. The debate on land reforms, feudalism and so on was not carried further particularly after the globalization theories gained momentum and marginalization of only Dalits and service castes. It is in the tradition of explaining the unexplored area of social formation in Indian society, an attempt is made here to formulate the CMOP as an important analytical tool to understand the Indian situation.

The concept of MOP as seen above is a dialectical method through which the structure of institutions and their relationships within a society can be explained in a historical outline. Scholars have so far identified nine MOPs.[28]

They are (a) communal, (b) simple property, (c) independent peasant, (d) state (Asiatic), (e) slave, (f) feudal, (g) capitalist, (h) socialist and (i) communist. Though MOP is a Marxist tool developed by Marx himself, the concept has been adopted by both Marxist and Non-Marxist scholars. It consists of four important analytical parts. One, in the process of production, people use different implements and tools, such as plough axe, lathe, labour, and so on. This is known as means of production. The second component is productive force. No machine or a single factor can produce anything by itself. It requires the power, skills, experience and knowledge to put the means of production in motion. In the process of production, people necessarily enter into certain social relations known as production relations. This third component is dictated by the ownership of the means of production. The fourth component is analysed by Jairus Banaji by distinguishing relations of exploitation and relations of production in his concept of colonial MOP. The surplus is appropriated from the labourers in colonial mode not as rent but rent in kind through extra economic coercion. This relationship is only a relationship of exploitation and it is a very important component to understand the MOP. All the above four components are combined together in explaining a historically determined society. The productive forces and the relations of production together comprise the concept of MOP. In each of the modes of production, a dominant class emerges and controls the means of production. For instance, in the state or Asiatic mode, state is the dominant category, while in slavery, the slave is the dominant category. Land is fundamental for feudalism as capital is for capitalism. Though Marx had listed Asiatic, ancient, feudal and modern bourgeois modes of production, now scholars are identifying independent peasant and simple property, socialist, lineage, colonial, state AMP, slave and so on modes. We are now using the dominant socio-economic category of caste in India as MOP by studying different phases of society within the Marxist mould. The studies of Frank, Amin, Weiskoff and other third-world economists have brought out clearly that the characterization of some of the Latin American countries as capitalist or pre-capitalist is not a satisfactory explanation.[29] They have significantly contributed to the Marxist intellectual tradition by introducing dependency theory along with the centre-periphery imagery to explain the specific conditions of their societies. Ashok Rudra[30] stated that why two different concepts, that is, MOP and social formation, are being used to describe the same phenomenon and surmised that it was due to lack of clarity on the concept of MOP. He has noted the disagreement between Gunder Frank and Laclau on a single worldwide capitalist mode as a case of vast differences among Marxists to capture the diversity of socio-economic formations in different parts of the world.

In India, attempts were made by Marxist scholars and activists to make India correspond with other European societies in its process of development by identifying similarities in these societies without recognizing the specificities. In fact, Marx himself was struck by the peculiarities of the Indian society with the limited information available with him and called the formation as an AMP. Later, economists and historians realized the distinguishing features by introducing concepts, such as colonial mode and Asiatic mode. Even these scholars have not been able to succeed in capturing the whole process of production in India. They hardly touch upon the rural India, particularly, the caste system. Social anthropologists have studied these problems as issues of social categories in village studies without an explanation why do they survive even today?

## Features of CMOP

It is necessary to identify the fundamental and differential features of CMOP. In order to characterize the CMOP, we need a dominant category to identify the mode along with other components. Throughout Indian history, we come across the category of caste (*varna* in the past) as a dominant player in social and economic life. Marx has recognized the economic influence of caste in manufacturing sector in India and recorded its dominance in *Capital* Vol I in his main text. It is at the stage of explaining division of labour and manufacture, Marx has mentioned about caste system.

He said that

> the whole mechanism discloses a systematic division of labour, but a division like that in *'manufacture is impossible'* [emphasis added], since the smith and the carpenter and so on find an unchanging market, and at the most there occur, according to the sizes of the villages, two or three of each, instead of one.[31]

He has further elaborated by saying that

> the law that regulates the division of labour in the community acts with the irresistible authority of law of nature at the same time that each individual artificer, the smith, the carpenter and so on conducts in his workshop all the operations of his handicrafts in the traditional way but independently and without recognizing any authority ... this simplicity supplies the key to the secret of the *unchangeableness* [emphasis added] of Asiatic societies, an unchangeableness in such striking contrast with constant dissolution and

refounding of Asiatic States.... The structure of the economic elements of society remains untouched the storm clouds of the political sky.[32]

It can be noted from the above that the fundamental features of a CMOP is its *'unchangeable'* feature. It was recorded by Marx himself while explaining the division of labour. It is striking to notice that he has explained the above under a separate section on 'Division of Labour in Manufacture and Division of Labour in Society' to indicate the link between the two in India. The importance of unchangeableness and its relation within accumulation of capital is explained by Marx with an interesting example.

> On the whole, the labourer and his means of production remained closely united, like the snail with its shell, and thus there was wanting the principal basis of manufacture, the separation of the labourer from the means of production, and the conversion of these means in to capital.

Interestingly, Marxist historians who have picked some of his ideas relating to unchangeableness did not comment on the social division of labour in terms of caste as the principal reason for this with the example of snail given by Marx himself. May be some of the historians did not want to explain about the economic significance of this in their writings or could not get into the economic significance of accumulation of capital and the 'problem of caste snail' as hurdle to tear asunder the feudal system to usher in capitalism. Some scholars have written extensively on transition from feudalism to capitalism and we have noted above the debate on semi-feudal or colonial MOP in India. Interestingly, unchangeableness is understood as stagnation. In Economics, stagnation is different from unchangeableness. Stagnation occurs when the rate of growth of the economy remains slow with unemployment. But the unchangeableness is a socio-economic character of labour in manufacturing sector as noted by Marx. It remains the same irrespective of the change in the structure of the economy. Employment in India in the past seems to have not been studied properly in relation to caste-based occupations that were by and large reservation of jobs with little upward mobility of labour. Precisely for this reason to maintain unchangeableness in the socio-economic formation, *dharmashastras* (for instance Manu Dharma) are called in to brutally suppress any kind of breach to supply free labour and services to the *Dvijas*. In a different context, Wittfogel[33] has elaborated in the 'Oriental Despotism' under *dharmashastras* and *grihya sutras* to maintain total (caste) terror in India.

Anne Bailey edited a volume on AMP illustrated in the extensive literature on the subject to show the relevance of AMP to non-European societies, particularly, India (with its unique caste system). The pre-capitalist socio-economic formations as explained by most of the Indian Marxists looked at the lower castes as either poor or working class, but never probed deep why they remained like that for generations. It was Marx who tried to understand the unchangeableness of manufacture with unique division of labour, while the 'chief inhabitant' (the *Dvija*), who is judge, police and tax-gatherer in one, the book-keeper, who keeps the accounts of the tillage, who prosecutes the economic elements of society remains untouched by the storm-clouds of the political sky. Strangely this description never attracted the attention of the (*Dvija*) Marxists who did not bring in the role of the *dharmashastras* even as superstructure and its economic base while critiquing Marx-AMP. Similarly, several scholars who were looking at India, through a window of their own, however, did not touch the 'untouchable'. Some even denied the existence of slavery in India. We can find in the Indian history that the occupational mobility of certain artisan castes (some are now considered as other backward castes (OBCs) and the conditions and lifestyles of the untouchables have remained the same through ages, which Marx observed from a distance and noted its 'unchangeableness' character.

Ambedkar[34] recognized this and identified the untouchables with slaves and related it with Hinduism. Had he used the economic explanation of its existence, such as the MOP or some other, he would have enhanced our understanding and a solution could have been found. He said that

> most parts of the world have had their type of what was called the lowly. The Romans had their slaves, the Spartans their helots, the British their Villains, the Americans their Negroes and the Germans their Jews. So, the Hindus have their untouchables. Slavery, serfdom, villainage have all vanished. But, untouchability still exists and bids to last as long as Hinduism will last.

While explaining the need for annihilation of castes, Ambedkar noted,

> Caste is not merely division of labour. It is also division of labourers ... it is an hierarchy in which the divisions of labourers are graded one above the other.... This division of labour is not spontaneous (as in Adam Smith), it is not based on natural aptitudes.

It is almost like Marx, Ambedkar said that the greatest evil in

> industrial system is not so much poverty and the suffering that it involves as the fact that so many persons have callings which make no appeal to those who are engaged in them. ...as an economic organization caste is therefore a harmful institution subordinating man's natural powers to social rules.

This is one way of explaining the existence of untouchability and discrimination. The unchangeableness of the conditions of the Dalits (untouchables, service castes and artisans) needs to be sought in the MOP. However, his explanation that castes are stagnant classes (borrowing it from Ketkar) or division of labourers does not directly explain the concept. Division of labour as elaborated by Adam Smith and explained by Marx is a practice where the process of production is divided into different stages, like 18 sequences for pin making, and each process is perfected by one. This raises productivity. But in India, each occupation is held by a caste and the finished product is produced by the family or caste by following all the processes by caste occupation (e.g. the carpenter caste or family makes legs, base and top of a table as finished product, while in division of labour, leg is made by one, top by another and the table by some other). This does not allow any change as noted by Marx above. Interestingly, this problem has not been considered by Indian scholars for further study, perhaps limiting our understanding of CMOP.

No human being survives without food and it is to be produced. Dalits or other socially marginalized groups are involved in the process of production not only as food gatherers, but even remain the means of production. They never refused to accept modern methods of production as some historians characterized their backwardness, but the mainstream society made them to survive without any change. It is necessary here to bring in history. The Indus and Harappan civilizations, which were basically urban and river valley in origin have provided evidence on the lifestyles and social institutions. There was no trace of untouchability and a group of citizens living outside the mainstream. It was only after the destruction (collapse) of the urban culture and the introduction of alien or Aryan 'gram' or village mode of living that the caste system started developing as a gigantic social formation. But those who survived the onslaught remained outside as an independent social group and those who opposed the mainstream within its structure have also been thrown into this category. As a result, Dalits emerged as a 'residual' or as an experimental group. The social relations between the mainstream and the untouchables have been maintained through an MOP, otherwise they would have emerged as an independent social group as observed in the case of artisan communities in the mainstream. They are deliberately maintained as untouchables. But social interaction continued to make use of their productive forces. That is why, untouchables have found to be surviving yet without any improvements in their living conditions. As the productive forces play a dominant role in the MOP, they are used, yet the developments in the mainstream are restricted through extra economic coercion known as caste restrictions. The productive forces of Dalits remained constant as they were forbidden to enter the mainstream, enter literate learning and own property. These three important restrictions made them to stagnate with what they originally possessed as an 'indigenous community'. The situation did not alter very much as anticipated by Marx in the British Raj. It was said that the British, 'fulfil a double mission in India: One destructive, the other regenerating—the annihilation of Asiatic society and the laying of the material foundation of western society'.[35] The British in fact recreated and strengthened the caste discrimination by rediscovering their Aryan roots in Hinduism and improved the productive forces of Brahmans and other *Dvijas*. Therefore, we can see in India, the development of different modes of production existing side by side without any contradiction, but at the same time replacing one after the other without any difficulty. As characterized in the colonial MOP, the economy and the productive forces were drained without affecting the mainstream elite. The colonial mode as analysed by scholars did not identify the groups who were responsible in collaborating with the British as 'agents' or managing agents. It was the same *Dvija* communities which have acted as 'collaborating elite' by making use of English education, technology, western culture and so on. At the same time, the artisans, the Dalits have been exploited and their capacities have been drained. However, no scholar of repute has elaborated these peculiarities as unique features of India.

The CMOP was sustained with the 'Jajmani' system and the unequal exchange between different communities in the village. Most of the social anthropologists have examined the self-sufficient nature of the village. But the village was never self-sufficient. It was the self-sufficient agriculture that was sustained by the Dalit labour and the labour of artisan communities in providing infrastructure for the self-sufficiency of agriculture. There were interactions between villages (gramam) and occasionally resulted in 'sangramam' (disputes) due to unsettled issues. The remarks of some scholars that there was no interaction among villages are not well founded. The rent on caste is devised in a meticulous way through the restriction of numbers of *Dvijas*. In the Hindu social order, there is no possibility of entering the *Dvijahood* by others. One may aspire or even use the symbols to call themselves with pseudonym called 'Viswa Brahmin' and so on. But the change is never accepted. The number of untouchables keeps on increasing as it is a residual category and anyone can be thrown into it (we are not entering into a debate on socially necessary labour power to produce wage goods and the Malthusian theory here). This has created surplus people and the premium has remained constant, and a subsistence wage is paid. While the Brahmins keep on enjoying a higher premium with all the advantages, including their number, they have extracted rents with the increase in the population and demand for their services. One can see the constant and sometimes ever-increasing demand for the services of Brahmins in Hindu order and their entry to secular occupations in modern India. Therefore, the occupation of the Brahmin remains untouched by others and their mobility is unrestricted due to the premium. The Dalits and others were pushed into 354 occupations, mostly into lowly paid jobs in the post-independent period. Even today, the untouchables are not allowed to share (a) crematorium, (b) water and (c) shrines indicating the continuation of the CMOP. The argument that some positions in public sector are occupied by the Dalits through reservation is an indicator of occupational mobility that is to be understood as an external force (political) and not as an autonomous act of the CMOP. Further, the number of such positions held by the Dalits is estimated to be 1.01 per cent of the total Dalit population (15 per cent of 1.75 crore jobs in government) as compared to the total control of the means of production and their upgradation over a period of time by the *Dvija* communities. The situation has not changed even after globalization. Out of $609,838 million foreign direct investment (FDI) proposals (by 2019), no Dalit is benefited by the process of globalization as not even a single individual was accorded FDI.[36] All the benefits of globalization, including shares in multi-national companies (MNCs), disinvestments, scams and the like, are appropriated by the Brahmins and other *Dvijas* indicating the strength of the CMOP even in the 21st century. It is symbolically noted that out of 100 board of directors of corporate bodies, 44.6 per cent are held by Brahmins, 46 per cent by Vaishyas and the remaining by OBC and scheduled caste (SC) members.[37] It reflects the reverse dividend profile of the country (*Dvijas* include Brahmin, Kshatriya and Vaisya). It means the so-called demographic dividend will help the *dvijas* in reverse proportion to that of lower castes.

## Characteristics of CMOP

The foregoing discussion on the nature of CMOP in India can be summarized under the basic features or characteristics noted below. Ever since the Portuguese recognized the division of society consisting of different castes, the Indian caste system has been commented by both ordinary travellers and experts as a typical social category. It was only Marx who, in a reference to division of labour in his *Capital* as noted above, elaborated the economic significance of it as a distinctive AMP. Unfortunately, it was never discussed in that light by the mainstream Marxists, particularly the party functionaries, derogating it as an aberration. However, it has received the attention of scholars as it is a dominant category in all aspects relating to India and can never be veiled. Apart from the studies of social anthropologists, economists like George Akerlof[38] have tried to capture the apparently social category in a neoclassical economic model of equilibrium to understand its significance in economic operations in India. As Akerlof conducted studies in Punjab, he knew the importance of caste and hiring practices that lead to lower-level equilibrium once the other party learns about the low 'caste' members and predicted that those who do not follow the caste code will be known in the community and will be treated as outcastes.

> An outcaste in India is permitted to hold only scavenging (or other polluting) jobs. He is not allowed to eat with caste members, to touch them, or to touch their food, which in the case of someone outcasted includes his own parents and siblings. Of course, his own children will be outcastes and will suffer the same prohibitions.[39]

Perhaps Akerlof is one of the few economists who had recognized the economic importance of caste and the discriminatory practices used in labour relations in India during 20th century. Akerlof concluded that,

> in a segregationist society they follow the caste code. While not denying the possible returns to the arbitrageur and social deviant, the models of statistical discrimination and caste explain why economic rewards may favor those who follow prevailing social custom; and in so doing, they give economic reasons why such social customs may endure.

Though caste is not explained by Akerlof in the Marxian MOP analysis, he has substantiated its economic value in socio-economic transactions in India. We have cited the study to show that caste is not just a super structure but an infrastructure that links economic base with the so-called super structure of beliefs, religion, ideology, institutions and so on. Further, caste is characterized by Kane, Ambedkar and others as division of labourers that has not fully captured the economic significance as enunciated by Adam Smith as a spontaneous realization of self-interest that Ambedkar has partly admitted. The real issue is that 'social division of labour in essence is a vast network of interrelations among specialized producers held together by the propensity to truck, barter and exchange'.[40] This is limited by the extent of market. In other words, the characterization of caste as division of labourers does not fully explain the discriminatory and unpaid labour of untouchables and artisan castes in the process of production. They are segregated, and codes and customs are imposed not to rebel and demand wages or remuneration equal to that of other caste labourers in the market. In fact, they are kept outside the secular market. This is perpetuated in a systematic basis under the paradigm of past karma and worth by birth limited to few who are termed as twice born or *Dvija*, *Brahmin*, *Kshatriya* and *Vaishya*. They are exempt from manual labour and each caste is given a rank starting from Brahmin down to the untouchable whose value starts with zero. Therefore, any transactions between a Brahmin and others is always fixed at a higher premium for the Brahmin. For instance, if an SC labourer exchanges his product with another (say Xl and Yl) with the same quantity of labour power, the exchange value goes in inverse proportion (X1 $\alpha$ X2) to the status of untouchable. That is, if a Brahmin puts one hour of labour power and produces a commodity (service), it can be exchanged with a commodity produced with more than one hour of labour power of others. In other words, the economic value of labour power is determined in relation to the social and ritual status of caste and the supply of labour is regulated by the system of caste rules. It can be seen that while the labour supply of Brahmin and other *Dvijas* are limited by prohibiting others to enter, the SCs and artisans do not have any serious restrictions to supply their labour. Thus, scarcity of Brahmin labour gives him the opportunity to collect rent that enters into price of commodity, while labour of Dalits does not matter. This is a simple model of operation of CMOP that remained immutable in a state that is regulated by caste. Caste plays a dominant role in the creation of state apparatus, as caste itself is a state like the class is a state in other societies.

Caste is ubiquitous and all pervasive from the post-Vedic period.

> The twice born were entitled to Vedic studies and investiture with the sacred thread, and fourth *varna* or the *Shudras* were excluded from it. They were meant to serve the higher orders and were branded as born slaves. Thus, in the Greco-Roman context the twice born can roughly be called citizens and the *Shudras* non-citizens.[41]

The fifth *varna* seems to be not part of this scheme and had remained outside as outcastes to serve the whole system, including the fourth *varna*. R. S. Sharma concluded his study that,

> the process of state formation and social stratification gathered momentum and assumed significance in the middle of first millennium BC and later ... primary producers were gradually separated socially and politically from those who collected and consumed taxes, tributes, gifts and so on. This separation represented as division of labour, found juridical and ideological articulation in the form of *varna* system, which became the hallmark of state and society in post-Vedic times.[42]

This has remained as an 'unchangeable' formation to use Marx's term, in the years to come, tinkering here and there. The relations of production in CMOP as noted above remained caste based.

## Marxian Political Economy and Caste

Though MOP is a Marxian concept, it has certain structural interlinks that are not generally taken into consideration by some experts and rely heavily on the production process for their analysis. It is said that

> the objective material relations that exist in any society independently of human consciousness, formed between all people in the process of social production, exchange, and distribution of material wealth. Production is not possible without relations of production—humans cannot produce outside of a social structure, whether a nation or a family—relations of production exist for all producers. The basis of the relations of production is ownership of the 'means of production'.

When the means of production become public property, then all people are able to exercise their freedom in relation to the productive forces through the social and political structures of society.[43] In the Indian (caste-based) society, everything is owned by the *Dvijas*, including the labourers as force of production. This needs to be taken into consideration along with other economic operations, such as exchange, distribution and international division of labour.

The forces of production in such a system continue to be Dalit labour power that is ranked zero. It gained momentum with P. V. Narasimha Rao's New Economic Policy (NEP) in 1991 and has become a strong and stable model after 2014, repeating some of the past methods of regulation of the *varna* MOP. The internal differentiation in each *varna* as invented by some scholars and critiques is not a serious problem as the *Dvija* constellation has always remained at the apex without much change in their ranks, and some groups from among the *Shudras* are co-opted in the modern period when they wanted physical support. This happened by way of land reforms and tenancy restructuring, keeping the untouchables away from ownership of land in majority of the states (except Bengal and Andhra Pradesh) after 1948. But the basic structure and asset ownership of the dominant castes did not alter; may be some Brahmins entered secular lucrative occupations after displaced from *Agraharas*. *Kshatriyas* entered business, while *Vaishyas* strengthened their hold over the economy with political manipulations from the time of Bombay plan. In other words, caste never retreated from its traditional role in keeping the state, resources and lower castes under its control. This has happened with the help of the following manoeuvring.

1. Discrimination and denial of right to own property
2. Untouchability and physical alienation
3. Offences and atrocities to create terror not to cross social borders
4. Economic deprivation by denying access to public and common property
5. Using judiciary as a source of deprivation of rights
6. Promoting division and fragmentation within to suppress protest

We are going to discuss each one of the issues in the following chapters to substantiate the uniformity and continuance of CMOP in India as a socio-economic formation.

## Caste and Class

CMOP assumes that at every stage of social and economic development in India, caste has played a dominant role and the European category of class is out of sync here. However, the Marxist literature on classes that takes into consideration the Hegelian 'class in itself' and 'class for itself' are being understood as economic class situation and class consciousness, respectively, can be related to caste. In fact, caste consciousness as 'caste for itself' is taught to every sibling at home and as a part of childhood formation, and the person realizes its importance first within as a social category and then draws rent in public life (economic) as per his rank attached, as noted above, that is, he or she gets into 'caste in itself' once encounters with a dominant caste. Therefore, class analysis in India should be in the form of caste so that the contradictions can be understood and resolved. In fact, caste relations in the country, particularly, in the rural areas are only production relations. The social relations between Dalits, Adivasis and service castes are related to production as they do not have any family or community links except on the job. The dominant or to use Mao Zedong's[44] concept of primary contradiction is between the upper castes and lower castes (as in bourgeois and the proletariat), and the secondary contradiction is understood as one moves into the larger space of occupying different places he or she gets in to sub-caste and inter-caste and intra-caste contradictions (as in Mao, the secondary contradiction between bourgeois and feudal becomes primary if feudals threaten bourgeois progress and the primary contradiction between bourgeois and proletariat will be temporarily relegated to secondary contradiction). It is noted that the relationship between primary and secondary contradictions is not static and they remain dynamic, as secondary contradiction sometimes becomes primary, such as the anti-Mandal or anti-reservation movements in India, and becomes secondary once economic criterion is applied by the judiciary (as advocated by a section of leftists for reservations) in jobs to upper castes. These contradictions keep on changing, but the primary contradiction of the upper caste or class and the proletariat or social proletariat of lower castes remains to be resolved at an appropriate stage. The major problem with class analysis is that of categorization of classes into three divisions as bourgeois, petty bourgeois and the proletariat, while castes are around 5,000. There is a slow process of resolving some of the secondary contradictions when groups of lower castes are united to fight for their rights against the dominant castes. Here, we may concede that all the *Dvija* castes are economically dominant in terms of their resource base and command over state for the last hundreds of years. In fact, the non-Brahmin movement initiated by the lower caste peasants in the beginning by Ezhavas in Madras and appropriated (?) by *shudra* landed gentry was actually a peasant struggle against the landed proprietary class who owned land in the form of *Brahmadeya* (to Brahmins), *Devadana* (donated to gods) and *Agrahara* (settlement of priests) for generations and held in common possession that Marx was referring to. It was only after 1793, permanent settlement of lands was allocated to individuals. Even after such allocation, lower castes, particularly untouchables and artisans, have remained attached labourers. There are several institutional structures that caste system has developed, such as the *Jajmani*, as an agency to distribute resources as per caste ranks studied by social anthropologists. It is unusual to notice some scholars did not recognize chattel slavery and analysed class relations of production with sophisticated theoretical framework that is by and large not directly related to facts on the ground. The untouchables were not allowed to own land for instance in Punjab until 1947, and in many parts of India they were not sharecroppers, just 'bonded labourers'. It seems the experts take recourse like the NDA government that denied the existence of untouchability in India at World Conference against Racism (WCAR) 2001 by citing Art 17 and declared that bonded labour is abolished by law. In fact, the first bonded labour Act was passed by the British India government under 'The Bengal Bonded Warehouse Association Act 1838, Indian Slavery Act 1843 and later Payment of Wages Act 1936, Watandari Abolition Act, etc.' only to mitigate chattel slavery. They are all related to untouchable castes and Adivasis who constitute around one-third of our population and in some regions like Bengal more. It is likely that some scholars may not be aware of the fact that there are two categories of agricultural labourers, touchable and untouchable, in rural India. They are given differential wages. It may be due to the caste blind approach of class analysis by some Marxists who tried to relate our social formation to the analysis of abolition of serfdom through peasant class struggle. Some scholars, such as Ramakrishna Mukherjee,[45] who was critical to M. N. Srinivas and Andre Beteille, recognized caste but tried to complicate it by saying 'caste in class' that has cut across the caste hierarchy, without providing empirical evidence as to how to accommodate the fifth *varna* and Adivasis (who are poor and marginalized) in the threefold division of classes. Further, the emergence of new petty bourgeoisie is characterized by Poulantazas[46] as those white-collar employees, technicians, supervisors, civil servants and so on and now ICT and employees of the financial institutions who are mostly drawn from *Dvijas*. As these jobs exist in the private sector, they are not accommodated in class analysis. The politicization of castes and the entry of Dalits in civil service and modern occupations as noted above is limited to about 1 per cent of their population, which may not alter the traditional classification of castes as four *varnas* and an appendage panchama and Adivasi in the Indian social formation, and it needs to be reckoned with to grip the contemporary reality after 2014. The role of religion in India as a form of accumulation of wealth in precious metals was recognized by Marx when he referred to the Anantha Padmanabha Swamy temple in one of his articles to *New-York Daily Tribune* around 1855. The strength of religion and *Dvija* in getting financial and, thus, political support came out openly when the Supreme Court abruptly closed the remaining vaults after discovering lakhs of crores of rupees worth of precious metals in vaults A, C and so on in the Anantha Padmanabha Swamy Temple in 2012.[47] The episode of Martanda Varma who was the custodian of the wealth killed 42 rebels around the 1730s in his princely state and declared them as outcastes signified the link between caste, religion and accumulation of wealth in modern period.[48] Thus, caste particularly the *Dvija* group controlling the wealth in the past and appropriating public and private resources after 1991 resulted in the emergence of crony capitalism, which is in essence caste (upper) capitalism. Therefore, it is possible to examine the social formation of CMOP with the category of caste.

Scholars such as Anand Teltumbde[49] and others have raised the dichotomous nature of social categories in India as classes and castes leading to disastrous consequences in fight against imperialism. Anand noted that, 'these erroneous outlooks have bifurcated the movements of proletarians in India into two parallel streams, viz., a communist movement and a Dalit movement. In the ensuing debate, the two sides, instead of seeking common grounds between them, vehemently distanced themselves further.' In other words, the polemics of a century-old caste class in India did not yield any positive ground for the unity among the oppressed and perhaps have helped the Hindu stratagem of divide and rule that became the order of the day by 2020. Instead, it is necessary to incorporate not only the economic bearings of different SCs and artisan castes as analogous and use the same terms as castes not only to make clear that we are addressing the objective reality, but also satisfy the subjective experiences of majority of the population in India. Perhaps the use of 'class' as an analytical category today satisfies none other than the tiny minority of the *Dvijas* whether Marxist or non-Marxist to hoodwink lower caste proletariat. In fact, this did not help the experts and activists to relate the kind of studies made in the West about the contemporary social classes to India for arriving at a theory of praxis to halt the onslaught of the united force of fundamentalism and imperialism.

## Caste and Race

The notions of race, caste, gender, nation, ethnic group, indigenous people and so on have engaged the attention of social scientists as serious issues of contemporary relevance for quite some time at the international level. The notion of racial superiority has brought unprecedented human suffering and a world war during the last century. But, the humankind has not learnt lessons. Racism and racial discrimination continued to haunt both the gullible and the enlightened public resulting in crisis in the society. Racial discrimination and the related intolerances have brought an international upsurge when a parliamentarian in the UK uttered something that evoked racial feelings during the last week of April 2001. Yet, some sociologists, particularly the Indian brand, refused to recognize the fact that people still carry notions of racism and continue to discriminate people on the basis of these false beliefs. The argument that racism does not stand for scientific reasoning even after human genome project only sounds academic, but the fact of the matter is that people believe in wrong and unscientific notions and act accordingly. That does not mean that there is no discrimination based on racism. The United Nations (UN) Human Rights Commission has published reports of brutal killings in Germany, in the USA and in other parts of Western Europe during 1998, 1999 based on racial beliefs of people. It is in this context the UN has taken serious note of it and geared the world to combat this human tragedy through WCAR.

The concept of race is a European invention and caste is an Indian social institution. There are several parameters, which are common for both the categories. One important factor that is common to both the categories is the concept of inequality based on birth and or descent. In fact, the International Convention on the Elimination of All Forms of Racism (ICERD) has clearly defined what discrimination is and how it is practiced. In article 1, para 1, it defines the concept of racial discrimination as,

> any distinction, exclusion, restriction or preference based on race, colour, *descent* or national ethnic origin which has the purpose or effect of nullifying or improving the recognition, enjoyment or exercise, on an equal footing, of human rights and fundamental freedom in the political, economic, social, cultural or any other field of public life.

The definition includes descent, ethnic origin and colour. This is applicable to the Indian caste system devised by Indo-Europeans to perpetuate slavery and discrimination against the native populations who were called as *Dasyus, Panchamas* and outcastes. There is now sufficient literature that indicates almost all the Dalits belong to the native Indians (NIs) and the non-Dalit *Dvija* populations belong to the Indo-European Caucasian in terms of research in physical anthropology and genetics. One study indicated that, 'differences in social rank between castes correspond to mitochondrial DNA (mtDNA) distances between castes, but not genetic distances, as estimated from y-chromosome data'.[50]

There is also an argument that racism spread from the tenets of Hindu caste system as enunciated by Manu and popularized by European Indologists during the 18th century. But, the Indian government because of its own reasons has not reconciled to the fact that caste discrimination exists even in the 21st century. Interestingly, the international Dalit networks have succeeded in establishing a common link wherever there is untouchability based on descent and work. It is estimated that there are around 260 million people who are affected by this inhuman practice of untouchability and discrimination based on birth in south Asia. This belief, it is said, is widely disseminated by the Hindu customs of purity and pollution. This is found to be prevalent in countries where the Indian diaspora spread. It is observed during WCAR at Durban that representatives from Nepal, Sri Lanka, Malaysia, Thailand and Japan have formed into an international Dalit human rights network to fight against the evil of caste discrimination. This has set aside the argument of the Government of India that it is an 'internal issue'. In fact, racism, apartheid and so on are specific to certain countries, but they are considered as a crime against humanity because of their evil designs. Indian government knows about it. But the NDA regime put up its arguments in consonance with their social philosophy and not as per the secular traditions of the Constitution. It is no more an internal problem as the Dalits of Nepal and India, Barukuman of Japan with similar social disabilities and Dalits in Sri Lanka, Malaysia and Thailand have joined together to fight against this evil at the international forum. In fact, the Dalit groups of Nepal who constitute around 15 per cent of the Nepal population have succeeded in making the Nepal government to recognize this problem and persuaded the government to make a declaration at the Tehran conference even at the discomfiture of the Indian government. The Bangladesh representative spoke against caste in the government representatives' session at Tehran. The three-day meeting discussed the issues from various dimensions and the issue of caste discrimination has been incorporated not only under the theme, but it has gone into other themes of the WCAR, including globalization, gender, indigenous people and refugees. This has further strengthened the issue of caste discrimination as an important point to be discussed at Durban, South Africa, in August 2001. Interestingly, the representatives who were elected by the non-governmental organization (NGO) forum to represent various issues at WCAR are found to be more in number for the caste issue out of the 20 from the South Asia Pacific at the Kathmandu meeting.[51] The argument that caste and race are two different notions and do not qualify to get included in the agenda of WCAR did not carry strength of conviction in its argument. ICERD has recognized caste discrimination as an important form of discrimination in 1996 (CERD Doc A151/18). Further, the WCAR is concerned not only about the discrimination, but even interested to probe into the intensity of it through the observation of the practices which indicate intolerance. Untouchability is an extreme form of intolerance observed by many in India today. The government of Andhra Pradesh has appointed Justice Punnaiah Committee to enquire into this problem and the findings of the report have further strengthened the veracity of practicing caste discrimination today (see Chapter 10).

The question whether caste discrimination be equated with racial discrimination needs to be answered. What is the moral sanction of the UN to discuss any form of discrimination, be it racial, caste, ethnic or some other category? It appears that its strength is derived from the universal declaration of human rights in 1948, which has been accepted by many countries including India. The first article in the declaration reiterates that 'all human beings are born free and equal' and any form of discrimination based on birth, sex, belief and so on is a violation of human right. If caste discrimination, for that matter racial discrimination, is looked at from this background, it is clear that any form of discrimination based on birth or work is against the principle of equity. Since caste discrimination, particularly the inhuman practice of untouchability, negated the principle of equity as enshrined in the universal declaration of human rights, it is same as that of racial discrimination. In fact, caste discrimination is much worse than racial discrimination as the institution of caste carries an intolerant practice of untouchability. No activist says that race and caste are the same. But, the practice of discrimination based on one's birth in a race or caste is to be condemned. At this stage, both are equated for condemnation for similar crime against humanity.

Feminists have long been arguing to establish a link between feminism and Marxism. It is alleged that the 'Orthodox Marxists' consider race only as false. It is noted that consciousness (Leonardo 2003) and Feminism can be subsumed under modes of production. But studies by African–American Scholars, Bowles and Gintis have proved that race plays an important role in the creation of human capital and the resultant lifelong earnings of racial social groups in the USA.[52] Neo-Marxists like Bourdieu[53] and Lareau have developed concepts, such as cultural capital, and habitus, to link economic capital with cultural practices. Further, Hall,[54] using Gramscian narrative, describes 'relations of force' as an important factor to be considered in a social formation. Thus, caste as a socio-economic category can be used as a set in MOP analysis as an approach to study political economy of caste.

# Notes

1. T. S. Kuhn, *The Structure of Scientific Revolution* (Chicago, IL: University of Chicago Press, 1970).
2. Martin Hollis, *The Philosophy of Social Science: An Introduction* (New Delhi: Cambridge University Press), 15.
3. Antonio Gramsci, *Selections from the Prison Note Books* (Chennai: Orient Longman, 1996).
4. Michel Foucault, *The Archaeology of Knowledge* (London: Routledge, 1989).
5. S. A. Dange, *India: From Primitive Communism to Slavery: A Marxist Study of Ancient History in Outline* (Delhi: People's Publishing House, 1958).
6. D. D. Kosambi, *An Introduction to the Study of Indian History* (Bombay: Popular Prakashan, 1956).
7. R. S. Sarma, *Indian Feudalism* (Delhi: Mac Millan, 1965).
8. Prabhat Patnaik, 'EMS Namboodripad's Perception of History', *The Marxist* 25, no. 34 (July–September 2009).
9. Murzaban Jal, 'Marx and Ambedkar: Reflecting on the Deflecting Indian Emancipation', *IIAS Review* 11, no. 2 (2005).
10. Utsa Patnaik, ed., *Agrarian Relations and Accumulation: The Mode of Production Debate in India* (Delhi: Oxford University Press, 1990).
11. E. Varga, 'La Situation Economic en Chine, International Correspondence', 16 December 1925.
12. K. A. Wittfogel, *Oriental Despotism: A Comparative Study of Total Power* (New Haven, CT: Yale University Press, 1964).
13. Harbans Mukhia, 'Was There Federalism in Indian History', *The Journal of Peasant Studies* 8, no. 3 (1981): 273–310.
14. Shakti Padhi, 'Asiatic Mode of Production and Indian History', in *Readings in Political Economy*, ed. K. S. Chalam (Hyderabad: Orient Longman, 1999), 408–431.
15. Kosambi, *An Introduction*, 16.
16. S. A. Dange, *India: From Primitive Communism to Slavery: A Marxist Study of Ancient History in Outline*, 3rd ed. (Delhi: People's Publishing House, 1972).
17. Anne M. Bailey and Joseph R. Llobera, eds., *The Asiatic Mode of Production: Science and Politics* (London: Routledge and Kegan Paul, 1981).
18. K. Marx, *A Contribution to the Critique of Political Economy*, Introduction by M. Dobb (Moscow: Progress Publishers, 1977).

19. Ibid, 11.
20. Ibid, 33.
21. L. Krader, ed., *The Ethnological Note Books of Karl Marx* (Assen: Von Gorcum, 1972).
22. Baily and Llobera, *Asiatic Mode of Production*, 37.
23. Jal, 'Marx and Ambedkar', 48.
24. Kosambi, *An Introduction*, 12.
25. K. S. Chalam, *Education and Weaker Sections* (New Delhi: Inter India Publications, 1988), chap. 3.
26. Jairus Banaji, 'For a Theory of Colonial Mode of Production', in *Agrarian Relations and Accumulation: The Mode of Production Debate in India*, ed. Utsa Patnaik (New Delhi: Oxford University, 1990); Jairus Banaji, *Theory as History: Essays on Modes of Production and Exploitation* (Leiden/Boston, MA: Brill, 2010).
27. Patnaik, *Agrarian Relations*.
28. James Russell, *Modes of Production in the World History* (London: Routledge, 1989).
29. Bailey and Llobera, *Asiatic Mode of Production*.
30. Ashok Rudra, 'Class Relations in India Agriculture', in *Agrarian Relations and Accumulation: The Mode of Production Debate in India*, ed. Utsa Patnaik (New Delhi: Oxford University, 1990), 251–267.
31. Karl Marx, *The Capital Vol I* (Moscow: Progressive Publishers, 1977), 338.
32. Ibid.
33. Wittfogel, *Oriental Despotism*.
34. B. R. Ambedkar, *Babasaheb Ambedkar Writings and Speeches*, Vol. 1, ed., Vasant Moon (New Delhi: Dr Ambedkar Foundation, 1942).
35. Karl Marx and Frederick Engels, 'British rule in India', in *Selected Works*, vol. I (Moscow, Russia: Progress Publishers, 1969), 88–93.
36. Ministry of Industrial Development, Govt. of India Fact Sheet, FDI.
37. D. Ajit, Han Donker and Ravi Saxena, 'Corporate Boards in India—Blocked by Caste?', *Economic and Political Weekly*, 47, no. 32, 11 August 2012.
38. George Akerlof, 'The Economics of Caste and of the Rat Race and Other Woeful Tales', *The Quarterly Journal of Economics* 90, no. 4 (November 1976): 599–617.

39. Ibid.
40. Mark Blaug, *Economic Theory in Retrospect* (Hienmann Educational Books Ltd, 1968), 40, chap. 2.
41. R. S. Sharma, *Material Culture and Social Formations in Ancient India* (Delhi: MacMillan India, 1992), 163.
42. Ibid., 166.
43. MIA: Encyclopedia of Marxism, Glossary of Terms.
44. Mao Tse-Tung, *Selected Writings of Mao*, August 1937. www.marxist.org/reference/archive/Mao
45. Ramakrishna Mukherjee, 'Caste in Itself, Caste and Class, or Caste in Class', *Economic and Political Weekly* 34, no. 27 (3 July 1999): 1759–1761.
46. Nicos Poulantzas, *Classes in Contemporary Capitalism* (London: New Left Books, 1975).
47. R. Krishna Kumar, 'Treasures of History', *Frontline*, 29 July 2011. https://frontline.thehindu.com/the-nation/article30176370.ece
48. Jake Halpern, 'The Secrete of the Temple: The Discovery of Treasure Worth Billions of Dollars Shakes Southern India', *The New Yorker*, 23 April 2012.
49. Anand Teltumbde, *Anti-Imperialism and Annihilation of Castes* (Thane: Ramai Prakashan, 2005).
50. Michael Bamshed, et al. 'Genetic Evidence on the Origins of Indian Caste Populations', *Genome Research* 11, no. 6 (June 2001): 994–1004. https://www.ncbi.nlm.nih.gov/pmc/articles/PMC311057/; David Reich, 'The Collision That Found India', *Caravan* (1 October 2018).
51. K. S. Chalam, *Caste Discrimination as an Issue before WCAR* (Hyderabad: Centre for Dalit Studies, 2001).
52. Zeus Leonardo, 'The Unhappy Marriage between Marxism and Race Critique: Political Economy and the Production of Racialized Knowledge', *Public Futures in Education* 2, nos. 3–4 (2004): 483–493.
53. P. Bourdieu, 'Cultural Reproduction and Social Reproduction', in *Power and Ideology in Education*, ed. J. Krabel (New York: Oxford, 1977).
54. S. Hall, 'New Ethnicities', in *Critical Dialogues in Cultural Studies*, ed. David Morly Kuan Hsing Chen (New York: Routledge, 1996).

# 2

# Colonial Approach to Hindutva and Marxist Writing

The ideas and concepts relating to Hinduism, *varna*, caste, *atma*, *dharma* and so on that are popular today among the informed citizens seem to have been influenced by the writings and documents prepared by the East India Company and the British India colonial elite. Most of the Indologists, including Indian Marxists, relied on some of their sources from these writings on India. It is time that one should look at the sources and the purpose of such material in the context of attempts of internationalizing certain ideas that are against the identity of NIs (Dalit and others).[1] It is noted by scholars like Kosambi,[2] Basham,[3] Kulke[4] and Jha[5] that several bands of alien uncivilized groups or races entered India in the process of their search for settled life here in the past. It is perhaps due to the fact that India is strategically and geographically located in the Southern hemisphere in such a manner that the most diversified and naturally sustainable resources are available here both in temperate and cold climates to sustain any form of life. It is this unique advantage of India in the world that did attract human immigration from different areas of the ancient world. However, the scholars and Indologists have been concentrating only on those who had migrated from the Mediterranean region and Central Asia, basically for two reasons. First, most of the experts, including those who were trained by them, have come from the so-called Indo-European background. Second, among the groups who have migrated into the country, the bands that have come from the West are notorious and ruthless in morals and also in their modes of cruel repression of enemies (it is still displayed in the cruelty of Talibans). Therefore, the aliens who are called as Aryans had developed the competence and connection, continuously arriving into the country from the time of *panchajanas* (*Yadus, Turvasus, Anus, Dhruyus* and *Purus*) down to *kushan*s and Europeans.[6] It appears that the aliens had been invited with open hands by those who settled here, considering them as their long-lost kin. Unfortunately, the so-called NIs did not have any friendly contacts outside the country like that of the Maya and Inca people. The Africans had the advantage of colour and compose to easily connect with their brethren in any part of the world while the dark and brown NIs were shy of such contacts. It is increasingly believed that none of the alien faiths, mostly Aryan or Indo-European, did protect either physical extinction or social or cultural alienation of NI in the past. The same is true even in the modern period. The literacy rate was just 0.53 per cent when the enlightenment project of untouchables started in the 19th century, which now stands at 66 per cent. The conditions have changed since the time of B. R. Ambedkar who was supported by two princely states of Baroda and Kolhapur, and now no one is uttering about the upliftment if not amelioration of the poor NIs. The reason being that Dalits have developed a 15 per cent reservation syndrome of infighting among themselves for the crumbs of reservation, forgetting the democratic right of getting proportional representation in every aspect of public and private endeavours in the country. It is necessary to understand the background of the present backwardness of certain castes that are called as SCs and OBCs, the constitutional categories that are given special protection under the Constitution. This has happened due to the legal framework developed by colonial rulers who looked at the caste discrimination, sati and other social practices as archaic under Hinduism.

The notion of Hindutva or Hinduism seems to be a colonial discovery, as the term did not exist either in the *puranas* or in the Vedic corpus as per some scholars. Noted historians like Romila Thapar[7] have analysed that the term was manufactured by the pundits in the 19th century based on the missionary presence in India. In fact, the so-called Boston Brahmin, Ananda Coomaraswamy (defender of Suttee), has explained in his book 'The Dance of Siva' that 'Indian philosophy is essentially the creation of the two upper classes of society, the Brahmins and the Kshatriyas'.[8] Radhakrishnan[9] has ardently lived to this description through his colossal rewriting of Indian philosophy under the benevolent guidance of his missionary teachers. There is perfect understanding among the votaries of both the religions that there is a hidden Vedanta in Christianity and hidden Christ in Hinduism.[10] This is basically the opinion of the colonial masters who under the influence of their missionaries developed a sceptical view of Indian philosophy and Religion. But, they have not done any sympathetic study of the NI belief systems and have considered all the religious practices of natives (and not the Brahminical component) as superstitious and black magic and so on. Some of the missionaries have studied the belief systems of the lower caste people and untouchables and considered all of their beliefs not only irrational but barbaric to be condemned by a civilized society. Henry Whitehead, one of the missionaries who had published on 'Village Gods of South India',[11] categorically called the belief systems of the lower castes as archaic and uncivilized and wanted that the believers are to be relieved of this so that Christ can replace the vacuum. He has narrated how in Telugu districts SCs have destroyed idols and erected cross. In some of their writings and reports, it is found that their ultimate aim was to create space for conversion and this would be possible once their small gods and goblins, mostly village goddesses are considered as trivial so that spiritual space would be created for the Abrahamic pantheon to enter. The materialistic world view and practices of *Lokayata, Ajivikas, Tantrics* and so on are dissented as local and heretical. It seems the same kind of opinion was held by some of the Muslim scholars who considered that the lower castes did not possess any tangible faith and were longing for a spiritual solace that was provided by Islam. The lower castes of East Bengal, mostly animists, joined Islam not out of coercion but by their own volition to relish equality. Thus, the NIs are deprived of any spiritual or materialistic identity of their own as if they are barbarians, believed then and even now.

The analysis of the belief systems of the natives by the company officials seem to had the support of the local clergy who were their translators and contrived to make their beliefs and faith were distinctly different and superior from the natives and untouchables. Though the so-called Sanatana Dharma was in existence as per the Vedic scholars, it did not speak about the local and native systems of faith or socio-religious practices. If there were any references to such phenomenon, it was deliberated out of contempt. Sanatana as endless or *Anadi* refers to something that is alien to Aryan and, therefore, is not part of the *Dvija* categories that were according to some adherents, the main inhabitants of the country (later some of the epistemics appropriated). This was true even at the time of Muslim and European onslaughts. Interestingly, none of the so-called Hindu critiques have pointed out any contradictions in their metaphysics and practices. No one has ever raised how an animal could be despised at one stage and became an Avatar at another. How the names of places and Gods, such as Agni and Indra, keep changing from time to time and place to place and the pundits interpret as per their convenience to make the gullible to worship in the name of *puranas* and get rewarded. They never thought that there was no unanimity among the *Shaivas, Vaishnavas, Advaitas, Dvaitas* and *Vishishtadvaita* and try to bridge the gap under the garb of abstract reasoning and overwhelm with state support. Interestingly, all of them parade in tandem and remain pious and twice born despite of several inconsistencies in their behaviour and paradoxes in their *dharmashastras*. There is no uniformity even in the *dharmashastras*, as there is a difference between North and East, South and West. It is precisely for this reason and to bring standardization, Macaulay, a Tory, was brought to India. Yet, the hegemony of the Brahmin pundit continued as if they alone preserved the values of Vedic religion or what is called way of life. It was not Hinduism or Hindutva as depicted by some scholars now, but it was alleged to be pure Brahminism (not Brahmaism). Hinduism as propagated by a section of the militant Hindu organizations today consists of several practices assimilating from the natives, while the converted natives and their missionaries disown the foundations. That is why the devout Brahmin as well as the convert despises the practices of the NI beliefs as superstition, but do not dare to question the contradictions in Hinduism. Jyothi Rao Phuley[12] started the denigration and questioned the prima facie of the Bhats and simultaneously indicated the sacrifices of NIs like Bali Raja in the 19th century while Ambedkar critiqued Rama and Krishna.[13] Very few of the mainstream scholars of Indology or South Asian studies seemed to have observed the distinction between Brahminism and Hinduism in the first phase and Hindutva in the later stages. The recent language jingoism in the name of *Hindusthani* or Hindi as the only language of India originating from Sanskrit that should be promoted as a national language, if not official language, is another aspect of so-called Indo-European project. It is said that there was no language like Hindi before the 16th century except Persian or Urdu with Indo-European connection and the

British promoted *khari boli* of North East of Delhi as *Hindusthani* in public affairs. Therefore, the fundamentalists wanted only Hindi to be promoted even in states, such as Maharashtra where Marathi is hardly found in their communication.[14] The so-called Maratha pride is never seen using the people's language and only observed in a cursory manner at the time of taking oath of office of government. It is alleged that Hindi as an offshoot of Sanskrit is being used as a symbol of hegemony by few groups who continue to practice a language full of Sanskrit even in the South. There is no contradiction between English and Hindi as many of them know the 'virtue' and 'Varchus' are the same and lend their support even from the opposition camp to protect the hegemony.

The so-called Indo-European term for Sanskrit was coined by Thomas Young in 1813 was most likely influenced by the local linguists and William Jones.[15] But linguists in general say that Afro-Asiatic languages are ancient followed by Pre-Anatolian and Proto-Indic in the form of Vedic Sanskrit. It seems the technique of Srauta tradition/oral recitation to inherit the language without leakages for thousands of years with the introduction of grammar first time in history to codify it around fourth century BC is unique. But its relation with Avestan lingua and its European origin is now being confirmed by genetic studies.[16] If we look at the Indo-European language speakers in retrospect, it would indicate how they were very brainy in foreseeing the importance of language and had operated through grammar to regulate the culture in their own terms. It is brilliant of Dignaga the fourth century AD Buddhist Philosopher to critique the discovery of grammar as a method to control thought process of common people.[17] It is still the same in India, as none of the local dialects/languages were promoted and some appropriated. Interestingly, a particular social group and their adherents are the only ones who defend the Hindutva and Hindi in various forums, including the horrid social network/Internet. This has exposed the one-side view or egocentric elucidations of the defenders of fundamentalism. The media that had been under the authority of traditional literati class from time immemorial is inconspicuous by its absence on these issues.

There seem to be some kind of a craving for the esoteric India in the past that was perhaps built by bands of vagrants in their travelogues who explored the mysteries of the unique country from time immemorial. It is due to the biodiversity in its geography and passive nature of the inhabitants who never bothered about outlandish invasions of any kind. It seems they have given way for aliens to enter without much resistance and with accommodative spirit. We do not have yet a comprehensive history and pre-history of the country recording the developments at the grassroots. Though the Indus Valley Civilization was brought into focus only in the 20th century by colonial explorers/archaeologists, no finality is reached. We do not know what is holding the assertion to declare that Sanskritized Hinduism was alien or Indo-European, such as the genetic studies on haplogroup R1a1a establishing ancestral north Indians (ANIs) as Caucasus/European (noted above). There seem to be an anxiety among the Indo-Europeans that once the Indus Valley or Saraswati Civilization is popularized, the ancient Egypt, Greek, Iran and Sumerian either would become unimportant or parallel which perhaps they do not wish to happen. This is also convenient for the fundamentalist apologetics of India who try to link the NI culture and civilization with their alien cultural pedigrees. It is at this stage, history has become once again a force to reckon with both in academics and in public life. Though some of the Marxist historians declared that they are following relations of production thesis to ascertain the type of society prevailing in different periods, they have, however, ultimately come to the conclusion that do not debunk fundamentalists, as noted in the previous chapter.

The colonial rulers, including William Jones, were not interested to confront the onslaught of Vedic or so-called Brahminical Hinduism of the few with whom they had transacted in the process of governance. They were not interested perhaps in converting them as long as they served their purpose and were interested in proselytization among the poor untouchables and artisans. Some had allegedthat they wanted untouchables be kept as servants and menials in the household. Those who had embraced them for purposes of sharing power and prestige (mostly *Dvijas*) of a ruling class were hugged, assimilated and perhaps became Anglicans. They sailed together and the question of alien faith did not isolate them, and, in fact, colonial officers helped to collect and translate the ancient texts into English. We have today prestigious universities in the West offering courses on Hinduism with chairs mostly seized by *Dvijas*. It is reported that USA alone has 500 Hindu places of worship with billions of dollars' worth of properties and lobbies in the senate and white House in the USA. In other words, the apparently open conflict between Hindu fundamentalism and Christian faith depicted by a section of the media is not coming in the way of capitalist expansion.[18] It is an open invitation now with direct command of the policies by the few *chenchas* of MNCs but pose Christian baiting to divert attention of the public. There seems to be a similar understanding with the Muslim *bhadralok* taking part in active politics of the right. This is happening perhaps due to the internal differentiation of each religious group divided on the basis of the origin of their caste alignments. This was deliberately promoted by the colonial powers or at least one could see that they knew it and kept inconspicuous.

It is interesting to find that Sharad Patil, a Marxist by training and *bahujan* by persuasion, with profound scholarship in ancient literature has continued the discourse by analysing the caste conflicts within Brahmin domain in Maharashtra among Chitpavan and Saraswat and Deshastha to show how the debates were subjective. He said, if the revivalism of non-Chitpavan brahmins, such as Bhandarkar, led them to take anti-Brahminic and pro-Kshatriya stand on the problem of the origin and development of Indian philosophy, the revivalism of Chitpavan Brahmins such as Kane led them to take anti-Kshatriya and pro-Brahminic stand on the same problem.[19]

The Upanishads are known as *up-ni-sad* as secrete knowledge in the ancient past. This phenomenon could be construed as the covert technique of borrowing the knowledge systems of the NIs by the aliens and cultured it as a thought in Sanskrit language that was guarded by the chosen few through rote memory (Sanskrit seems to be a code language that was kept on refined and reformed by select few as *sanskara bhasa*). It was, thus, given a status by the mainstream society as it is now being paraded as Brahminical wisdom in a secure language. In the case of Lokayata or Charvaka philosophy as a rustic reaction to the alien and debasing schools of thought and practices as were current at that time, seemed to have been questioned by Jabali, Makkali Ghosal, Kapalika, Ajitakesa Kambal and others in the epic tradition. The above formulation is supported by an authority on History of Indian Philosophy by S. N. Dasgupta, through his elucidations on the subject. He said that

> it may therefore be presumed that a good number of Atharvanic hymns were current when most of the Rigvedic hymns were not yet composed. By the time, however, that the Atharvaveda was compiled in its present form, some new hymns were incorporated in it, the philosophic character of which does not tally with the outlook of the majority of the hymns.[20]

This suggests that several ideas, notions, scientific practices were adopted from the NIs. This was further supported by the studies of D. P. Chattopadhyay,[21] K. B. Krishna,[22] Sharad Patil and others. It is disheartening to note that the kind of scholarship that we had in our country to make an objective analysis of the facts of the matter particularly with reference to philosophy is being slowly disappeared. It seems the post-modern scholars consider these issues petty and have not done much on the origin of the Indian thought rather they appear to be secure and comfortable with the European and Anglo-Saxon discourse studies. Further, some of the Indian scholars have accepted the damaging nomenclatures ascribed to the NI thought and practice as 'Little culture' by American social anthropologists with their limited field work knowledge in cities, such as Chennai. It is also accused that some of the anthropologists themselves were misguided by the same inherited Brahminical scholarship (with English education) that had called the native thought as useless and stupid. A section of the English-educated enlightened Brahmins who carry democratic spirit in their enquiry seem to have started epitomizing Savarkar as a proponent of Hindutva. But Savarkar who was under the regime of the British used the same colonial categories to elucidate his ideas of Hindutva with little credit to NIs. Commoners in the rural areas and illiterates in the urban *bastis* were never bothered about what Vivekananda, Aurobindo, Dayanand and others thought about their gods or practices. It was for the educated and the political workers, Hindutva and the so called cultural nationalism was a concern during elections. Therefore, it is alleged that no permanent or structured organizations has emerged from the so-called left or secular organizations to encounter the organized robust Hindutva. However, the fundamentalist ideas are not very popular among the common people of non-*Dvijas* whose religious practices are sporadic until the advent of militant Hindu missionary work during the last half a century perhaps with tacit support of the ruling elite. It is irony that the *Shudras*, particularly the OBCs, who were denounced as half animals and wretched by the priest class are now made to carry them on their heads. Yet, the democratization of education and the written word had enabled a minuscule number of scholars to protest against this *adharma* and recorded the significant contributions of the NI thought. Their number is very small and insignificant as of now, but it needs to be recognized and promoted for the benefit of posterity and diversity in India.

The colonial inquiry into the social structure of the country was recorded as they understood it when they first entered the country and perhaps translated into their own culture of classes in the beginning. Later some anthropologists have tried to identify the groups with mistaken identity of Aryan origin of some of the *Dvijas* as pronounced by William Jones as their long-lost kin. But they never looked at the folks, the untouchables, and artisans and so on who were in distant contact in their everyday life. It was perhaps the missionaries who were searching for gaps in the spiritual life of the common man for an opportunity to proselytization got influenced by the upper caste accounts of the practices of the lower castes demonizing them as barbarian. Why is it that they have not adopted similar attitude towards the contradictions in the Brahminical rituals? In fact, they have eulogized the scriptures and traditions as the greatest contributions of human will and translated them into European languages. The protagonists of Hindutva seem to have not been ashamed of or embarrassed to use the colonial epithets of Jones and Lord Curzon who had said that India was the original country of Indo-Europeans. Now the same rhetoric is repeated time and again both in India and elsewhere. But, Indologists like Schlgel,[23] Muller,[24] Weber[25] and Muir[26] contradicted the idea and have elaborated the common ancestry of Aryans (North West India), Persians, Greeks, Romans and Germans as one that might have originated in central Asia. In fact, Muir in his monumental 5 volume work on 'Original Sanskrit Texts on the Origin and History of the People of India, their Religion and Institutions' explained the systems with authentic citations from Vedic literature and published them in 1860. B. R. Ambedkar has used extensively this work in his studies and cited him authoritatively. Therefore, it is not true that caste, as per some sociologists, was created by the colonial powers through census in 1881. In fact, there have been always a section of the learned men who stood for truth and one among them is Kamalakar Bhatt whose *Sudra Kamalakaram* was compiled in the 19th century to indicate how castes are created in a matrix form explaining the intermixing of *varnas* through anuloma and viloma forms of marriages.[27] Interestingly, the number of castes among the *Dvijas* have remained the same or reduced through caste consolidation, whereas the number of lower castes multiplied through a process of subdivision and fragmentation of each social group. However, it is not uniform throughout the country. The number of castes is low in the North and Northeast India and higher in number as one moves from North to South or the route through which the Aryan incursion of the South took place from Varanasi down to Kanyakumari. Both the colonial masters and the modern scholars rely on their source material as the British India documents speak about untouchables or SCs when it comes to the question of social division in Hindu India, but not so much of other castes like the backward castes (BCs) and castes in other faiths in India. This has limited the scope and depth of analysis of social transformation in India particularly after independence. The democratic process of first-past-the-post electoral system in electing leaders to govern people has strengthened the caste cleavages making caste as an important factor to consolidate power on the basis of unity among the ruling castes and division and despair among the lower castes to keep the traditional *varna* system in order. It is interesting to notice that those who fought against the so-called Brahminical social order have assimilated their values and ultimately succumbed to their charm and became their protectors by the end of the 20th century. The trend reminds of a system that was perhaps in vogue in the past in keeping the majority under check through the process of division and subdivision among the masses the so-called 'divide and rule' a technique unique to India.

The issue now is how to annihilate caste and reduce caste-based discrimination in public and private life of Indians. How is it possible? The issues that Phuley, Ambedkar to some extent and Lohia encountered in the past were different from what is observed today. The economic system was not so strong, dissipated and was under the control of the state to manipulate for the benefit of the masses. Now the system is under the control of a few private players consisting of the *Dvija* conglomerate with co-option of upper caste *Shudras* through bureaucratic and media manipulation to herald crony capitalism (They are reported to have emerged as the *vishwa guru* with command over the economic, political and cultural resources not only to sustain the Brahminical order, but also to expand on a world scale, such as that of Hitler with compromises with Jews.). The Dalits and BCs who are entering into the private sector lost their identity, and the younger generation under the lure of Western and market enchantments do not intend to link with their past. There was a systematic process of acculturation of non-Dalit masses to accept the hegemony of Brahminical Hindutva over a period of time. The emergence of present dispensation as per some analysts is not a sudden outcome. It has a long history.

In fact, D. R. Bhandarkar in his lectures at Madras University in 1940 perhaps for the first time explained the Aryanization, Brahminization and Indianization.[28] He has noted 'What Hellenism was to Asia minor, Syria, Iran and Babylon, Aryanism, that is, the Aryan Culture, proved itself to India and greater India'.[29] He has explained with literary sources how Aryans became Brahminized and carried 'the historical memory from the time of 'Rigveda', the cow was considered sacramental efficacy … shared with their Iranian brothers … old Avestic literature and even in the mind of the modern Parsi.[30] Interestingly, the colonial masters and their agents propagated that the land of the Baratas (Baratavassa)—or 'land of the Baratas which (I) have proved to be the original form of the name Brit-ain'.[31] Though Waddle argument was not taken seriously by some historians, the Hindu fundamentalists are arguing that Aryans migrated from Saraswati valley. This is not new as Curzon long ago popularized the same opinion that was noted by Muir[32] and others (noted in previous chapter).

The influence of Marxism on Indian scholars can be formally traced to B. R. Ambedkar who studied Marxism and Post-Marxian Socialism as a paper for his degree course in Columbia University during 1913–1916. M. N. Roy had excellent links with the international communist movement, including Lenin, and wrote on Marxism. K. B. Krishna wrote dissertations in Harvard on Hindu (Indian) materialism and imperialism among others in the 1930s. He taught Marxism to political detunes in the prison after he landed in India and was sent to jail after some time. K. B. Krishna, the first generation Marxist scholar, who had written on the materialist traditions of India did not get adequate attention by the established party functionaries. His writings have seen the light of the day only during the centenary year in 2006. But the crop of historical writings from the time of D. D. Kosambi and other professional historians who claimed to have used dialectical historical materialism or MOP to understand India from primitive times to the present cataleptically dropped the caste particularly the untouchables and their contribution to material production. In fact, the volume of literature on the MOP and the materialist interpretation of Indian society produced by historians outwitted the economists who are supposed to examine the forces of production and their role in the relations of production that is generally seen in our caste transactions both under *jajamani* in the past and the reincarnation of the same after 1990 with the advent of *Dvija*-based capitalism in India. We have noted the reservations expressed by Prabhat Patnaik and Murza ban Jal (previous chapter) about the limitations, if not lapses of Marxist scholars in grappling with reality that created perhaps space for the present dispensation to occupy.[33]

## Notes

1. Mahatma Phule's description of shudras and ati shudras as native to India and Bhats or Brahmins as aliens in his *Gulamgiri* is well known that D. N. Jha noted that he was the first to term the Aryans as aliens.
2. Kosambi, *Introduction to the Study*.
3. A. L. Basham, *The Wonder That Was India* (Delhi: Rupa, 1970).
4. H. Kulke and D. Rothermund, *A History of India* (Delhi: Rupa & Co, 1986).
5. D. N. Jha, *Ancient India in Historical Outline* (Delhi: Manohar, 2018).
6. K. S. Chalam, 'Native Schools of Thought and Dominant Philosophies in India'. Center for Studies in Afro-Asian Philosophies, Nagarjuna University, Guntur, Lecture Series 1 (2012).
7. Romila Thapar, *Early India* (Delhi: Penguin, 2003).
8. Ananda Coomaraswamy, *Dance of Shiva* (New York: The Sunwise Turn, 1904, reissued 2003), 4.
9. S. Radha Krishna, *Indian Philosophy* (Oxford, UK: Oxford University Press; Vol. I, 1923; Vol. II, 1927).
10. K. M. Banerjea, *The Relation between Christianity and Hinduism* (Calcutta: Oxford Mission Press, 1881).
11. H. Whitehead, *Village Gods of South India* (Ithaca, NY: Cornell University; Kolkata: Associated Press, 1921, reprint 2014).
12. Joythi Rao Phuley, *Gulamgiri* [Slavery] (New Delhi: Gautam Book Center, 2007).
13. B. R. Ambedkar, *Babasaheb Writings and Speeches*, Vols. 3–5 (Delhi: Ambedkar Foundation, 2010).
14. Home Minister of India, Shri Amit Shah who spoke about the introduction of Hindi in all states at the Hindi Divas meeting in 2019 retracted his statement when Tamils, Kannadas and others reacted to this proposal.
15. Thapar, *Early India*.
16. Reich, 'Collision That Found India'.
17. Rahul Sankrityayan, *Darshan and Digdarsan* (Kolkata: Chirayat Prakashan, 1989).
18. The recent 'Howdy Modi' Programme in Houston on 22 September 2019 is a continuation of the legacy built in the

USA. It is strange that none of the events that protested against the programme were reported in Indian media as per *The Wire,* September 2019.
19. Sharad Patil, *Dasa Sudra Slavery II* (Pune: Sugawa Prakashan, 1999), 230–231.
20. S. N. Das Gupta, *A History of Indian Philosophy,* Vols. 1–5 (Cambridge: Cambridge University Press, 1963).
21. D. P. Chattopadhyay, *Lokayata* (Delhi: People's Publishing House, 1959).
22. K. B. Krishna, *Studies in Hindu Imperialism* (Guntur: Dr K. B. Krishna Birth Centenary Celebration Committee, 2007).
23. K. W. F. Schlegel, German Indologist 1772–1829 published on the language and wisdom of India.
24. Max Muller, *India: What It Can Teach Us* (London: Funk & Wagnalls, 1883).
25. Max Weber, *The Religion of India: The Sociology of Hinduism and Buddhism,* Reissued (Delhi: Munshiram M, 2000).
26. J. Muir, *Original Sanskrit Texts on the Origin and History of People of India,* 5 volumes (London: Trubnes & Co, 1860).
27. Kamalakar Bhatt, *Sudra Kamala Karanm,* Telugu Translation (Vizianagaram, 1891).
28. D. R. Bhandarkar, *Some Aspects of Ancient India Culture* (Madras: Madras University, 1940).
29. Bhandarkar, *Aspects of Ancient India,* 25.
30. Ibid., 72.
31. L. A. Waddell, *The Indo-Sumerian Seals Deciphered* (London: Luzac & Co, 1925), 10.
32. J. Muir, *Original Sanskrit Texts on the Origin and History of the People of India, Their Religion and Institutions* (London: Trübner, 1868).
33. The allegation that Marx relied on colonial sources for his analysis is not supported by facts. Marx had used both East India Company Documents and other writings, including German, French and so on, sources to arrive at certain conclusions. In fact, he has used his dialectical method of induction under the framework of a structured theory to scrutinize caste and other features of India that are not being referred to. There is likely scope for misunderstanding or understatement.

# 3

# Caste and Economic Power in India

We have seen how a section of social scientists overlooked the caste question in economic analysis and in MOP debates in the previous chapter. We discuss below the economic power of caste in India. Caste has surfaced once again as an important unit of social and political mobilization. The NDA occupied the seat of power in Delhi symbolizing the re-emergence of a new category of alliances of upper castes. It is very clear now that some middle castes and the *Dvija* collective have determined to get the resources and opportunities distributed among themselves. No significant move has been made to uphold the spirit of the Constitution to provide opportunities to the 'backward class of citizens which, in the opinion of the state, is not adequately represented in the services under the state'. Already, the Supreme Court gave a judgement which appears to strengthen the spirit of the NDA with regard to reservations and atrocities (see Chapter 8). The fourth part of the Constitution is made infructuous; it may be repealed in due course as indicated by statements of some political parties. At the same time, the first thing that the NDA coalition did in co-opting the opportunist elements among the Dalits is by extending political reservations to Schedule Castes (SCs) and Schedule Tribes (STs) for another 10 years. This will help strengthen the NDA in getting political support from these sections. The traditional Hindu tactics of co-option is being enacted once again. That is the reason why 100 and odd MPs belonging to SCs and STs do not have any voice in a parliament of several coalitions. They do not have either social or political power. But, a group of 10 or 15 MPs belonging to upper castes or *Dvija* collective can wield positions of cabinet berths and can get contracts worth rupees hundreds and thousands of crores. How is this happening? Is it due to the fact that the power of these castes is higher than that of others? How did they get this power? This needs to be probed.

The concept of 'power' in social sciences is understood as the capacity of a subject to have his own way. Power takes into account the social relationship between two individuals or groups of individuals. Power is always exercised through domination and subordination. It depends upon the historical setting, social structure, nature of the state and economy. Economists have neglected analysing the nature of power until Galbraith developed the theory of countervailing power as a socio-economic phenomenon.[1] Some economists have no doubt discussed about it as a technical relation in the theory of competition. There are theories that discuss about the monopoly power in capturing the market demand and so on. But what is important here is that power appears in varied forms. J. Pen[2] classifies seven categories of non-economic power, such as (a) physical power: threat of use of physical force, (b) personal power: personal ascendancy, father–child relationship, (c) social power: respect for the social position of the subject, (d) administrative and organizational power: based on the rules of an organization and administrative body, (c) state power: based on the sanctions which the state has at its disposal, (d) legal power: legal relationship based on an agreement, and (e) political power: this is the exercise of power by citizens in respect of the state.

In the theory of power, social scientists have analysed how a person's power over another person is affected in terms of the behaviour pattern. In order to analyse it, the constituents of power need to be examined in terms of the base, means, scope and amount. The base of power is considered as the resources, such as economic assets, constitutional prerogatives and military force. The means of power is exercised through specific actions, such as promises and threats. The scope of power lies in the specifications of the subject. The amount of power is measured in terms of the increase in the probability of performing some specific action.

## Economic Power

Economic power has been defined in terms of the economic situation. J. Pen defined it by saying that

> in which the subject who has a series of unsatisfied wants is faced with the relatively scarce means of satisfying these wants. In this situation, economic power can be exercised if the means on which the subject must rely for the satisfaction of his wants are in the hands of another subject.[3]

For example, if the resources are in the hands of A, then A is powerful, as B depends on A. But, the dependence of power on resources is not a simple preposition. It needs to be analysed in terms of power structures, such as liberal democratic state, patriarchal family, capitalist economy and the caste system. These power structures influence not only the base, but even the means of power. Our concern here is to examine up to what extent caste system as a power structure influenced the base and means of economic power in India. It is very difficult to analyse this problem in the Indian context, as there are very few studies available now to undertake this exercise.

No economist has so far examined the Indian caste system as an economic power relation. It is always considered as a social institution wielding no economic power. But, the past experience in the country in terms of ascendancy of certain castes and the subjugation of several other castes as dependents has not been analysed in the purely economic terms. Attempts have been, however, made to measure power in terms of concentration of economic resources.[4] In an attempt to measure the power monopoly of big business houses, three criteria have been followed that include (a) the share of the largest companies in industrial output, (b) concentration of ownership of capital and (c) concentration of management of companies in the economy. Though similar attempts have been made by economists to measure the economic power even after NEP, no attempt seems to have been made to examine the social background of the people who wield this economic power. It is noted by the commission that four business houses, Birla, J. K., Tata and Shreeram had an approved investment of 39 per cent of the total in 1964–1966. None of them was from lower castes. The proportion of the group in the power structure of the state has increased in NDA II.

Caste has been considered as an economic asset of a group of individuals in the Indian context. It is a property. The value of the property is raised or reduced directly in proportion to the ritual status in the social order of the Hindu society. Wiser,[5] a Christian missionary, has attempted to measure the economic relations between different castes considering the 'jajamani' system in a village in 1935. No serious attempt has been made by social scientists to measure the economic power as defined above, in terms of the Indian caste system. No one has ever bothered to examine why the upper castes particularly the *Dvija* castes of Brahmin, Kshatriya and Vaisya have always remained in the higher echelon of economic power and the Dalits at the lower rung. Some attempts have been made in the West by sociologists to examine the social background of top decision-makers in the corporate sector. The study of C. S. Wilson and T. Lupton brought out clearly the connections between directors of merchant banks, and between merchant banks and directors of the Bank of England. Nor is it surprising that we find that positions in certain firms are occupied by adjacent generations of the same family....

What might seem surprising is that kinship connections of this kind have persisted through many changes in the scale and functioning of banking, in the organization of industry and, in the complexity of politics.[6]

What is found in the English system of kinship relations is inherently naturalized in the Indian caste system.

The development of the elite class from among the *Dvijas* and more particularly among the Brahmins took place during the 1960s. In fact, the criteria used by M. N. Srinivas[7] to call a caste dominant are not appropriate to capture all castes in a village or region, because landholdings are no more an important base for economic mobility. It is now subsidized higher education, access to banks and credit institutions, contracts, public sector sales outlets and so on that make a caste dominant. The opportunities created by the public sector of Nehruvian era were systematically grabbed by the educated *Dvijas*. That is why Periyar called the bank nationalization as bank Brahminization. There is nothing wrong in it, because Brahmins were the only group that was eminently qualified at that time to enter into public sector. Several of the Indian doctors, engineers, scientists and technocrats migrated to the USA, the UK and other industrialized countries. Most of them got absorbed in the multinational companies and developed close contacts. Some of them have also occupied important positions in Fund Bank institutions. In other words, a separate caste, a universal dominant caste, crossing across the narrow geographical boundaries of state emerged like that of Zionism. A Pandit of Kashmir, a Shastri of Tamil Nadu and a Sharma of Uttar Pradesh carved out a pan-Indian collectivity. They have started teaching Hindi and Sanskrit to local Americans and revived the Vedic rituals in New York, Delhi, London and elsewhere to 'share common culture and way of life'. For the first time in the history of India, Brahmins as a group started entering into economic sphere and have been using the bureaucracy for the accumulation of capital, human and physical. The tycoons of public sector started ploughing the money into private coffers.[8] They have used their positions for contacts with multinationals to establish units in India either in their name or with a *benami* to start with. Once the blood of the public sector unit is totally sucked, they left it. Several of the neo-rich industrialists of the pre- and post-liberal period belongs to this genre. They are supported by NRIs. The formation of this internationalized elite has been taking place, not out of isolation of the nationalist pan-Aryan or Vedic revivalism in India and abroad. In fact, one should not forget the fact that more amount of money and bricks for Ram temple poured into India from the USA and other developed countries in the 1990s. This could not have been possible without a systematic networking. The so-called pseudo religious secularists (*sarva dharma samabhava* type) in Congress, some United Front constituents and others did not take this trend very seriously. It was this universal dominant caste with pan-Aryan identity that wanted the country to be liberal. It was they who wanted Narasimha Rao to open up the economy. It was ultimately they who appropriated the opportunities created in the economy. The small conglomerations of regional entities became pygmies or *Balis* once the *Virat* or Brahmin capitalist with his 1,000 faces and hands came on to the horizon. They have started surrendering to the Brahmin one after the other to seek refuge in him. Vaishyas being the traditional trading community have been co-opted into the new corporate-Hindutva alliance and started 'shock and awe' to capture economic power.[9]

## Caste as an Oppressive Force

Race is used in the West, particularly in the USA, to intensify discrimination and segregation. This is done not on the premise of social and psychological advantages. It is perpetuated according to P. A. Baran and P. M. Sweezy[9] to gain economic advantages in the capitalist America. Baran and Sweezy have listed five economic interests in the existence of Negro sub-proletariat.

1. Employers benefit from divisions in the labour force which enable them to play one group off against another, thus weakening all.
2. Owners of ghetto real estate are able to overcrowd and overcharge.
3. Middle- and upper-income groups benefit from having at their disposal a large supply of cheap domestic labour.
4. Many small marginal businesses, especially in the service trade, can operate profitably only if cheap labour is available to them, and
5. White workers benefit by being protected from Negro competition for the more desirable and higher paying jobs.

The situation in India is not different from what has happened in the USA. Here the Dalits take the role of Negros. Interestingly, India entered the liberal capitalist frame in the 1990s to perpetuate the differences between *Dvijas* and Dalits. The rulers in 1990 realized that the feudal system was not giving economic benefit as the influence of power was limited largely to social sphere. Therefore, the economy was linked to the international market and the market forces are brought in to develop several agencies to exercise economic power. It is the capitalist MOP that perpetuated the CMOP in India without any serious problems of adjustment. K. S. Chalam noted this phenomenon in the 1992 and has provided empirical evidence in 2017 to substantiate his argument.[10]

## Caste as a Source of Economic Power

Caste has been used as a source of social and economic power ever since it was discovered in the Indian soil. The *Dvija* castes have used caste as property of the group of people who inherit a particular caste by birth. The *Dvija* caste power per se as domination is exercised through social action. The social action in India is implemented through the operation of upper caste cleavages. These cleavages have been in existence in India as they do in the English society (mentioned elsewhere) in a subtle manner before 1990. It is a known fact that all public sector undertakings, particularly the powerful banking sector, is under the control of 'Brahmin power'. It is difficult to explain how the financial institutions used by an ordinary person, such as Harshad Mehta, to the extent of thousands of crores of rupees remained unpunished for a long time.[11] Why is it that civil servants in the administrative cadre, belonging to lower castes, such as SCs and STs, are punished some allege, for smaller offences?

The NEP has provided opportunities to the upper castes to consolidate their social and economic power by deals and mergers. The public money in the form of forced savings of the middle castes and Dalits is being diverted to private individuals belonging to upper castes in the name of disinvestment. The recent publication of 100 rich persons in India by an agency does not contain even a single person belonging to Dalits. The emergence of upper caste multi-caste corporations (MCC) in metropolitan centres in the area of financial companies, agri-business and other sectors are providing unlimited opportunities only to the *Dvija* castes and similar opportunities are denied to Dalits and Adivasis. The issue of merit became a smoke screen to deny opportunities to *bahujans*. This is happening because of the fact that caste has re-emerged as a powerful economic weapon after the NEP. It is systematically planned to leave the urban service sector and the unremunerative traditional agriculture to the Dalits and artisan castes and capture all the coveted investments by the upper castes. Even the UPA I 'telecom scam' is a pointer to indicate the exercise of power by upper castes in India. It is not strange to find the reasons how upper caste investors emerge as billionaires overnight without any initial investment while similar opportunities are not available for equally qualified and talented Dalits and *bahujans*. This difference in opportunities and market efficiency is to be found not in the abilities of the persons but their social background of belonging to different castes. The present economic policies of all the political parties as mentioned in their election manifestos clearly indicate that they are interested in market efficiency through privatization. The policies will definitely provide opportunities to Dalits and others not in the primary and secondary sectors of the economy, but in the tertiary sector, particularly in the service sector. The traditional caste system provided space for the non-*Dvijas*, particularly Dalits and service castes (who are supposed), to serve the *Dvijas*.

Now the space created by service sector will be filled by the Dalits and BCs. In other words, the *varnashrama dharma* will be recreated in the 21st century where 90 per cent of the population should serve around 10 per cent of *Dvijas* (more detail is given in Chapters 6 and 7).

## Notes

1. K. J. Garbraith, *American Capitalism: The concept of Countervailing Power* (Boston, MA: Houghton Mifflin, 1952).
2. J. Pen, *The Wage Rate under Collective Bargaining* (Cambridge, MA: Harvard University Press, 1959), 91–105.
3. J. Pen, 'Bilateral Monopoly, Bargaining and the Concept of Economic Power', in *Power in Economics*, ed. K. W. Rothschild (Halmondsworth: Penguin Books, 1979), 110.
4. R. K. Hazari, *Industrial Planning and Licensing Policy* (New Delhi: Government of India, 1967).
5. Wiser William Henricks, *The Hindi Jajmani System* (Lucknow: The Lucknow Publishing House, 1936).

6. C. S. Wison and T. Lupton, 'The Social Background of Top Decision Makers', In *Power in Economics*, ed. K. W. Rothschild (Halmondsworth: Penguin Books, 1979).
7. Hazari report noted how the select few Industrial houses captured the investments in priority sectors and all of them belong to either Bania or Brahmin caste.
8. Prabat Patnaik, 'Decoding the Corporate Hindutva Alliance', *The Hindu*, 3 October 2019.
9. P. A. Baran and P. M. Sweezy 'The Socio-Economic Background of the Negro Question', in *Power in Economics*, ed. Rothschild (Harmondsworth: Penguin Books, 1971).
10. K. S. Chalam, *Economic Reforms and Missing Safety Nets* (Mumbai: Vikas Addyankendra, 1999).
11. Pravin Palande, *Economic Milestone: Stock Market Scam, 1992* (India: Forbes, 20 August 2011).

# 4

# Inequity in the Development of Human Capital in India

Education and Schooling are two different concepts that are alien to the social life of lower castes for a long time. It was only during the British India, government schools were thrown open to all.[1] Education being a component of the concept of human capital is as old as the discipline of political economy.[2] It is a common knowledge of every parent that children with more education earn higher incomes than those who have less education. But it was Adam Smith, the father of political economy, who discussed about the economic behaviour of an educated man in his 'Wealth of Nations'.[3] He has said that 'a man educated at the expense of much labour and time to any of those employments which require extraordinary dexterity and skill, may be compared to one of those expensive machines. The amount earned through work which he learns to perform must be expected over and above the usual wages of common labours that will replace to him the whole expenses of his education with at least the ordinary profit of an equally valuable capital'.[4] Though scholars in economic discipline date the concept implicitly to Sir William Petty,[5] it was, however, Adam Smith who had explicitly explained the economic value of education. Alfred Marshall[6] who was familiar with the definition of capital of Irving Fisher, 'as simply any stock at any given point of time that yields a stream of services whose value is calculated by capitalizing the income flow',[7] did mention about economic value of education in the first edition of his 'Principles'. But later, he dropped the idea, thinking that the individual is his own inalienable property in a non-slave society and, therefore, cannot be compared with a machine. It is, however, realized that human beings cannot be treated as produced means of production in the full sense that capital goods are considered. Because a non-slave society prohibits people from contracting to deliver their future services, 'free' people must keep their human wealth tied up in the form of labour services and cannot hedge against unforeseen changes in the future demand for their services.[8] But, the situation has undergone a change in the hands of neoclassical economists, such as T. W. Schultz, the noble laureate. The concept is further strengthened with the indulgence of modern economics and management experts who consider 'human beings' as experts and skilled personnel and can be traded in the market in the name of body shopping, franchise players and so on.

Thomas Piketty in his *Capital in the Twenty-first Century* argued against the concept of human capital as, attributing a monetary value to the stock of human capital makes sense only in society which it is actually possible to own other individuals fully and entirely.[9] It is exactly for this reason Marshall dropped the idea in the later edition of his 'Principles'. However, Piketty has attributed other reasons as well since the concept does not explain inequality in the USA after 1980. He was of the opinion that 'if the supply of skills does not increase at the same space as the needs of technology then groups whose training is not sufficiently advanced will earn less'. But some scholars with Marxist persuasion did not agree with Piketty for assuming some neoclassical assumptions like full employment and his assumptions of capital investment in each country and so on.[10] However, Prabhat Patnaik agreed with the diagnosis of the capitalist system that created and widened inequalities. Daniel Kuehn[11] and Murphy and Topel[12] have contended that even if we use human capital as distinguished from that of labour the inequalities can be measured. Thus, the theory of human capital that gave birth to the popular human development Index (HDI) and the United Nations Organization (UNO) reports has provided sufficient ground that the provision of the constituents of human capital including education that takes a share of two-thirds of its weight in HDI is very important for development. We have noted the reservations and limitations of the concept of human capital expressed by scholars above. However, the fact remains that it is an important concept to reckon with to understand the historically deprived castes who were structurally denied access to it. Denial of education, particularly formal schooling to a select few based on their birth, is crucial to understand how systematic the CMOP in India was. We have selected education here to substantiate our argument to understand the unique character of education. Education is considered as an important item of investment that leads to both consumption expenditure and investment benefits simultaneously. The investor gets consumption benefit in the form of psychic income. At the same time, it provides investment return through a stream of life-long earnings. It is to be noted that the consumption and investment effects of education are inseparable, and investors are invariably conditioned by social, cultural and other factors. However, T. W. Schultz[13] has observed that the consumption element in education in modern times seems to be of minor importance and the future consumption element is consistent with an investment view of education. It was T.W. Schultz again who made an attempt to link the concepts of physical capital and human capital in his study on 'Investment in Human Capital'. He is regarded as the pioneer of the theoretical study with his estimate of stock of human capital in the USA for 1900 and 1957 and its overall contribution to growth. There are several such studies on every country today linking education, as one of the important investments in human capital, to economic growth, measured in gross domestic product (GDP).

## Human Capital and Human Development

The concept of human development evolved in 1990 by the United Nations Development Programme (UNDP) is different from human capital. The concept is defined as, 'the process of enlarging the range of people's choices, increasing their opportunities for education, health care and income and employment and covering the full range of human choices from sound physical environment to economic and political freedom'.[14] Human development is used as an alternative measure of GDP to measure development. It is the end of human capital, while human capital is a means to achieve human development. Concepts such as social capital, finance capital and cultural capital are being used by social scientists to convey the stream of benefits that one gets once these are acquired. It seems the concept of social capital is being used to explain the caste networks of social relations which are characterized by norms of trust and reciprocity that lead to outcomes of mutual benefit in India. It is more pronounced in India after liberalization particularly among the *Dvija* castes.

## Human Capital Formation

T. W. Schultz in his presidential address to the American Economic Association in 1961 identified five major categories as investment in human capital.[15] They are (a) health facilities and services broadly conceived to include all expenditures that affect life expectancy, strength and stamina, and vigour and vanity of people; (b) on-the-job training, including old style apprenticeship, organized by firms; (c) formally organized education at elementary, secondary and higher levels; (d) study programmes for adults that are organized by firms, including extension programmes, notably in agriculture; and (e) migration of individuals and families to adjust to changing job opportunities. Gary Becker, who has produced a monograph on 'Economics of Discrimination',[16] in 1957 constructed a general theory of investment in human capital based on conventional neoclassical capital theory. He has provided the methods to calculate costs of education and training and the total returns as the present value of the income differentials occurring in each period during the active life of workers in the relevant occupation. He has concluded in his study that the increased supply of skills in the USA during the past century was induced by higher returns to education. He has developed the theory under the neoclassical assumptions of perfect competition, marginal 'product equals wage at equilibrium', technical progress as neutral and so on. The empirical studies have so far provided four important measures of human capital. They are all related to education.

The measures of human capital are (a) The number of school years adjusted for a length of year. It is also necessary to adjust the content, structure and type of education, (b) the productivity of earnings of appropriate members of the labour force with weight for years of schooling, (c) the present value of the expected lifetime income yield of education, and (d) the costs of education measured with base year prices, including the earnings forgone or opportunity cost. The stock of human capital can be estimated by using any one of the measurements. (e) There are several limitations in the measurement of human capital. The difficulties pointed out by Professor Joan Robinson[17] with reference to the measurement of physical capital are equally applicable to the concept of human capital. However, economics by now have accepted the above measures as a useful tool to estimate the stock or flow of human capital in terms of educations and training provided in a country. The stock of human capital is measured on the basis of data on the education already attained by people during a period of time, while enrolments at different levels of education are considered as a flow of human capital. There are several issues involved in the measurement of these concepts as pointed out by scholars like Sen,[18] Bowman,[19] Scaffer[20] and others. It can be seen from the survey of literature on the concept of human capital that investment in duration and training is given primacy over other aspects of investment in people. Therefore, human capital is broadly equated with education, though expenditure on health and migration would equally contribute to the flow or stock of human capital. Education is broadly defined as formal or informal schooling, including time spent on research, extension and other activities of higher education.

## The Stock of Human Capital in India

There are various studies available on the measurement of stock of human capital in India. The study conducted by a young European scholar on the stock of human capital and economic growth in Japan, Indonesia and India for the period 1890–2000 is fascinating.[21] It is found that the value of stock of human capital in India was $81.64 billion US dollars in 1890 compared to $2.4 billion in Indonesia. In 1895, Japan had a stock of human capital of $120.8 billion compared to India with $84.1 billion, a difference of around $40 billion. By the time India attained its independence in 1947, Japan had a value of $2,090.8 billions while India had only $224.5 billion. It is found that the increase in the stock of human capital between 1895 and 1947 was 166.9 per cent in India while it was 1630.7 per cent in Japan. The value of the stock was doubled in Japan with $4,805 billion between 1947 and 1980 while it was a five-time increase in India ($1,037 billion) during the same period. The stock of human capital was found to be $8,641 billion in 2000 in Japan while it was $2,064 billion in India.

Economists have established that the rate of growth of an economy is related to the availability of human capital in a country. Therefore, the rate of economic growth of India and Japan are found to be very diverse as were their stock of human capital. It is very interesting to see that India had invested heavily on education, during the post-independence period up to 1980 when education, including higher education, research and training, in the quality institutions was subsidized by the state.[22] This is the period in which the elite of the country were educated at the cost of ignorant masses, particularly those who have not seen the doors of higher education.[23] The policy of education in India seems to be lopsided and prejudiced against some groups and heavily inclined towards few. It is here that we can reflect whether education was universal from the beginning of the East India Company rule in India or parochial from the beginning? What is the modernist project of the British? Whether the criticism that Lord Macaulay system of education had replaced indigenous education is misplaced or genuine? What has happened to the policy of education that made only 16 per cent of the population literate by the time we attained independence? What is the social base of the underdevelopment of education of certain social groups who have remained poor, ignorant and disadvantaged? A brief account of the history of our educational policy will throw light on the problem.

## A Brief History of Educational Policy

There are several scholarly studies on the history of education in India emphasizing that the modernist project in education was ushered in through the so-called Anglican or English education.[24] But only a few of these studies have indicated that education was available to all castes or social groups during different periods of Indian history. Except the 'beautiful tree' of Dharmpal[25] that recount the spread of universal education in the 18th century, no study has supported the argument that education was universal in pre-British India. It is strange that no critical study on the educational policy of ancient period particularly with reference to Buddhist principles of equality of access to *viharas* and the Muslim education of Madarasas for common folk vis-à-vis the unlettered classes or castes has been made available. Though the study of Radhakumud Mookerji[26] mentioned about the availability of knowledge of Samkhya and non-Vedic agamas to all castes and women, it was based on evidences from scriptures and studies of scholars, such as A. B. Keith.[27] They are not based on historical data. According to the travelogues of Hiuen Tsang[28] and I-Tsing,[29] admission into university education was based on entrance examination of high standard. It was secular education and, therefore, no distinction of caste was observed at Nalanda. We have evidences from medieval period that great saint poets, such as Ravidas,[30] Kabir,[31] Thukaram,[32] Vemana[33] and others from lower castes, have composed great libertarian poetry. They were all literate emancipators and educators.[34] Then, why the literacy rates of non-Brahmins, particularly the so-called SCs and backwards, were found to be low during the British period and thereafter?

The educational policy of the East India Company was primarily aimed to educate Indians in English to be interpreters between the company and the people they governed. This created a modern educated class. But social reformers like Jyotirao Phule[35] had to contest this policy before the Hunter Commission in 1882 as it was not made democratic.[36] He was the first leader in modern India who demanded universal primary education. The British India government had tried some changes thereafter. But the re-organized education had neither destroyed the oriental learning nor provided a restrictive curriculum for the elite particularly in the colleges and institutes of higher learning sponsored by them. The curriculum and syllabus used in most of the colleges during the period consisted of both the traditional Vedic education and English education that was prevalent in contemporary England. Several leaders and scholars, including Ram Mohan Roy,[37] Gandhi,[38] Nehru,[39] B. R. Ambedkar[40], S. Chandrasekhar,[41] Jagdish Chandra Bose,[42] C. V. Raman,[43] Tagore,[44] Meghnad Saha[45] and several scientists, were trained by them. It was this system that has produced the first three Indian noble laureates. Interestingly, some scholars while appreciating the liberal education of the British critiqued it by saying that it was introduced to exploit India[46]. If that was so, why the policies and reforms that were attempted by the government after independence have not substantially overhauled the system? The state has invested in public higher education at the cost of primary and secondary education. It is clear from the allocation of funds for different levels of education during the plan period 1951–2010.[47] This is also reflected in the estimates of stock of human capital noted above.

## National Policy of Education

The major concern of the post-independence period was to rebuild India. The University Education Commission (1948–1949)[48], the Secondary Education Commission (1952–1953)[49] and the Kothari Commission (1964–1966)[50] made several recommendations to realize the socialistic pattern of society. A national policy of education was declared in 1968. The policy has deliberately proclaimed that it was for national development. The first sentence of the report had emphasized that the future of India would be shaped in the classrooms. The commission spoke about free and compulsory education, equalization of educational opportunity, common school, science education and research, education for agriculture and industry, establishment of new universities with adequate funds, education of the minorities, distance (correspondence) education, examination reforms and above all a new educational structure of 10 + 2 + 3. This was for the first time a comprehensive review of education from nursery to university research covering almost every aspect of education was made. The commission has utilized the services of great educationists of the time involving both American and Russian experts. It was in this report a progressive direction of investing 6 per cent of GDP on public education was made. The commission report was extensively debated in all forums throughout the country. Intriguingly, it is still being debated indicating how the sage advice of the commission was trivialized.

The emergence of the 21st century was considered by all developed societies as an opportunity to reform their existing systems of education. India has also reflected and introduced the challenge of education in 1986.[51] A programme of action based on the recommendations of the 1986 policy was formulated. Thereafter, two review committees headed by Acharya Ram Murty[52] and N. Janardhana Reddy[53] made about 100 suggestions for implementation. The 1986 policy document, in fact, has honestly looked at every weakness of our system and made comprehensive recommendations for a technological society. The recommendations and advice of the committees were kept aside while the Ambani and Birla committee[54] was made to recommend privatization of Higher Education in 2000. A knowledge commission was appointed under the chairmanship of a technocrat Sam Pitroda in 2006[55] to make recommendations to reform higher education for a knowledge-based economy. The planning commission has incorporated in its Eleventh Five-Year Plan some programmes for an inclusive education. Finally, the Right to Education Act was passed in 2009. The implementation of the Act will have far-reaching consequences for massification of higher education in future. Thus, the national policies of education in India have a long list of expert advice almost on every aspect of education during the post-independence period. Therefore, we cannot say that there was no intention or policy to reform education in India. They are always available in print.

## Westernization of Higher Education

Sociologists have developed the concepts of modernization, Westernization and even Sanskritization to describe how the Indian society has undergone the process of change. Srinivas[56] has brought in the concept of Westernization in 1962. It was noted by him that English as a medium of instruction and opening of schools to all with the secular orientation of education among other things has brought Westernization. He has elaborated the concepts of Westernization and Sanskritization as opposite notions in understanding the process of social change. The concepts can be applied to education. But, the system of higher education that was prevalent during the East India Company, after independence in 1968 or 1986 or 2010 has almost remained the same. In fact, the use of English as a medium of education and the clamour for American slang is widened today than ever before. A number of courses, such as business management, fashion technology, soft skills, Information Communication Technology (ICT) and other courses that are popular and in great demand in the USA, Australia and other English-speaking countries were introduced not only in the private sector and in non-formal educational institutions, but even in university departments and in deemed universities.[57] A cursory look at the courses designed by the deemed universities and private institutes and the twining programmes of Western universities with Indian institutes clearly indicate the deep involvement of Indian higher education with American sentiment. The state has remained helpless spectator if not a facilitator. The issue is how these reforms or developments are taking place in education if there is already a national policy? Do the above-mentioned developments and the declared and undeclared policies that are forthcoming correspond with Indian ethos or Western sentiment or a continuation of the East India Company project of modernization? Those who are interested in Indian education or at least indigenization of education have ever tried to change the trend? It appears that all those who are benefited by the system either in the past or in its present form have facilitated it to continue while debating vociferously against it. The elite and the governing classes or social groups who are benefited by English education have perhaps taken the education to its logical end-Westernization? Why do the disadvantaged groups, such as Adivasis, Dalits and service castes have still remained outside the system of higher education, particularly in the quality institutes, established in the private sector? Why has the disparity between Adivasis, Dalits and the *Dvijas* remained the same? What is the role of judiciary in facilitating social justice in education? These are some of the questions that need to be addressed in light of the theories of social justice.

## Disparities and Divides

The development of education in India over the years is closely associated with the structure of society. The inequitable instinct is manifested here. India was literate to the extent of 10 per cent in 1931, of which the literacy rates for SCs and tribes were only 1.9 per cent and 0.7 per cent, respectively.[58] The disparity between SCs, tribes, service castes and others has remained the same in terms of literacy rates. The gap is much wider if the enrolment rates in quality institutes are considered. The disparity has increased during the last one decade due to the emergence of private sector where the so-called reserved categories do not have access. The policymakers have been emphasizing on the creation of equality of opportunity in education, a term seems to have been derived from the American experience to bridge the gap. It is pointed out by scholars that the concept of equality of opportunity is possible within a stratification that has high degree of inequality with a tall and narrow pyramid of society. But India has a graded social inequality and it is structurally built into the caste system. Further, the term opportunity contains a grain of colonial arrogance as if someone is providing a chance to some other to gain entry into education even though they do not deserve it. The American experience is related to settlers and natives. Therefore, the educational opportunities were created there to reduce the racial inequalities between African Americans and whites. Thus, their entry into education is not a right may be charity.

Though, the educational differences have slowly declined due to the opportunities created, the class inequalities have continued to exist and have in fact raised the so-called status anxiety. It is pointed out by scholars, such as Murray Milner Jr[59] that it is through redistribution of wealth and income rather than through equality of opportunity in education that inequalities can be reduced. It is an illusion to reduce inequalities through education. On the other hand, the distribution of income would sufficiently create equality of opportunity in education and eliminate inequalities both in education and income. It is established by research studies both in the USA and India that the educational performance of students is broadly influenced by the prestige of the college and the socio-economic status of the students. Therefore, the so-called merit is not just based on the numerical marks obtained in an examination, but due to a host of other contributing factors that need to be taken into consideration in judging the worth of a candidate.[60]

The concepts of merit and efficiency have a historical context. I think they are not timeless concepts. Some of the present-day business houses were considered inferior to the English or European corporations before independence. They were provided with state support and protection in the initial period to achieve the present commanding heights in their own fields. In fact, the strategy of planning adopted in India has transformed several feudal lords into capitalists. This has facilitated the abolition of *varna* category at least among the *Dvijas* to transform them as upper classes. It is made possible by providing opportunities to utilize their capital, both physical and human. The state support for education and subsidies for industry helped them to emerge as great economic players over a period of five decades.[61] But this did not percolate down to lower castes and they have remained as castes both in rural and urban areas. This is recognized by the planning commission through the identification of the social divides in the Eleventh Five-Year Plan.[62] In fact, the divides are so flagrant that it is the creamy layer in each caste, particularly among the *Dvija* castes, that are stonkingly benefitted by the state policies. The recent media reports about the Wealth of the top 100 or 500 billionaires or the occasional outbursts of scams in the parliament show the inequality of distribution of opportunities.[63] This has once again shown that equality of opportunity is an illusion. The concept may be useful to employ it as an ideological smokescreen, but may not help reduce inequalities. In other words, Matsyanyaya is in operation in modern India. Is it in harmony with the social justice rhetoric of a democratic state?

There are several studies to prove that the rate of return on higher education from Adivasis and Dalits are higher than that of other categories due to minimum opportunity cost of education. Naturally, the returns, particularly the social returns from education of the reservation groups, will be maximized, if the limited opportunity is given to them; of course, the institutions will take care of remedial measures to bring them on par with their peers. This is fait accompli in rate of return studies on education.[64] The principle should guide the educational policy of the government in the formation of human capital in India. Education and training are the important sources or means through which a person can enter into an organized service in a modern society. In fact, education is essential for survival. The history of education in India has shown that some social groups have remained outside the formal system and, therefore, persisted for ages as underdeveloped. It is necessary that they are brought into the mainstream. But social litigation has prevented the state to formulate radical policies of reform. We have scrutinized (Chapter 8) some relevant theories of justice to be adopted by the state so as to help in formulating a sound social policy.

## Democratization of Education and Derision of Knowledge

The social philosophy of India in the past and its continuation in different guises today consist of several dichotomies. One of the blatant dichotomies can be seen in the government policy on education. It is a known fact that the non-*Dvijas* were denied not only formal education and even access to *dharmashastra* in the past. In the modern period, it was Jyotirao Phuley who fought with the East India Company to provide access to schooling to *Shudras* and *Atishudras* (Dalits) through his memorandum to Hunter Commission in 1882. We have noted from the previous section the history of struggle for democratization of education in India that became a right only in 2010. The ruling castes, if not the political class, are intelligent enough to enact laws to satisfy the anxious low-caste groups and work quite opposite to nullify the results to maintain a status on. This is visible in the educational policies of the union and state governments except states, such as Kerala. Even in Kerala and West Bengal, scholars have pointed out the 'systematic exclusion'[65] of lower castes in educational pursuits.[66,67] Studies undertaken by Chalam have established that the process of inequality continues in education at all levels, particularly in quality higher educational institutions. But the data collected by government sources show that the social gap is being reduced between lower castes and others. This is the real dichotomy in education. In order to satisfy the constitutional and social obligations, enrolments and retention through non-detention system are obtained. The Association for the Study of Higher Education (ASHE) Report indicates that the GRE is 25.8 per cent for general and almost the same for SC, ST and others.[163] Interestingly, 11 per cent of the enrolment or nearly 42 per cent are in distance education mode. The quality of education and the knowledge base of the students from these institutes is miserable with few exceptions. Kanti Bajpai[68] noted that the language and mathematical skills are tragic as half of our class 5th students can read text of class 2 and 40 per cent students in class 8 can do long division. Most of the reservation category students who are pushed into government colleges get the BTech, BA and even PhD degrees, but the knowledge base as seen from their test scores of public examinations is appalling as the institutes in which they study are in need of trained teachers, infrastructure and a systematic teaching–learning process which the governments do not wish to improve. It means that they satisfy the constitutional obligation of providing places in educational institutional, but do not care to improve the knowledge base. The dropout and pushout rates at higher educational institutions, such as the Indian Institute of Technology (IIT), the Indian Institutes of Management (IIMS) for Dalit, Adivasis and other socially marginalized sections, speak for itself as several young boys and girls committed suicide.[69]

## Notes

1. Government of India, *Compilation on 50 Years of Indian Education 1947–1997* (New Delhi: Ministry of Human Resources Development, 1947). http://www.nic.in
2. M. Blaug, *An Introduction to Economic of Education* (New York: Penguin, 1976).
3. Adam Smith, *An Enquiry with the Nature and Causes of Wealth of Nation*, ed. Edward Cannan (London: Methuen & Co., 1904).
4. Ibid.
5. William Petty, *Essay Concerning the Multiplication of Mankind*, 2nd ed. (1698).

6. A. Marshall, *Principles of Economics*, vol. 1, ed. Sh. Guillebaud (London: Macmillan, 1906).
7. I. Fisher, *The Nature of Capital and Income* (MacMillon, 1906).
8. Blaug, *Introduction to Economic of Education*.
9. Thomas Piketty, *Capital in the Twenty-First Century* (Cambridge, MA: Harvard University, 2014), 163.
10. Prabhat Patnaik, 'Capitalism, Inequality and Globalization: Thomas Piketty's Capital in the Twenty-First Century', *Marxist*, April–June 2014.
11. Daniel Kuen, 'Human Capital in the Twenty First Century', *European Journal of Comparative Economics* 15 (2018): 3–9.
12. Kevin M. Murphy and Robert H. Topel, 'Human Capital Investment and Economic Growth', *Journal of Labour Economics* 34, no. S2 (February 2016): S99–S127.
13. T. W. Schultz, 'Investment in Human Capital', *American Economic Review* 21 (1961): 4.
14. UNDP, *Human Development Report, 1990* (New York: Oxford University Press, 1991).
15. UNDP, 1990.
16. Becker Gary, *The Economic of Discrimination* (Chicago, IL: The University of Chicago Press, 1957).
17. Joan Robinson, *The Accumulation of Capital* (London: Macmillan, 1956).
18. A. K. Seth, 'Economic Approaches to Education and Manpower Planning', *Indian Economic Review* (April 1966).
19. Mans T. Bronar, 'Human Capital: Concepts and Measure', in *The Economics of Higher Education*, ed. Selma J. Muslins (Washington, 1962).
20. H. G. Schoffer, 'Investment in Human Capital: Confute', *American Economic Review* L11, no. 4 (1961).
21. Bas Leevwen Van, 'The Role of Human Capital in Endogenous Growth in India, Indonesia and Japan, 1890–2000', International Economic History Conference, Helsinki, August 2006.
22. K. S. Chalam, *Introduction to Educational Planning and Management* (New Delhi: Anmol, 2004).
23. Chalam, *Education and Weaker Sections*.
24. K. S. Chalam, *Modernisation and Dalit Education: Ambedkar's Vision* (Jaipur: Rawat, 2008).

25. A. Dharampal, *The Beautiful Tree: Indigenous India Education in Eighteenth Century* (New Delhi: Biblia Impex, 1983).
26. Radhakumud Mookerj, *Ancient India Education: Brahminical and Buddhist* (Delhi: Motilal Banarsidass, 1989).
27. A. B. Keith, *The Religion and Philosophy of the Vedas and Upanishads: A History of Sanskrit Literature*, 2 vol. (New Delhi: Moti Lal Banarasidas, 1924).
28. Huen Tsang, a Chinese scholar came to study Buddhism in India in 633 AD.
29. I-Tsing, a Chinese Buddhist who lived in India during 671–695 AD.
30. Ravidas was a 15th-century mystic of the Bhakti movement from North India. He was from a poor shoemaker family.
31. Kabir harmonized Hindu and Muslim philosophies and was a predecessor of Guru Nanak. He belonged to 1440–1518. He was a low-caste mystic.
32. Thukaram, a prominent Marathi sant who contributed 4,500 abhangs. He belonged to the period 1577–1650.
33. Vermana belonged to the 14th-century Andhra. He composed poetry in simple language with satire on the existing social system and norms.
34. Gail Omvedt, *Seeking Begumpura Navayana* (New Delhi: Navayana Publishers, 2008).
35. Phooley Jyoti Rao, *Gulamgiri*, trans. N. D. Phadke (Mumbai: Government of Maharashtra, 1999).
36. Government of India, Hunter Commission, 1882. http://www.education.nic.in
37. Ram Mohan Roy was the leader of social reforms in India. He promoted English education.
38. M. K. Gandhi, Mahatma and father of India, brought freedom from the colonial rule.
39. Jawaharlal Nehru, the first prime minister of India, a modernist and true scholar.
40. B. R. Ambedkar, finally was called the father of the nation by the people of India and Dalits, a constitution maker (as per a survey conducted by a TV channel).
41. S. Chandrasekhar, a Noble laureate in physics.
42. Jagdish Chandra Bose, a scientist, the father of radio science and plant research in India.
43. C. V. Raman, a Noble laureate.

44. Rabindranath Tagore, a great poet and the first Noble laureate of India.
45. Meghnad Saha, a great scientist who started the Indian science movement.
46. Bipin Chandra, *Modern India* (New Delhi: NCERT, 1980).
47. Chalam, *Educational Planning*.
48. S. Radhakrishnan, The University Education Commission. www.education.nic.in
49. Government of India, Secondary Education Commission. www.education.nic.in
50. Government of India, 'Kothari Commission Report, 1968'. www.education.nic.in
51. Government of India, 'Challenge of Education, 1986'. www.education.in
52. Government of India, 'Acharya Rammurty Committee Report'. www.education.nic.in
53. Government of India, 'N. Janardhana Reddy Committee Report'. www.education.nic.in
54. Government of India, 'Ambani and Birla Report on Education'. www.education.nic.in
55. Government of India, Knowledge Commission. www.education.nic.in
56. M. N. Srinivas, *Caste in Modern India* (Bombay: Asia Publishing House, 1962).
57. The Ministry of HRD has abolished the grant of deemed university status to more than 45 institutes on the ground that they have not been able to fulfil the standards and norms as prescribed by University Grants Commission (UGC).
58. Government of India, Education in India. www.education.nic.in
59. Murray Milner Jr., *The Illusion of Equality: The Effects of Education Opportunity on Inequality* (Sanfransico, CA: Jossey Bass, 1972).
60. The SAT scores in the USA are being commented as the smokescreen to eliminate the poor and the underprivileged blacks and other minorities to enter into higher education.
61. U. Tataji, ed., *Fifty Years of Planned Development in India* (Visakhapatnam: Andhra University Press, 2005).
62. Government of India, *Eleventh Five Year Plan: Inclusive Growth* (Delhi: Planning Commission, 2010).

63. *The Times of India* has published a series of scams during the budget session of parliament in 2010.
64. Smrutirekha Sinshari and S. Maheswaram, 'The Changing Rates of Return to Education in India: Evidence, from NSS data', Institute for Social and Economic Change, Bangalore, 2016 paper 538.
65. 'Systematic Exclusion: Why Kerala's School and Colleges Have Few Dalit Teachers', *Scroll in* 5 October 2019.
66. Geetha B. Nambissan, 'Equality in Education: Schooling of Dalit Children in India', *Economic and Political Weekly* 3, no. 10/17 (1996): 1011–1024.
67. Government of India, *All India Survey of Higher Education*, 2017–2018 (Delhi: GOI, 2018).
68. Kanti Bajpai, 'Educating for Growth', *The Times of India*, 5 October 2019.
69. Abhinav Malhotra, 'Dalit Student Commits Suicide at IIT Kapur Hostel Room', *The Times of India*, 18 April 2018.

# 5

# Economic Deprivation and Social Exclusion of Marginalized Castes

Caste in India is a multidimensional category not easily amenable to a single disciplinary knowledge. It has been in existence for several centuries with ups and downs for different castes with a steady growth only for the *Dvijas*. The *Dvija* project is in supreme command of the social and economic dimensions of the country now and, therefore, is in the saddle of political power. But, majority of the castes particularly the ex-untouchables or adi-Hindus/adi-dharmi, service castes and the converts from these castes to Islam and Christianity are still on the margins of the society with crony capitalism co-opting groups that subscribe to Manu philosophy of graded inequality. It is now found that the Manu ideology and the Capitalist ideology are in sink without any contradictions as both believe in the merit of inequality and discrimination. We are going to examine here how this has affected the living conditions of the most marginalized social group, fisher folk who are still in the stage of food gathering with mechanization and capitalist entrenchment in deep sea fishing.

## Caste as a Source of Deprivation

Caste is considered by a section of scholars as a social category at the most as a class without defining the boundaries of each caste or class. The use of terms likes 'class in itself' and 'class for itself' may not directly guide our understanding of caste through economic scrutiny. Therefore, caste is to be considered as an MOP where the economic significance of each vocational caste, their skills, the unchangeableness of the skill (as used by Marx in Vol. I) would help us to ponder over why certain castes remain backward while few others flourish irrespective of the type of economy and society in which they function. Though we have around 5,000 castes that have become mutually exclusive due to the tyranny of 'Manu Dharma' reinforced by successive *Dvija* regimes, the economic status of the so-called Dalits, ex-untouchables, service castes and artisans, which is categorized and called with different names, had remained backward.

Caste is being used as a source of exploitation as each caste in the social and economic system, particularly in the rural and semi-urban areas, carry a rank and value. The caste system, including its original version of *varna*, is so rigid that any subversion is dealt with severe penalty including death. One may mention cases of how *Shudras* changing ranks or some lower castes crossing boundaries with state support, but the proportion of such cases is found to be less than 1 per cent and do not have any impact on the annihilation of castes. In fact, there are studies to prove that the social norms have economic basis to keep the value of the *Dvija* high and the lower caste lesser in value not only in social relations, but also in economic transactions (previous chapters). The recent lynching of Dalits, Muslims and lower castes is a significant display of caste (state) power to force them to supply cheap labour and accept the social obligation to serve the upper castes. It is also a harsh warning to them not to enter the leather and beef business of around ₹60,000 crores of exports. The produces of these communities are devalued by labelling them even in a capitalist market with discrimination and violence, often seen to be projected as communal violence. The economic undercurrent in these transactions is disguised in social and cultural stances that need to be deciphered for a proper understanding of economic basis of caste.

The concept of deprivation is being used by social scientists ever since the paradigm of human rights has emerged as an issue of public discourse. Scholars such as John Rawls, Amartya Sen and the constitutional experts, including some enlightened judges of Indian apex court, upheld the view that it is the duty of the state to protect inalienable rights of the citizens for they have surrendered their liberty to the state anticipating protection. Thus, 'human right' is an important constituent of human existence not only in terms of Thomas Paine's elucidation of natural right, but also under the aegis of UNO mandate. Now several independent nations do strive to reach out the people through the paradigm of rights. The development goals prescribed by UNO, including the present sustainable goals, are described within this broad framework. Therefore, the idea of deprivation is necessarily obliged to answer questions of rights. We are concerned here about the economic deprivations meted out to a backward fisher community; an index of deprivation specific to the living conditions of fishermen of North Coast of Andhra Pradesh is developed here.

## Economic Deprivation

Economic deprivation is defined as the lack of sufficient income for people to play roles, participate in the relationships, and take part in the accepted behaviour expected of them by the society. Economic deprivation is a state of income inequality wherein income generated by one individual is not enough to cover his basic needs. It has increased the gap between the rich and the poor, where the rich become richer and the poor become poorer. The economic resources on the coast, including fish, marine underwater resources, mangroves, reefs, and ecology, which the traditional fisher folk used to possess, are now alleged to be denied due to special economic zones (SEZ) and other liberalization policies. This is so because the rich have the financial means to create more wealth, while economically deprived people, on the other hand, barely have enough for subsistence. Peter Townsend[1] has pioneered a relative deprivation approach to poverty that covered a wide range of aspects of living standards, both material and social. For Townsend,[2] individuals, families and groups in the population can be said to be in poverty when they lack the resources to obtain the types of diet, participate in the activities and have the living conditions and amenities which are customary or at least widely encouraged or approved in the societies to which they belong; their resources are so seriously below those commanded by the average individual or family that they are, in effect, excluded from ordinary patterns, customs and activities.

Measures of deprivation are not the same as measures of income—they are related to how people live. Deprivation is the consequence of a lack of income and other resources, which cumulatively can be seen as living in poverty. The relative deprivation approach to poverty examines the indicators of deprivation. Townsend developed a list of 60 indicators of style of living for a survey into standards of living in the UK in 1968/1969, which was later revised.

The lack of or non-participation in the provision of adequate food, clothing recitation, education, health, social relations and environment at home is considered as deprivation. A 'score' for different forms of deprivation could be ascertained and related to household income. Townsend has kept on working on the theme and improved his method of calculating Deprivation Index. We have taken the improved method of calculation of indices used in 2010.

## Indicators of Deprivation for Fisher Folk

We have identified some specific indicators or factors that inhibit fisher folk to actively participate in economic and social interaction in the coastal region. As noted above, we have taken the Rights Approach as a feature that shows how the prevailing situation fails to provide opportunity to the fisher folk to exercise their natural right, such as fishing, in the sea. Fisher folk on the coast are a distinct community and, therefore, we need to identify their immediate problems of existence and identity. Therefore, we have selected the following indicators to estimate the fisher folk multiple deprivation index (FMDI). While accepting some select indicators of Townsend, we have added the following indicators for our study of fisher folk of north coastal Andhra Pradesh.

1. The main source of living is fishing in the sea and their right to do so is well protected by the government. But due to over-exploitation and industrialization on the coast, fishery resources have been dwindled. This has resulted in the fisher folk returning empty-handed after going into the sea, which is a violation of their natural right. It happens not once but several times in a month. We have noticed how many times in a month a fisherman returned empty handed as an indicator of deprivation.
2. The income of the fisher folk depends upon fishing for those who go for fishing and for others who are employed in organized and unorganized sectors. Therefore, per capita income is considered as a factor of deprivation if it is below the poverty line.
3. The government has passed the Right to Education Act, making it compulsory and free education up to the upper primary level of eight years of schooling. Those who do not complete or remain outside of this norm as a percentage of total are considered as deprived of education.

4. Healthcare is an important item of expenditure for the poor particularity fisher folk who live on the coast, away from the mainstream society. It is expected that government would provide facilities, such as hospitals, health centres in their habitations so that the expenditure on healthcare of the family be minimized. We have considered how many patients as proportion of total sufferers are going in for government doctors as an indicator of deprivation from healthcare.

Economic exploitation and deprivation are interrelated. We have taken into consideration the assets held by each household, income from different sources, such as wages, selling of milk, remittances from abroad, rents and income from agriculture. Fishing is a collective effort on the high seas. Even after landing, the boat needs the support of 10 people to anchor it on the shore as it weighs heavy. It is a known fact that a minimum of four males are necessary for fishing in an ordinary boat and if the size is bigger and a high horsepower (HP) motor is used, they may need more people either as partners or wage earners to do fishing. Trawler fishing is different, and we have not come across such owners among the fisher folk in our sample study area. We are providing empirical data culled out from a research study funded by Indian Council of Social Science Research (ICSSR) and conducted by Institute for Economic and Social Justice, Visakhapatnam. The study was undertaken in 3 districts of Srikakulam, Vizianagaram and Visakhapatnam on the coast of Bay of Bengal.

## Average Monthly per Capita Income

Per capita income has been used as a measure to learn about the economic status of a person or family if the income is expressed per household. The average per capita household and per person income in each *mandal* is estimated from the study. There are certain limitations in reading the data as we have estimated the per capita income as an average of the total number of people in each *mandal* and district. It is only an average that may not be directly related to every member of the household, as some members may be getting more than the average while some may be getting less than the average amount. It is noted that the region's average household income per month is ₹8,244, the highest being observed in Srikakulam Mandal and the lowest in Nakkapalli Mandal. The average income brackets of ₹960 and ₹960 to 1,500 are estimated to show that those who get less than this income are either under poverty line or just at the border. Generally, poverty levels are estimated on the basis of expenditure per capita. Experts and government statisticians have been using monthly per capita expenditure (MPCE) as a measure and have been revising the amount at different periods of time, such as ₹25 per capita per day once or ₹32 per capita per day in rural area and ₹47 per capita per day in urban areas on the basis of certain criteria as in 2014. Once the nutritional values of food items have been considered to determine whether a person is above or below a certain per capita some items have been given up and few essential items of expenditure for sustenance, such as gas, electricity, clothes, festivals and alcohol are considered here for fisher folk. Therefore, it is assumed that people who are getting less than ₹920 per capita per month are poor and those who are in the range of ₹920–1500 do experience the same conditions.

## Income from Non-fishing Activities

Fisher folk are now forced to enter into non-fishing activities, as fish resources are dwindling due to over-exploitation. It was noted in the previous sections that the proportion of fisher folk who are going in for fishing is limited to one-third of the population. They are seeking alternative sources of earnings to sustain. Those who are near the urban areas, such as

Pedagantyada Mandal of Visakhapatnam, Srikakulam, are able to get into informal sector, but those who are in the rural areas are getting into other jobs for wages or do petty jobs to earn something. As we have already explained in the previous chapter on occupational shift of the fisher folk, we confine here only to explain the earnings. The data need to be read with caution as the number of households involved in different jobs may not add to the total as the same household may be doing different jobs at the same time as secondary job/occupation. The purpose of the data noted above is to explain how the fishermen are getting different types of income doing non-traditional jobs.

Therefore, the incomes of different categories of jobs do not add up to the average income arrived. An aggregate income show how in each *mandal* incomes of fishermen vary. The present table shows incomes earned by different categories of people doing different jobs. It shows the average earnings of that particular job only.

Fishermen going in for fishing need not necessarily be in their own boats, it can be in others' boats for (a) wage and (b) sharing of catch. It is noted that 14 per cent of the households go in for fishing with their own boats. The average income of the family is estimated at ₹127,074 per annum. The average size of the family is 4 and it comes around ₹31,000 per capita per year. It is found that the highest amount of ₹181,305 income is recorded in Vajrapukotturu of Srikakulam district and the lowest is from Nakkapalli with ₹52,562. Fishermen who are going for wage in others boats is estimated at ₹150,842 and only 61 households or 6.6 per cent are in this category. The highest and lowest in this category is same as the previous one. There are many who go in for fishing as part of a group and they share the catch as per tradition. It is noted that the average income from this is ₹100,598 per annum. The highest and lowest amounts in the region differ widely under this category. It is now possible to compare the average income of a fisherman family, which is higher if he goes for a wage in a boat or ship and is lower if he goes for a sharing method of earnings from his catch. We have noted the earnings of some households from agriculture, rents and so on, but the proportion of households and the income is meagre. The average income from a household going in for services is ₹115,158. The ranks have changed here. Srikakulam Mandal fishermen are getting ₹175,597, the highest and the lowest is from Nakkapalli ₹25,907. About 27 per cent of the households involve in petty business and the average earnings are ₹48,945. Vajrapukotturu again comes first with ₹56,992. It is noticed that fishermen go for jobs or fishing in other areas or countries and send money back home. One hundred and ten households have such people remitting money. The average amount of remittances from outside/abroad is ₹19,290. Vajrapukotturu comes first with ₹18,809 here. The information gathered from the households clearly indicate that it is better for a fisherman to go for wages in a boat/ship rather than do it on his own or share it with others. This also indicates that the fisher folk are slowly disappearing as independent operators with their own boats as fishing is becoming a serious and costly business with new technology and fibre-mechanized boats with costly machines which they cannot afford.

## Average Savings and Income

The data from the households is culled out to estimate the average annual and monthly income and to find out the net disposable income after deducting savings from income. The average yearly income is estimated at ₹96,118 from all sources, and the highest is noted from Srikakulam district. However, the average monthly income is recorded as highest from Srikakulam with ₹10,309 and the lowest with ₹6,692 is found in Pusapatirega. The average savings from among the 635 household or 68 per cent of the household is 6,229. We have also found that the total income from all the households as reported by them comes to ₹89,198,076. Out of which

₹3,955,700 are saved. The savings are being put in banks as deposits by 15 per cent only and the remaining householders are using the savings to buy fishing gear, gold and so on. We have asked about their perception about their economic status based on their income and social standing. It is reported that around 20 per cent consider themselves as very poor and 56 per cent as poor, together making it 76 per cent. Twenty-two per cent of the fisher folk consider themselves as average and only 2 per cent perceive that they are rich. These figures seem to be as close to truth as we see from our expenditure data presented in the next section.

It is reported that 90 per cent of the households have bank accounts, may be due to Jan Dhan scheme. The total savings of the sample households amount to ₹3,433,100 that works out to be ₹4,097 as average savings. Only two households reported that they have invested in shares and the amount is ₹140,000. Four households reported that they have cooperative bank accounts. Interestingly, 17 per cent of households put their money in chit funds. Around 11 per cent have Life Insurance Corporation (LIC) accounts and only 1 person has post office savings; 9 households reported that they go to local pawnbrokers. Interestingly, 81 per cent are members of self-help groups (SHGs) and some NGOs are working among them to popularize the habit of savings and thrift.

## Highly Indebted Fisher Folk

The expenditure habits of people of low socio-economic status in general and the isolated fisher folk in a particular area typical in terms of their ecological conditions are often conditioned by their culture of poverty. After independence, the Reserve Bank of India conducted the first All-India Rural Credit Survey in 1951 to understand the indebtedness and credit needs of the people and found the high incidence of rural indebtedness. The National Sample Survey Office (NSSO) has been conducting surveys on debt and investment occasionally and the latest 70th survey of 2013 indicated the average amount of debt per household. The average value is expressed separately for cultivators and non-cultivators in rural area. It is estimated that the value of debt for cultivators is ₹110,438 and that for non-cultivators is ₹87,938. Further, it is noted that the incidence of debt is 31.4 per cent in rural areas. The data is cited here to show the circumstances of debt among fisher folk in our study region.

The indebtedness of fisher folk in the region and the sources of debt are obtained from the study. We have observed that there are 10 centres of sources of debt for fisher folk. They are (a) institutional loans from commercial banks, (b) rural banks, (c) cooperative banks, (d) Development of women and children in rural areas (DWCRA) or SHG, (e) money lenders or pawnbrokers, (f) traders or fish market brokers, (g) friends and relatives, (h) microfinance and call money dealers, (i) chits and (j) others. Every household of the fisher folk is involved in some kind of engagement with loans or debt. They are considered to be perpetual borrowers in the sense that they keep on borrowing from one source or the other to clear some persistent lender. There can be restriction in a formal institutional lending, such as a bank, but in informal sources, where the interest rate is high, there seems to be no limit.

We have noticed in our study that there is more number of households reporting as debtors than the households indicating that at least 10 per cent of them are repeaters. A total of 63 per cent of the borrowers are from SHG groups followed by 40 per cent borrowers from friends and relatives. Loans taken from banks are limited to 5 per cent and nearly half of that comes from other sources, such as microfinance and brokers. However, the situation seems to have improved due to the presence of some NGOs encouraging SHG, DWCRA and formalizing the channels of repayment and repeat of loan.

The data on outstanding amount of loan (as estimated in the study cited above) show that an amount of ₹141,910 per household is the highest and is from informal source of friends and relatives as estimated in the study cited above. Next comes ₹127,683 from banks and the lowest amount is that from SHG with ₹25,881. There are other sources in between. Similarly, the outstanding amount to be paid to the lenders is found to be maximum amount of ₹267,026 being recorded for banks, followed by ₹128,516 from the category of friends and relatives, and that from others come within these ranges. In other words, the average debt is ₹73,881 and the outstanding loan is ₹62,790. These amounts are close to the all-India averages arrived at by the NSS survey for 2013.

The rates of interest at which they take loans suggest the pressure of their needs to go for a debt. The rate of interest varies from 9 per cent to 72 per cent in the region. Banks charge reasonable rates of interest within 24 per cent. The data show that 2.6 per cent of the debtors take loan at 12 per cent and less than 1 per cent of the household take loan at 24 per cent. The rate of interest is very high if it is from non-institutional sources, such as friends, where 32 per cent of households take loan at 24 per cent and some 13 families' borrowed at above 25 per cent. There is one household in Srikakulam district who has barrowed at 72 per cent interest. We have also culled out information about the reasons that prompted them to borrow. It is noted that 41 per cent reported that they borrowed the money to meet the consumption needs of the family, 15 per cent reported that they borrowed it for business and 13 per cent borrowed for education of children, 10 per cent borrowed to meet health expenditure and only 11 per cent took loans to buy gear and so on for fishing. This is a reflection of the erratic conditions of their habits of savings and expenditure that needs to be further probed to find out solutions for their indebtedness.

We can notice from the data on income, savings, investment and expenditure of fisher folk revealing some inherent mechanism. The fisher folk do not have control over their items of expenditure, particularly the culture specific items, such as festivals, alcohol, menarche, consumption and other conspicuous items, that are not directly related to improve their productivity as fisher folk. The indebtedness show the trend of low-income groups tending to go for loans from whatever source that is available without considering the price, that is, interest on loans that make them bonded borrowers. It is a vicious circle and difficult for certain families to come out of it if they are caught again by natural calamities and forced to become paupers.

## Marketing of Fish by Fisherwomen

Selling of fish in the market, curing and processing are done by fisher folk women. Even if the family is not going for fishing as a primary occupation, fisherwomen go for selling fish, engage in processing and other allied activities either in a formal centre or informally in a nearby fish market. The price of fish is still determined in the traditional form of higgling and bargaining. The popular adage in civilized conversations referring to marketplace is the term used 'it is not a fish market' suggesting that it is most archaic and unorganized. It also shows how the toiling fishermen product is priced and exploited like the tribe's minor forest products, such as tamarind, nuts and so on, are appropriated at a very ridiculous price. There are broadly two categories of sellers in the fish market. The women of the families going for fishing get the product directly to the market and the other type is one where women from non-fishing families acquire fish through formal and informal contracts from the fisher folk and sell it in the market. It is noted that 91 per cent of fisher folk in rural area directly market them as seen from Nakkapalli, while this figure is 12 per cent in Peda Gantyada of Visakhapatnam city. It is around 55 per cent in Srikakulam district. Those who do not market their fish through their family members give it to merchants and others.

They get the fish from other family members. Their figure is about 80 per cent, while 4 to 21 per cent reported to have acquired fish through contractors and very few from brokers.

The interesting part of the table is given at the second part on how the weight/quantity of fish is measured. It is noted that in less than 5 per cent of the cases, fish is weighed in kilograms. In 97 per cent cases in Nakkapalli Mandal and in the same proportion in other areas except in Pedagantyada, fish is bought in bulk quantity in baskets. The role of the middleman, contractor and so on who provide loans and short-term hand loans use the situation to determine the price. Though 80 to 90 per cent cases in rural mandals of Nakkapalli, Bhogapuram and Srikakulam fix the price themselves, still 10 per cent of the price is a prerogative of the contractor cum money lender. Sometimes, they become the price leaders in terms of deciding the price to be followed by others. As noted in the second part, the price of fish, a perishable good, is determined immediately after landing at the respective centres. The role of the contractor and the middleman cannot be wished away. This shows that the pricing of fish both at the landing and in the informal market still rely on tradition. But when we go to a fish selling unit in a super market, the price is predetermined and is higher than what we see at the landing centres. This unorganized nature of marketing of fish deprives the fisher folk the proper remuneration to their labour leading to exploitation and non-remunerative prices.

## Poverty among Marine Fisher Folk

Poverty estimates have become a routine exercise by scholars whenever they embark upon economic analysis of a group, class, caste or state or a nation. This is being done in India ever since Dandekar and Rath brought out a monograph using nutritional levels, linking it to per capita expenditure in the 1970s. The government has been using the statistics for policy formulation and in providing assistance or subsidies to the poor. Therefore, poverty lines are being drawn based on sample surveys conducted by agencies, such as NSSO on a regular basis. Economists, mostly statisticians, are involved in the explanations and argue as to the quantity and quality of the measure, dimensions and so on with little regard for human element, such as diversity and ecology of the people living in different ecosystems in the deliberations. Fisher folk have been living in utter destitution, particularly those who are away from urban areas and in remote places due to several factors of mindless development projects on the coast. We have estimated per capita income and expenditure from the survey data. It is necessary to know how much money out of their earnings goes in for food and non-food due to several leakages in the households or fisher folk's behaviour pattern and habits and customs. We cannot rely simply on their statement of earnings to measure poverty. Before we examine the items of expenditure, the sources of income and expenditure, we need to identify that expenditure of fisher folk household involves the following:

$$E = \Sigma i - (s + e_a + e_f + l_r) + d$$

where $E$ is the per capita expenditure, $i$ is the per capita income, $s$ is the savings, $e_a$ is the expenditure on alcohol, $e_f$ is the expenditure on festivals, $l_r$ is the loan repayment, and $d$ is the debt or hand loan.

In other words, the per capita expenditure of a fisherman is not determined on the basis of his earnings through income from fishing, wage labour or regular job, but he has the habit of borrowing from different sources to meet the traditional customs like performing or participating in a *jatara* (festival), performing puberty (menarche) function of a daughter and attending to such functions in relatives homes that are customary by tradition. This signifies their identity as an important element of their life. The expenditure and income of fisher folk and other lower-caste households from traditional families are not generally interrelated. They do not know how to adjust their expenditure to the source of income and the pawnbrokers and call money sharks are always present in the habitations to help them to get hand loans or debts at a short notice, mostly for consumption purposes.

If there are few households among the fisher folk who would have taken loans for construction of a house or extension of a room or buying a boat, they are guided by their will and not by community traditions. We have identified the sources of income apart from the primary occupation of fishing. As noted earlier, the occupation of fishing is dwindling due to several factors and excessive exploitation of marine and living resources of the coast. There are only 30 per cent of the families going for fishing as a primary occupation and the rest depend upon other activities. Therefore, family income includes income not only from fish catch, but also from other sources, such as wages by labourers, income from agriculture, working outside and remitting money home and others, as well as women serving either as labourers or housemaids.

## Studies on Poverty in India

Ever since Dandekar and Rath studied the levels of poverty on the basis of nutritional value translated into expenditure, there has been a big debate in the academic circles about the methods of estimation of poverty in India. The World Bank teams were also involved in the debate. World Bank criteria of $1.25 per capita per day expenditure translated as ₹45 did not define the items. The 9th plan has commissioned study on below poverty line (BPL) families and listed criteria of 13 indicators that included landlessness, indebtedness, literacy, clothing, sanitation, housing and so on to arrive at the number. Reviewing the reports, the Ministry of Rural Development has appointed a Committee under N. C. Saxena to suggest measures to estimate poverty. After reviewing all the hitherto studies, Saxena has proposed 10-point criteria based on 5 indicators with weightage to consider a household as poor or non-poor. They are (a) SC, ST with weightage 3 and BC with weightage 1,

(b) landlessness with weightage 4, (c) below primary education with weightage 1, (d) tuberculosis (TB) patient with weightage 1 and (e) age above 60 with weightage 1. Based on the score, it is suggested that those who get the maximum score will be included first as BPL family and so on. Saxena has arrived at a figure of 50 per cent as the proportion of poor in India that is higher than that reported by the Tendulkar Committee. After examining all the issues, we have noticed that the fisher folk on the coast do come automatically under poor category as they are landless, illiterate, and under BC and SC categories. Therefore, we have made a preliminary scouting of the data to know whether any of the fisher folk possess sufficient land to come under the category and the results are discussed below. Finally, we have decided to take the per capita household expenditure that is devoid of any superficial items and contains just items for survival, which are taken to estimate the poor. Therefore, the data from the study indicate the actual figures of the poor among the fisher folk. It is different from the poverty definition of nutrition criteria given by some economists. According to Saxena, the concept given by some is a *kutta–billi* criteria as the amounts are just sufficient for dogs and cats to survive and, therefore, he included shelter, clothing, education, medicine and so on in his concept of poverty. In fact, the data on MPCE of fisher folk indicated exactly the same and nothing more than that. Therefore, we have taken the food and non-food items of expenditure to estimate the poor.

The per capita expenditure per month MPCE on food and non-food items of fisher folk in the study area are obtained. We have followed the NSS method in presenting the data after culling it from the survey data. The data is presented in rupees at the current prices. It is noted that the average per capita expenditure of the study area is ₹248.75. There are slight variations among the mandals. The highest amount of ₹270.54 is found in Pusapatirega and the lowest of ₹230.60 is reported from Nakkapalli. We have also given the breakup of expenditure on each item. Rice, the staple food, constitutes 24 per cent, while fish, eggs and so on constitute 20 per cent of the total food expenditure (we have imputed the price of fish consumed by those who use it from their own catch). Interestingly, alcohol constitutes 12.2 per cent and it varies from 7 per cent in Pedagantyada to 24 per cent in Nakkapalli. It is noted that expenditure on festivals and customs include on average around 12 per cent spent on alcohol in the same mandal. In other words, unproductive expenditure either on alcohol or festivals is a menacing preference of fisher folk. We have estimated MPCE for non-food items, including the item on festivals, which is being considered by them as an issue of identity and therefore essential. Some of the items noted are derived from the NSSS survey. The highest expenditure of ₹293 is noted in Pedagantyada mandal and the lowest is from Pusapatirega. The former is part of an urban area while the latter is from rural setting. The total per capita per month expenditure for food and non-food items is given at the end of the table. It is noted that the average expenditure comes to ₹486.12; in Pedagantyada, spending is more at ₹527.34 and Bhogapuram has the lowest spending of ₹425.96.

It is noted that non-food items of expenditure, such as alcohol, medicines and festivals, constitute a major component of the total per capita expenditure. We have estimated that they constitute 25 per cent and 28 per cent of total non-food items respectively. The total expenditure on these items is 26 per cent of the total MPCE. Had government schemes of free education, healthcare and prohibition are implemented effectively, the fisher folk would have crossed poverty.

The data indicate the average expenditure obtained from 928 households with a population of 3,792 of the sample. Therefore, we have rearranged the data in class intervals by taking into account the per capita per day expenditure fixed by the Rangarajan committee on poverty. The norm of ₹32 makes it ₹960 per month to determine those who are below that norm as poor. We have also taken the next category of ₹961–1500 for those who are on the margin and to account for the current prices as the norm was given in 2014. In fact, the expenditure on festivals puts them under this category. It is noted that 61.31 per cent of the population in the study area fall below poverty category. However, there are variations; a population of 73.53 per cent in Bhogapuram and only 32.67 per cent in Nakkapalli come under this category. But, if the norm of ₹961+ is taken, 93 per cent of the population in Nakkapalli come below the poverty line.

It is noted that if both the categories are combined, around 92 per cent of the fisher folk are categorized under BPL. The Central Marine Fisheries Research Institute (CMFRI) study on East Coast of Andhra Pradesh in 2010 has concluded that 93 per cent of the fisher folk of north coastal Andhra Pradesh come under BPL.[3]

## Regression Results

We have run a simple regression to test the reliability of our above figures.

$$Pe = a + \beta_1 Fe + \beta_2 d + \beta_3 Pi$$

where *Pe* is the per capita expenditure, *Fe* is the per capita food expenditure, *d* is the per capita debts or hand loans, *Pi* is the per capita income, and $\beta$ is the dependent variable.

$$Pe = 258.531 + 0.970 + 0.002 + 1.587$$
$$(-0.347) \ (1.822)^* \ (1.236)^* \ (0.148)^{**}$$
$$\bar{R}^2 = 0.556$$

*Significant at 5%.
**Significant at 10%.

The results of regression as noted above show that the model explains 56 per cent of the per capita expenditure, and the coefficients are significant.

## Multiple Deprivations of Marine Fisher Folk

We have adopted the UK method of estimation of deprivations here. The English Indices of Deprivation 2010 are measures of multiple deprivations at the small area level. The model of multiple deprivations, which underpins the Indices of Deprivation 2010 is based on the idea of distinct domains of deprivation which can be recognized and measured separately. These domains are experienced by individuals living in an area.[4] People may be counted in one or more of the domains, depending on the number of types of deprivation that they experience. Each domain represents a specific form of deprivation experienced by people and each can be measured individually using a number of indicators. Seven distinct domains have been identified in the English Indices of Deprivation, namely, Income Deprivation, Employment Deprivation, Health Deprivation and Disability, Education Skills and Training Deprivation, Barriers to Housing and Services, Living Environment Deprivation and Crime. Individual domains can be used in isolation as measures of each specific form of deprivation. They can also be combined, using appropriate weights, into a single overall Index of Multiple Deprivation, which can be used to rank every small area in England according to the deprivation experienced by the people living there. Along with two supplementary indices, Income Deprivation Affecting Children Index and Income Deprivation Affecting Older People Index, they form the English Indices of Deprivation. These statistics allow the most- and least-deprived areas of the country to be identified as well as provide information about the issues faced by people living in different parts of the country. The Townsend score is a summation of the standardized scores ($Z$ scores) for each variable (scores greater than zero indicate greater levels of material deprivation). The Townsend score was considered the best indicator of material deprivation available. The variables that make up the Townsend score are combined together in an overall deprivation index, with each variable being given an equal weightage. The variables selected are direct indicators of deprivation, that is, they represent the condition or state of deprivation. Z scores express each variable in terms of its mean value in the population and its standard error. If this were not done then variables with longer scales would have more weightage than variables with shorter scales in the overall score. For example, the number of children in a household could vary from 0 to 10, while the number of cars could range from 0 to 3. Simply adding these together would give children more weightage than cars—standardization is intended to avoid this problem. This index has been the most widely used and has been considered as one of the best indices available. We have adopted the methodology to estimate the MDI for each village, *mandal* and district of our sample study. However, we have given different weights to the variables as explained earlier based on the type of index we have selected for the marine fisher folk.

$Z$ score formula:

$$Z = \frac{X - \mu}{\sigma}$$

where $X$ is the score, $\mu$ is the mean and $\sigma$ is the standard deviation.

We have noted in the beginning the concept of economic deprivations experienced by the marine fisher folk of north coastal Andhra Pradesh. The weighted $Z$ scores for each item of deprivation and the sum of it is adjusted for 100 as multiple deprivations is noted. Each item is given a weightage depending upon its importance. Fishing is given a weightage of 50, income 25, education 15 and health 10. The results show that deprivations are uniform among all the *mandals* with little variation from combined score. However, Nakkapalli has a higher score of 74.97 on education while Srikakulam in health issue scored differently. The aggregate score of 74.97 and the same for all the *mandals* clearly indicates that marine fisher folk of north coastal Andhra Pradesh are subjected to multiple economic deprivations. (However, there are villages, such as Rajayyapeta, Bangaramma peta in Nakkapalli rural *mandal* and strangely all the three villages of urban Pedagantyada mandal have scores less than the regional and district average scores.)

## Social Exclusion

Economic deprivations generally lead to social exclusion if the group is on the margins of the society, such as the marine fisher folk. In the present study of north coastal Andhra Pradesh, the fisher folk are found to live and subsist far away from the mainstream society. We have noted in the previous chapters that fisher folk suffer from several discriminations. The village level survey of the 26 villages on the coast of North Andhra provide us information about the kind of infrastructure available to show that they are physically excluded from the mainstream society.

Social exclusion is a complex and multi-dimensional process. It involves the lack of or denial of resources, rights, goods and services, and the inability to participate in the normal relationships and activities, available to the majority of people in a society, whether in economic, social, cultural or political arenas. It affects both the quality of individual and the equity and cohesion of society as a whole.

Social exclusion is defined as a multi-dimensional process in which various forms of exclusion are continued. Participation in decision-making and political processes, access to employment and material resources and integration into common cultural processes denied are part of social exclusion. When combined, they create acute forms of exclusion that find a spatial manifestation in particular neighbourhoods.

This concept of social exclusion has been extensively put into practice in Indian society. Here, 'social exclusion' is based on caste, patriarchy and gender. The obvious excluded are those of caste and community groups along with gender. Exclusions are of two forms, one is exclusion from access to or denial of rights to various services, such as health, education, housing and water; sanitation is also more recently included as an essential service. The other form by exclusion is that of deprivation of the right to express ones' views of representation and voice as per Hirschman (1970).[5] It can be passive or active exclusion as explained by Amartya Sen (2000).[6] Social inequality, isolation and discrimination are the hallmarks of social exclusion. Inequality is essentially relational and can be the basis for a form of deprivation linked with poverty, experienced by the specifically disadvantaged, marginalized weaker sections of Indian society, including the marine fisher folk of different geographical and ecological zones across the country.

## Isolated Villages

The village level survey collected information on availability of 31 items of minimum infrastructure facilities in the habitations from the head of the village either panchayat president or community leader. The multiple Index of deprivations of each village scores is also estimated for the study. It shows wide variations in the region. It is noted that drinking water is available in 100 per cent of the villages. In the Vizianagaram district, 60 per cent of the villages do not have primary schools within the habitation while the figure is 30 per cent in Visakhapatnam. No residential school is located within the habitation in any of the villages and they are required to go long distances of about 14 km to get their children admitted in BC welfare hostels or *ashram* schools. Ninety per cent of villages in Srikakulam,

75 per cent in Vizianagaram and none in Visakhapatnam rural have primary health centres within the village. But, health subcentres are present in 40 per cent of the villages. Even private hospitals are not available in majority of the villages and they need to travel 11 km to get healthcare. Drainage system is not available in 56 per cent of the villages. Interestingly, community toilets are not available in 80 per cent of the villages. Interestingly, 66 per cent of the villages have an arrack/alcohol shop. However, a commercial bank office, cold storage and so on that are essential facilities for marine fisher folk are not available in any of the villages.

The participation of fisher folk in group activities, such as cultural meets and political participation in decision making process, is obtained from the village heads and presented in the report.[7] We have ascertained how they interact with non-fishing community in the process of fishing through the participation of non-fishing community. It is reported that 30 per cent in Srikakulam district and 12.5 per cent in each in Vizianagaram and Visakhapatnam reported positively. It is noted that all the villages do have community meetings and the frequency of meeting as monthly, quarterly and so on vary from village to village. Though the fisher folk are interested in cultural activities, community halls are available in 38 per cent of the villages only. And there are no restrictions for non-fisher folk to visit their habitations or families. Cyclone shelters are not available in all the villages but available only in select villages.

The concept of social exclusion as noted above is a complex issue. We have noted on the basis of the village data that most of the villages are socially excluded from the mainstream society in terms of social and economic transactions as they are on the coast near the sea. However, most of the villages or habitations of the fisher folk are single community-based or single occupation-based habitats. Though some villages near the city are found to be mixed in nature, they are however inhabited by socially and educationally BCs and their locality becomes a slum in course of time. In the city of Visakhapatnam, there are around 750 slums and almost all the habitations of the fisher folk out of this number are declared slums. Therefore, it is found that in such multi-caste mixed villages or slums, social exclusion as a process is difficult to understand. The government schemes, such as DWCRA, skill development training, social welfare schemes of self-employment, are provided to all the inhabitants irrespective of the sub-caste. It has helped to a large extent to make the womenfolk come together to transact and interact to develop social communication among different sub-castes. However, it is doubtful to what extent other groups or castes do interact with them to shun social exclusion. We have provided data on how many members are there in DWCRA groups. The membership is found to be around 90 per cent in rural areas, such as Vajrapukotturu with 91.8 per cent, and lowest membership is observed in the city, such as Pedagantyada with 72.9 per cent. All of them have invariably noted that they have joined the groups for getting a loan. But very few, a negligible proportion of 0.4 per cent in Srikakulam and 1 per cent in Pedagantyada, reported that they attend caste meetings.

Social inclusion of a group expects that they participate in the conduct of collective activities, such as political participation, cooperative society, NGO/community-based organization (CBO) activities. Data from the study noted above show that around 60 people or 6.5 per cent are active in cooperative society for economic benefit, such as getting a loan. It is strange to notice that only four people in Srikakulam district have reported that they participate in activities of political parties. A total of 20 people, mostly from Vajrapukotturu, known for its community-based activities, reported that they are active in CBO/NGO activities. Important processes of collective actions, such as political participation, CBO, cultural gatherings and so on, where there shall not be any distinction based on social or economic background indicating the spirit of inclusiveness, is found to be absent in the villages of fisher folk of North Andhra Pradesh. The recent collective effort of marine fisher folk of North costal Andhra Pradesh with a demand to get their community a ST status was received with rude shock. The tribal groups are up in arms against fisher folk claiming that they should not be included in the ST category of Andhra Pradesh. The social reality of exclusion has come out in open when none of the leaders of political parties looked at the congregation of fisher folk and the whole movement got dissolved gradually after a month.

## Conclusion

The case study of marine fisher folk, a listed backward class/caste in Andhra Pradesh but an SC on the same coast a few miles away in another state, is cited here to show that the economic deprivation and social exclusion of certain castes is perpetual whether it was in the past or in the present. The system of MOP seen as pre-capitalist or capitalist does not change the socio-economic status of the lower castes. The changes and alterations of ranks of certain castes in the new economy are only limited to non-*bahujan* castes or *Dvijas* and few upper *Shudras*. The lower castes continue to remain on the margin and subsist in the traditional mould.

The economic status and social resilience of the marine fisher folk studied here has given us insight that the economic status of the sample population has not improved over a period of time. We have used standard methods of estimation of poverty in terms of MPCE and developed a new methodology to estimate the multiple deprivations that the fisher folk suffer in our study area. It has come out clearly that the fisher folk of north coastal Andhra Pradesh spread in the three districts have almost the same characters and are subjected to economic exploitation in terms of determination of prices for their products and in getting meagre income as traditional fishermen. Those who have gone for mechanization seem to have not improved their fate as marine and living resources on north coastal Andhra Pradesh started dwindling due to excessive use of mechanized methods of fishing and over-industrialization on the coast mostly by the non-fisher folk caste. Most of the owners of trawlers and mechanized boats are non-fisher folk. The data on indebtedness of fisher folk have indicated that every household has one or the other kind of credit taken from institutions or mostly from friends and relatives. Therefore, the income and expenditure figures do not match as major chunk of income goes for repayment. The culture of profligacy among fisher folk is so vile that they remain perpetual barrowers.

The multiple deprivation indices calculated for the study region based on right to fishing on the sea and other parameters have shown that they all are deprived in the same manner and not without any distinction as rural and urban dwellers. Poverty levels estimated on the basis of per capita expenditure have shown that 93 per cent of them are living BPL, a comparable statistic arrived by CMFRI for coastal Andhra Pradesh. We have tried to see how the community is interacting with outside the world to learn about the process of social exclusion. It is noted with regret that social exclusion of the villages in terms of distance and infrastructure remained the same with some sprinkles of government schemes, such as public distribution system, primary school and so on, coming within the habitations. Interestingly, more number of habitations is served by alcoholic shops than by healthcare centres. However, mixed habitations, particularly in urban areas, show that majority of the womenfolk join DWCRA to get loans, which may be for consumption purposes. In that process there is a likelihood of inclusive communication within the community, but their external and durable benefit leading to social inclusion need to be studied further. In other words, the marine fisher folk of north coastal Andhra Pradesh are subjected to multiple deprivations and are socially excluded from the process of development in the civilized society. The recent upsurge of fisher folk demanding ST status for the community received little attention from the public in general and OBCs in particular to which they belong now. The study indicates that caste is predominantly used here to discriminate and deprive the basic rights of a social group on the caste basis. The data noted in the text are drawn from a study conducted with ICSSR support, which consists of about 400 pages, and the tables are available with the author.

## Notes

1. P. Townsend, P. Phillimore and A. Beattie, *Health and Deprivation: Inequality and the North* (London: Croom Helm, 1988).
2. Ibid.
3. CMFRI, 'Marine Fisheries Survey: Andhra Pradesh', Delhi, 2010, Summary, 4.
4. Ibid.
5. A. O. Hirschman, *Bias for Hope-Essays on Development and Latin America,* (New Haven, CT: Yale University Press), 1971.
6. A. Sen, Social Exclusion: *Concept, Application and Scrutiny*, (Mandaluyong, Philippines: Asian Development Bank), 2000.
7. K. S. Chalam and U. Tataji, *Marginalization Economic Deprivation and social Exclusion of Marine Fisher folk of North Costal Andhra Pradesh*, Vol. I and Vol. II, (Visakhapatnam: Institute for Economic and Social Justice, 2016. ICSSR funded.

# 6

# New Economic Policy
## *The Dvija Project*

'I reincarnate myself when dharma is in danger'—asserted Lord Krishna in the Bhagavad Gita. It is said that he has so far reincarnated 10 times to restore peace and caste tranquillity. During the Kaliyuga and particularly after the *mlecchas* left the Aryavartha, the caste order seems to have been disturbed. It is only to restore the order; successive governments in the Republic have been trying to implement policies that correspond to the *dharma*, the order in society.

The social order in the Indian society reckons with the *varnashrama dharma* in which the four *varnas* shall always perform their assigned duties so as to keep equilibrium. The first three *varnas* are called the *Dvijas*, the twice born, and the fourth *varna* is put in a position to serve the *Dvijas*. Therefore, they are called the *Shudras*. There are several layers among the *Shudras* and they are manipulated and ordered to work as per the requirements of the *Dvijas*. The panchamas, the fifth category has always been outside the order as an experimental group. Keeping this social structure in view, several attempts have been made to develop the socio-economic conditions of the people. Interestingly, those who have migrated to other faiths over centuries ago have not behaved very differently and therefore fit into the *varnadharma*. There seems to be an agenda hidden or public according to which the social and economic processes take place in India. Unless one understands this, it is very difficult to analyse any developments in the country, be it contemporary or historical. An attempt is made here to analyse how the NEP has reinforced the *varnadharma*.

## Caste as Property

Caste in the Indian subcontinent is considered as an important social category. But, caste is hardly analysed by social scientists as an economic category. Though its manifestation is social, its essence is found to be purely economic. In fact, the first social anthropologist, H. W. Wiser, who examined caste and introduced the concept of 'Jajmani' for the first time in the 1930s, had analysed the transactions among different castes in a village and found them as purely economic. The real transactions between Brahmins and Kshatriyas, the '*Dvijas*' and other servile castes, and the servile castes and untouchable castes were found to be purely economic in nature. He even estimated the values of products and services transacted between castes in Kalimpur village. It was clearly established that the Brahmin gives only intangible service and takes the highest value of goods and services from others. At the lowest level, the untouchable provides the maximum value in terms of goods and services and in return receives the lowest value. If these values are translated as returns from each caste's property, the concept of caste as an economic category will be clear. Marx has mentioned that social relations are always embedded in economic relations. These relations are nothing but property relations. In this context, caste needs to be understood as property in India. However, considering the Hindu caste as property has certain limitations. The character of property as a thing to exchange with others or sell it to outsiders is very much limited here. Therefore, caste is to be considered as communal possession and not as private property. Wiser has mentioned in his study that caste was a corrupted form of ancient system of the custom of communal ownership directed by the Panchayat. In other words, caste is a Hindu category of property where the Brahmin possesses the highest value and the lowest value is assigned to untouchables. Viewed from this angle, caste system as described by Ketakar and adopted by Ambedkar is not just division of labourers. In the division of labourers, the individual labourer is considered as a unit of analysis. But the Indian caste system is a division of groups of people, each being assigned with a particular duty and economic value. That is why, the members of families in a caste produce finished goods and not parts of a good. This is generally understood as division of labour in economics. The castes being economic entities accumulate these values over a period of time. But, the Hindu super structure, which has been protecting this economic caste base, did not allow the non-*Dvija* castes to accumulate and capitalize their value. The *Dvija* castes of Brahmin, Kshatriya and Vaisya are given the right and opportunities to education, assets, weapons and so on, which naturally accumulate (may be primitive accumulation) capital over a period of time and improve their value of human capital. But it is denied to the *Shudras* and untouchables. As a result, the social manifestation of unequal exchange between castes is now synthesized as property relations.

Caste being a property of a group of people can be utilized for the advantage of the members of the group. This has also been used for the exploitation of others and also empowering of one's own group. These concepts have been used here to understand the economic power of the dominant *Dvija* castes, particularly Brahmin and Bania castes, in India today.

In a modern democratic society, the struggle among different political groups is aimed ultimately to distribute resources. Those who are the winners in the race will have control over the resources and provide opportunities for their supporters to have access to these. In the Indian situation, the Brahmins have remained arbiters and enjoyed the patronage of both the winners and also the runners. Kautilya, the Brahmin intellectual had laid a strong foundation for a Brahminical political economy as distinguished from Western political economic theory much before Western economic theory emerged. The basic principle on which Kautilya laid his political economic theory is that every person is dishonest as against the Western idea that man is rational. He mentioned in his *Arthashastra* how the state should get revenue and how it should spend the money. In the hierarchy of the state, the ministers, who were in general drawn from among the Brahmins, came first and then the *purohits* enjoyed the highest status. He had even gone to the extent of saying that the king can cheat gullible people in getting revenue for the exchequer. Kautilyan principles have been followed by almost all the kings in the country till the emergence of urban economy. The vaishyas have cooperated with the king in carrying out the internal and external trade. Thus, the *Dvijas* had the opportunity to run the state in the past and in the present.

### The *Dvija* Project

*Dvijas* as the twice born are basic pillars of the Indian society. There is absolute understanding and cooperation among the three groups to maintain equilibrium. It is found sometimes, that one category among the three is benefited, and it is their unwritten denotation that the other will not grudge. In times of crisis, they get united and share the pillage. This is abundantly clear in the economic reforms of post-independence period. There seems to be at least one adjustment and reform in a period of one decade starting with the first five-year plan. Each adjustment made the *Dvija* groups to modernize and mend to the changing times. They get dispensed among different groups and platforms and argue and speak differently ultimately to benefit the *Dvijas*. For instance, the abolition of privy purses made the Kshatriyas to turn out as capitalists, the public sector modernized the Brahmins, the license *raj* benefited the Vaishyas and so on. This is the *Dvija* project which has been in operation for quite some time. There are, however, certain aberrations here and there when some upper *Shudras* tried to climb the ladder in the guise of a *Dvija*. In such cases, they are either thrown out of the system or absorbed depending upon the circumstances and the strength of the beholder. The economic reforms or the so-called NEP required to be analysed from this perspective to draw meaningful conclusions.

It is said that after the advent of direct *Dvija* rule in 1947, India had abundant educated and skilled manpower to manage the affairs of the economy at that time. And around 90 per cent of these people came from Brahmin families. B. R. Ambedkar in his statement concerning the state of education of the depressed classes in the former Bombay Presidency submitted to the Indian Statutory Commission 1928 data to prove that more than 50 per cent of the enrolment in collegiate education was from Brahmins.[1] The unemployment rate among the educated was very high during the 1930s and the 1940s. Therefore, Nehru thought that these educated unemployed should be utilized for nation building. He was influenced by the British Labour Party Policy of industrialization and socialism. The Soviet model of commanding heights of public sector was adopted by Nehru. He modified the Soviet model to suit the Indian situation without nationalizing the means of production. Naturally, almost all the public sector undertakings were managed and operated by the then educated Brahmins. All important sectors of the economy were brought under the control of the bureaucracy through its License Permit Raj. The Brahmins started migrating from rural areas to urban centres leaving some of their lands and assets behind. Villages were deserted by Brahmins. In order to provide some relief to these people, land reforms were introduced when most of the Brahmins sold away their lands. Those who did not sell their lands and assets and clung to the tradition of priesthood had suffered. (The internal differentiation among Brahmins is not discussed here.) But most of them have converted their agricultural rural property into urban property. In this process some lands transferred into the hands of the hard-working *Shudras* and others. Some of them mostly the upward mobile *Shudras*, such as Reddy, Kamma, Mudaliar and so on, in the south occupied some positions of power in politics and contracts.

Majority of the Brahmins have started occupying modern secular jobs and enjoyed the highest security and economic privilege in the country. Planning was introduced in the country in the 1950s and investments to the extent of several thousands of crores during the plan periods were basically managed and enjoyed by the Brahmin and *Dvija* bureaucrats. Public property was slowly converted into private property through black money, scandals, bribes and other economic crimes. By the end of 1980, most of the upper castes acquired properties worth crores of rupees in the form of urban property, real estate, shares in private companies, and they were also in a position to develop an independent economy. Several studies in the area of social economy of Tamil Nadu revealed that the reservation policy of the DMK government weakened job opportunities to Brahmins. This made enterprising Brahmins, such as T. V. S. Iyengar, Sundaram Finance and so on, to develop private enterprises with public money (bank credits, investment capital, licenses and so on) from the centre. An impulsive observation of all our metropolis and urban areas reveal that posh localities and government-developed estates are occupied by the upper castes. All the banks in the country are either managed or owned by them. The recent non-performing assets (NPAs) of public sector banks and the frauds reported in the media indicate the nexus of upper castes.[2] Bank frauds are different from NPAs as noted by Raghuram Rajan, RBI governor in his note to parliament (as cited in the above paper of Ashwini Manikandan). Further, public higher education helped them to become most lucrative

NRIs. Most of the NRIs today are from *Dvija* groups. The Mandal Commission report has provided data on the numerical strength of the Brahmins in the Indian Bureaucracy and the time-to-time updates given in the parliament on the queries from members.

Meanwhile, the license *raj* helped the few to develop independent industry at the cost of public sector.[3] Some SC and STs have started entering into public sector employment through reservations to challenge the hegemony of *Dvijas*. In the south, OBCs have also joined the ranks of secular job seekers in the modern public sector. The *Dvijas* who have swelled private offers with public money thought that it would not be beneficial anymore if they continued in the public sector. They envisaged that it becomes risky if the public sector continues further as the Dalits, Adivasis and OBCs are emerging as a formidable force. The results of research and development (R&D) of public institutions have been slowly passed into private individuals or corporate bodies. The Official Secrets Act is being used by the bureaucrats to syphon off money and other resources for private gains. The so-called insider trading now popular in share market was inherent in the leakages of public policy for the *Dvijas*. This made the public sector dry and inefficient. The jolt given by the *Dvijas* public sector tycoons, such as Krishna Murthy, Harshad Mehta, Ketan Parekh, RBI, SEBI personnel and others, show the nexus between them and their control over the economy. The anti-Mandal clique perhaps thought that it is difficult to fight the massive *bahujans* if the struggle to control the economy is made an internal issue and conspired to link it with international market. The alleged international manoeuvring for an Aryan hegemony by combining Germany, Russia and India[4] is only a move to curb the emerging *bahujan* power and to get international support to crush the indigenous *bahujan* majority. The NEP and the World Trade Organization (WTO) must be seen in this context. This is the *Dvija* project in operation in an era of liberalization. The Cambridge project on 'Caste and the Indian Economy' undertaken by Kevin Munshi[5] substantiated the above argument with data by saying 'aggregate evidence indicates that there has been convergence in education, occupations, income and access to public resources across caste groups in the decades after the independence.[6] It has been made possible in the garb of liberalization, privatization and globalization.

## What Is New Economic Policy?

Liberty, the concept on which the whole edifice of NEP is built today was first enunciated by J. S. Mill to enhance individual choice and for the organization of production. Mill never advocated liberty for the sake of exploitation and profit making. The economic reforms of the Government of India in 1991 based on the principle of liberty, however, consisted of broadly two kinds of policies. First one was the stabilization policy, which was implemented in response to a payments crisis in 1991 as India was running a current account deficit of around $10 billion and the reserves were down to two weeks of imports. The second policy was the structural reforms, which were initiated in the early 1980s but slowed down later and again vigorously pursued as a package of economic reforms in 1991. The stabilization policy, which was purely on account of trade deficit and earlier policies of the government, was embarked upon as an inevitable strategy to come out of the crisis. In fact, the economy as a whole was not that bad and it was growing at 5.5 per cent just before the economic reforms (1980–1990) as compared to 3.6 per cent of the previous period (1965–1980). However, the economy slipped into a crisis in the later part of 1990 due to several factors that were not purely economic in nature. The liberal licensing policy of allowing foreign automobile manufacturers to start production of two wheelers and four wheelers that consume oil forced the country to import more oil straining the foreign reserves. It has been argued that India had entered the decade of nineties with large internal and external imbalances, which made the economy highly vulnerable for any kind of shocks. It is further elaborated that the gulf crisis added a serious blow to the system and its foreign reserves dropped dramatically and the international credit ratings placed India at a very low position particularly between August 1990 and July 1991. This situation has forced the government to adopt an adjustment strategy by borrowing heavily from the international agencies.[7] It has devalued its rupee three times during a period of two months and instilled confidence in foreign funding agencies and borrowed heavily from the World Bank and International Monetary Fund (IMF). Along with these changes, the country has also agreed to follow the economic prescriptions dictated by these agencies. Though the government may say that it is pursuing a structural reform, it was in fact providing opportunities to control the economy through market. Therefore, the following prescriptions were implemented.

1. In the realm of trade policy, the new policy replaced import licensing.
2. In the area of industrial policy, the system of licensing that regulated the entry and the expansion of firms was eliminated. The industrial policy of 1956 and 1980 that envisaged 'commanding heights' for public sector was given up.
3. In the area of public sector, the exclusive reservation of certain key industries has been curtailed and foreign investment in these areas has been openly invited.
4. Some of the public sector units are open for private initiative by slowly converting the equity and allowing private enterprises and business houses to hold the equity of public sector, including defence.
5. Reduction of fiscal deficit is envisaged by way of reducing aggregate expenditure in areas, such as the so-called unproductive items, which generally create scope for new jobs.
6. Encouraging the economy to link itself with global markets to improve competitiveness and efficiency.

## Macroeconomic Indicators

Despite the adverse effects of the policy, the government has vigorously implemented it, as there was no constructive opposition from political groups. It appears that there is almost an agreement among all the *Dvijas* spread in all political parties on this. Therefore, NEP continues. As seen from Table 6.1, the macroeconomic indicators show the results of the economic reforms. It is found that the economy is growing at an average rate of around 7 per cent after 1992–1993. It has slowed down after the NDA-II regime. The increase is found to be more in manufacturing and in services sectors. The inflation rate is now brought down to the single digit level from that of 12 per cent in 1990–1991. The fiscal deficit is also brought down to around 3.5 per cent of GDP from that of 8.3 per cent in 1990–1991. The savings and investment ratios as a per cent of GDP have, however, remained less than the pre-NDA period. The current account deficit remained at –2.5 per cent of GDP, though it is found to be less than what it was in 1990–1991 (3.2%). There are fluctuations over the years. But the government is able to manage with the flows in the invisibles particularly due to expatriate remittances. All these modest achievements of the economic reforms can be attributed to the sacrifices made in terms of the reduction in the domestic capital formation and the external debt remaining around 50 per cent of GDP. The fiscal deficit is covered by disinvestment of some of the profit-making public sector units and in reducing public expenditure on social sectors, such as education, health and welfare programmes. The impact of these changes needs to be examined in detail with reference to the socially disadvantaged groups who are more vulnerable than any other marginalized sections in the world. Out of the super 100 firms reported in Business India, none appears to be owned by a Dalit or Adivasi. The manifestation of caste power in terms of emergence of crony capitalism is discussed in Chapter 7.

**TABLE 6.1** Macroeconomics Indicators

| | 1990–1991 | 1991–1992 | 1992–1993 | 1993–1994 | 1994–1995 | 1995–1996 | 2001–2002 | 2010–2011 | 2017–2018 |
|---|---|---|---|---|---|---|---|---|---|
| 1. GDP (annual percentage change) | 5.2 | 0.5 | 5.3 | 6 | 7.2 | 7.1 | 5.4 | 8.5 | 6.9 |
| Agriculture and allied sectors | 4.2 | −1.8 | 6.1 | 3.6 | 4.6 | −0.1 | 5.7 | 8.3 | 5 |
| Manufacturing | 7 | −1.2 | 4.2 | 8.5 | 10.2 | 13.6 | 3.3 | 7.6 | 5 |
| Services | 4.3 | 4.1 | 5.5 | 7.3 | 7.5 | 8.8 | 6.5 | 12.2** | 8.1 |
| 2. Inflation (percentage per annum) | 12.1 | 13.6 | 7 | 10.8 | 10.4 | 4.4 | 7 | 8.87 | 4.3 |
| 3. Broad money M3 (annual percentage increase) | 15.1 | 18.5 | 11.2 | 18.2 | 14.9 | 13.2 | 11.2 | 16.5 | 9.2 |
| 4. Reverse money (annual percentage increase) | 19.7 | 12.9 | 10.4 | 15.6 | 5.7 | 19.6 | 5.6 | 15.45 | 10 |
| 5. Gross domestic investment (percentage to GDP) | 27.7 | 23.4 | 24 | 23.6 | 26 | 27.4 | 24.0* | 37 | 29.8 |
| 6. Gross domestic saving (percentage to GDP) | 24.3 | 22.8 | 22.1 | 23.1 | 24.9 | 25.6 | 23.4* | 34 | 30.5 |
| 7. Gross domestic capital formation | 27.7 | 23.4 | 24 | 23.6 | 26 | 27.4 | 26.3 | 36.8 | 28.6 |
| 8. Current account Deficit (percentage to GDP) | −3.2 | −0.4 | −1.8 | −0.5 | −0.9 | −1.7 | −0.5 | −2.6 | −2.4 |
| 9. Fiscal deficit (percentage to GDP) | 8.3 | 5.9 | 5.7 | 7.4 | 6.1 | 5.8 | 5.5 | 4.8 | 3.5 |
| 10. India's external debt (percentage to GDP) | 30.4 | 41 | 39.8 | 35.9 | 32.7 | 28.7 | 22.3* | 50.6 | 49.1 |

*Source*: Economic Survey of India, Government of India, Various Issues.

*Notes*: *Relates to 2000–2001; **Trade, hotel and cement.

# Manifestation of the *Dvija* Project in the Stock Market

The opening of the economy to global opportunities is a spout for the *Dvijas* to publicly acknowledge and declare their build-ups. In fact, the so-called technology transfer or foreign technology agreements and FDI approvals, all without any exception, benefited the *Dvijas* with a few spillovers to upper *Shudras* from regional groups. During the last two decades, investment approvals with a projected investment of ₹18.54 lakh crores are reported in the FDI factsheet of the ministry of commerce and industry for the year 2017.[8] Out of this, around 50 per cent came from Mauritius and Singapore, indicating the dubious nature of FDIs. These collaborations and technological transfers have taken place through informal sources. A *Dvija* NRI with the tacit approval of the foreign collaborators nominated his kith and kin as a promoter in India. The promoter with the help of brokers and fraudulent operators entered the stock market and manipulated the capital market to their advantage. For instance, if the Infosys hold about 29 per cent and Wipro 84 per cent of their shares, respectively, then the market capitalization naturally benefit them. Speaking on such manipulators Mr A. K. Gupta, Deputy Director, CBI said:

> The gullible public and the inefficient banking system provide ample opportunities for the financial institutions to play and squander the public funds. The overheated stock market and the laxity of the financial institutions and the watchdogs like SEBI are the other major contributory factors. The modus operandi is fairly simple. The investors are lured to part with their savings by promises of unrealistic returns. The banks and financial institutions are made to part with their funds either by misrepresentation or through forgery or by simply corrupting the bank officials. The funds are placed at the disposal of scamsters who use these in the stock market operations. As the bubble bursts, which is inevitable, everyone becomes a loser. Investigation, arrest and prosecution

deter them for some time but in due course new scamsters and new scams emerge.[9]

The so-called boom in software technology and the clamour for body shopping is said to result in the current crisis in IT-related services. It is reported that during the boom period, shares of even loss-making companies commanded with premium. Another major scandal of the initial period was that the promoters, especially multi-national companies (MNCs), issued preferential shares at prices far lower than the then prevailing market prices. All the operators in the stock market belong to the *Dvija* castes and manage the moneys of first-generation non-*Dvija* investors. In the USA, the stock market operators are professional managers; however, in India, caste, family and primordial relations entered the market. The data in Table 6.2 indicate the shares of different categories of shareholders in market capitalization. It is found that out of ₹8,221,592 crore total market capitalization as on April 2015, ₹2,428,669

**TABLE 6.2** *Top 10 Companies in India (₹ in Crores)*

| Category | Market Capitalization | |
|---|---|---|
| | 2015 | 2019 |
| 1. Tata Consultancy | 509,837 | 775,130 |
| 2. Reliance Industry | 285,051 | 893,819 |
| 3. ONGC | 278,994 | 179,268 |
| 4. HDFC Bank | 258,157 | 680,047 |
| 5. ITC | 257,137 | 309,066 |
| 6. Coal India | 242,137 | 129,139 |
| 7. Infosys | 23,160 | 277,648 |
| 8. Sun Pharma | 229,765 | 97,604 |
| 9. SBI | 210,037 | 246,408 |
| 10. Hindustan Lever | 183,101 | 454,913 |

*Source:* Author (estimates based on BSE data sources).

crores or 29 per cent are held by top 10 companies, which has remained almost the same even in 2019 when it has reached ₹14,002,664 crore. The total turnover of the stock market in a year is estimated to be ₹2,880,990 crores in the year 2000–2001, which is higher than that of the gross national product (GNP) during the year and it remains almost the same in 2019. The data presented by RBI show that it is only the West and Central India that hold the key. This indicates the economic size of the stock market and the *Dvija* project.

A new generation of journalists, academics, economic consultants, chartered accountants and so on has emerged during the post-liberalization period. The single point agenda of these people is to eulogize the benefits of liberalization and the efficiency of the market. Majority of these consultants are involved in government policymaking helping their own social groups to get benefitted. Few years ago, the government of the *Dvijas* has created a separate ministry of disinvestment to take control of the public sector units, where the poor and the Dalits have invested their future through the government. No one knows how the ownership of the private sector enterprises (PSEs) are transferred and to whom? Even the profit-making organizations are transferred to private individuals or companies. Invariably all the new owners are either the *Dvijas* or MNCs with *Dvija* control.[10] A new brand of MCCs have emerged with the *Dvija* agenda. Some academics like Bardhan,[11] Corbridge and Harris[12] and Jenkins[13] have recognized the fact that caste interests have played a role in the NEP in the backdrop of *mandal* and *bahujan* upsurge. However, no serious evaluation and discussion on the issues raised by the academics has taken place either in the mainstream academic discourse or in the media.

According to the NEP, market is given the supreme position in the allocation of resources to various sectors and groups. It is generally claimed that those sectors and groups, which are found to be efficient and competitive, would alone survive and those which are weak would perish in the market.[14] When this market strategy is translated into practice, it would be clear that those sections and sectors, which have been given importance in the policy formulation and implementation, will get strengthened.[15] They alone would stand in the competitive world now. And those sections/sectors which are given help or subsidy for sustenance would not be in a position to compete in the market. It means that the reservation groups will have to face a greater challenge than others.

The impact of the *Dvija* project in India is already experienced by the Dalit and service castes. First time in the history of this country, Brahmins have taken control over the economic resources along with *Banias* and therefore total control over the country. The God of the *Dvijas* reincarnates again and again to restore the social order in which the supreme position of the *Dvijas* is ensured. The NEP is one such act of the God supreme. Naturally, the Dalits and service castes are thrown into the emerging service sector that serves the *Dvijas*. Therefore, the *varnashrama dharma* is restored. The *Dvija* project is fructified within the CMOP.

## Notes

1. Ambedkar, *Babasaheb Writings and Speeches*, Vol. 2.
2. Ashwin Manikandan, 'Why Indian Bankers Are Hesitant to Report Frauds', *The Economic Times*, 9 October 2019.
3. R. K. Hazari, *Hazari Committee Report on Industrial Planning and Licensing Policy* (Delhi: Planning Commission, 1966).
4. K. S. Chalam, *Economic Reforms and Social Exclusion* (Delhi: SAGE Publications, 2011); B. Karl Blind, 'Does Russia represent Aryan Civilization?' *The North American Review* 571 (June 1904): 801–811.
5. Kevin Munshi, *Caste and the Indian Economy* (Cambridge, UK: University of Cambridge, June 2017).
6. Ibid, abstract.
7. S. Corbridge and John Hariss, *Reinventing India: Liberalization, Hindu Nationalism and Popular Democracy* (Cambridge, UK: Polity Press, 2000).

8. Government of India, Ministry of Commerce and Industry, Factsheet on FDI, 2017.
9. Alternative Economic Survey, 2001–2002, 124.
10. M. N. Panini, 'The Social Logic of liberalization', *Sociological Bulletin* 44 (1999), 33–62.
11. Pranab Bardhan, *The Political Economy of Development in India* (Oxford, UK: Basil Blackwell, 1998).
12. Corbridge and Harris, *Reinventing India*.
13. Jenkins Rob, *Democratic Politics and Economic Reforms in India* (Cambridge, UK: Cambridge University Press, 2000); Atul Kohli, 'Politics of Economic Liberalization in India'. *World Development* 17, no. 3 (1989), 305–328.
14. Anne O. Krueger, *Economic Policy Reforms and the Indian Economy* (Oxford: Oxford University Press, 2002).
15. Prabhat Patnaik, 'Notes on the Political Economy of Structural Adjustment'. *Social Scientist* 22 (1994), 4–17.

# 7

# Caste and the Advent of Crony Capitalism in India

The East Asian miracle eulogized by some group of economists in the 1997 has evoked interest in the growth trajectory of Asia. Some scholars argued that corruption and rent seeking can be damaging to growth in some countries, but not others; this impels us to have a clearer understanding what kind of corruption and rent seeking affect economic performance.[1] David C. Kang[2] who published a book on crony capitalism has earlier discussed the concept within the paradigm of neoclassical economics about the efficiency of market in a capitalism system. He was of the view that if there is a balance of power among a small and stable number of government and business actors, crony can actually reduce transaction costs and minimize dead weight losses.[3] This theoretical position did not hold good when Hunter Lewis[4] published his study on crony capitalism in America, depicting stories of how private interests enter government's policymaking to save Goldman Sachs and fail Lehman Brothers during the 2008 crisis. Back home, Paranjoy Guha Thakurtha[5] published an online book on the Indian version of crony capitalism with reference to Ambanis in natural gas allocations of KG-D6 (Krishna Godavari exploration). However, all these studies did not look at crony capitalism as a subset of capitalism, which is an avatar of capitalist exploitation based on the theory and practice of private property protected by institutions, such as judiciary, legislative and executive wings of modern capitalist state. Lenin in his *Imperialism, the Highest Stage of Capitalism* has elaborated on the role played by industrial cartels, finance capital, monopolist business companies and their social linkages and had anticipated crony capitalism in the 21st century.

The operation of CMOP as a universal system of economic and social structure was guarded by the *varna* and caste formations at different periods of history. It is in this context that economic reforms in India were officially declared through the revised industrial policy declared on 24 July 1991 with a statement by P. V. Narasimharao asserting that 'the sky is the limit' for foreign investments. There are studies to indicate the positive impact of reforms and few critical appraisals evaluating the depraved influence of the policies on the socio-economic status of the underprivileged and the value system or ethos of India. In fact, it was considered by many as an extension of capitalist expansion by the neoliberal forces in a post-colonial setting. We are, however, concerned here how it has imported and strengthened crony capitalism in India.

Capitalism is said to be an economic system based on the merit and creation of opportunities that sustain it, the protagonists assert. Critiques, however, say it is relied on extraction of surplus value from labour and exploitation of resources probably by deceit. The notion of capitalism had entered India with the English. There are now different varieties of concepts of capitalism in use in academic discussions (J. W. Baumol and others listed oligarchic, state-guided, big-firm and entrepreneurial capitalism). The classical economists, including Adam Smith, regarded capitalism as a natural form of economic organization based upon human's propensity to truck and barter in his or her own self-interest. They said the laissez-faire system of economic institutions will make the people achieve welfare for all. Marx contested this. He gave an elaborate analysis of the system in his magnum opus Das Kapital. Nevertheless, Marx did not explain directly what capitalism is? He has used a different method known as MOP to explain the different stages of socio-economic formations. Since the concept of capitalism is popularly known through the writings of Marx, it is better to look at his formulation. Edward Avelling,[6] his son-in-law, in the abridged edition of *Capital* reduced the formula to M-C-M'. It means that the capitalist goes to the market with his capital M and buys the labour C to produce and sell the commodity in the market at a price M'. The difference between M and M' is surplus value that is extracted from the labourer. The capitalist and the labourer belong to two different antagonistic classes. The dynamics of the capitalist system depends on the drive for surplus value, including the expansion of production for the market. The antagonistic contradictions of capitalism give rise to class struggles between the working class and the bourgeoisie.

The development and resilience of Capitalism in the 21st century (despite the prediction that it will disappear) has facilitated it to take different shapes and forms. In 1998, the capitalist system had undergone a terrible crisis in the East Asian economies. Scholars have started analysing it as a financial crisis and it was attributed to what is called cronyism prevailed in these economies as noted above. Few families and their cronies captured the state in these countries, particularly in Philippines, South Korea, Indonesia and Thailand. The cronies with the support of the bureaucracy get favours, such as permits, licenses to exploit natural resources and tax concessions, to remain successful in business. It is necessary to link capitalism as discussed above with cronyism as witnessed in the East Asia to arrive at the concept of crony capitalism. Crony capitalism in state-run systems, including state socialism, in Soviet Union had collapsed under its weight, which broadly might come under this category.

There seem to be four essential conditions to sustain crony capitalism.

1. The presence of opportunistic capitalists manipulating things in their favour rather than depending upon free competition.
2. Crony intellectuals or experts to defend and eulogize the significance of capitalism as a viable system.
3. The pliable bureaucrats who can crawl when the minister says bend the rules in favour of the few cronies.
4. A section of the media that survive on the spoils of the system and brazenly bring distorted stories to influence the public opinion in favour of crony capitalists. Crony capitalism takes place in the form of collusion, forming cartels, avoiding taxes or getting tax cuts and restricting others to enter the closely knitted networks of business.

It is in this context we can look at how the 20th century experts looked at it. Among many scholars, Hobson[7] is one who has analysed about the concept of imperialism as an oligarchy of few capitalists (cronies) who spread it to other countries due to the problems of mis-distribution of wealth in their own counties. It was Lenin[8] who had systematically studied the economies of the West in the early part of 20th century to present imperialism as the highest stage of capitalism. Lenin's explanation of imperialism is relevant here to understand the concept of crony capitalism as he was anticipating that such a thing would happen in future. If we look at the characterization of imperialism by Lenin, we come across five important issues.

1. The merging of bank capital with industrial capital would form finance capital and creation of financial oligarchy.

2. The concentration of production and capital has created monopolies, which play a dominant role in emerging economies.
3. The export of capital as distinguished from export of commodities.
4. The formation of international monopolist capitalist associations to apportion the world among themselves (cronies) and
5. Expansion and distribution of territorial division of labour among the biggest capitalist powers of the world.

This characterization of imperialism, particularly the emergence of finance capital through the operation of share markets, international financial institutions and so on, needs to be interpreted as crony capitalism as they were facilitated through the cronies and not due to free competition. We have witnessed today the phenomenon called insider trading, Wall Street operations and so on. They are all part of crony capitalism.

## Caste-based Cronyism

Crony capitalism is not new to modern India. The genesis was weaved with the formation of the East India Company of few Individuals who were closely related in England. It was the members of the company's families who were posted as officers to plunder India and take the booty back home as family income. After independence, the government has realized that there was concentration of wealth in the hands of a few. The Hazari Committee,[9] Mahalanobis Committee,[10] Monopolies Inquiry Commission[11] and so on appointed by the government during 1965–1969 have brought out the fact that the wealth was in fact concentrated in few business houses. Some of it might have been trashed in Swiss banks. The License-Permit raj was manipulated by the cronies in their favour and did not allow others to enter business. It is the same business houses and their extended families that are involved in the so-called soft scams of share market, spectrum license, oil and gas, coal and mining, body shopping and so on after liberalization. The non-traditional business families who have just acquired political power seem to have manipulated it to secure natural resources, real estate and so on in the name of permits and licenses for their cronies. The greatest advantage for the crony capitalism to thrive in India is the primordial relations of castes. This has strengthened the operation of crony capitalism with emotional appeal to castes in power. (But, one should realize that the cronies are not going to benefit the entire caste, but only few families in the caste.) This neophyte would facilitate the division of society to plunder without organized resistance that helps to maintain orthodoxy even in the 21st century. The sooner we appreciate the folly of caste politics and corporate-sponsored democracy to reinforce crony capitalism, the better for the country as a whole to realize the constitutional goals of socialism, secularism and democracy.

Crony capitalism as analysed by experts under neoclassical framework looked at it as a source of saving of transaction costs. Cronyism in India is ubiquitous in its presence as caste relations in all transactions, be it economic or social. Some of our scholars who had looked at the material base of our caste system did not throw light on the exchange relations and the differential terms of trade between lower castes and upper castes. Therefore, it has always been upheld and protected by the ruling castes, mostly the *Dvijas*. The supply and demand for labour and the products available in the market did carry a caste tag to regulate prices, wages and returns. Therefore, the surplus value that is so crucial in Marxist theory of capitalism could not be located here, as it is hidden under the caste rank. It was found to be a convenient structure to be used for the sustenance of political and economic power irrespective of who the ruler was. Caste system had continued regardless of the dynasty, including Gupta, Mughal, British or someone else. No ruling elite tinkered with it, lest the *virat purush* might crumble and create chaos. There were few intermittent changes. It was only some groups of people from the lower castes who tried to move the ladder of caste when there was some opportunity, but they soon reduced to a position that was not far from the original, as there was total prohibition to enter the privileged *Dvijahood*. It was perhaps never found to be a serious problem in transactions as the size of the population at any category was so huge, particularly at the lower levels. Thus, caste-based cronyism was cultivated and promoted.

### Inequality Widened through Trade

One of the important characters of crony capitalism is its reliance on trade and money. We know that money (including usury), banking and trade are traditionally confined to a particular social group in India. We have seen above that Hazari committee reported that four traditional businesses or Bania families had appropriated all the regulated licenses during 1960s. Thus, crony in India means caste networks, mostly the Brahmin, Bania, Kshatriya and *Dvija* group, appropriating anything. India has adopted a model based on foreign trade replacing its earlier model of import substitution after 1991. The volume of trade and value went up several times during the liberalization period and the so-called FDIs and foreign institutional investors (FIIs) are invested in sectors that are not identified as priority areas but are easy prey of political manipulation. The rate of growth and the sectorial contributions of GDP clearly show the trend in the Indian economy after the 1990s. The impact of trade on the economy and society are evaluated by the United Nations Conference on Trade and Development (UNCTAD).[12] The striking feature of the UNCTAD report on trade and development for 2012 is that it is dedicated to 'policies for inclusive and balanced growth' and devoted a separate chapter on how international trade has widened inequalities, in general, and in developing countries, in particular. Those who are familiar with the liberalization policies in India around 1990s do remember how vigorously some economists have championed free trade. Interestingly, neither the supporters nor the admirers have ever looked at the experiences in our neighbouring Southeast and Far East. But, for reasons better known to the elite of the political and bureaucratic executive, we have continued to follow the prescriptions of the West, particularly the Washington Consensus model. It has given an impression that globalization means contacts with a dozen countries, mostly English-speaking, and the cultural goods packaged and popularized through the media. Unfortunately, we know very little about China, Japan, Korea and other countries whose manufacturing goods are used every day. In other words, Western model, mostly American model of capitalist development, was popularized among certain serial groups. The ICT revolution and the educated upper castes' migration to the West is reflected in the remittances and culture of economic liberty, as a virtue has been popularized at home. This has to a large extent led to the political decimation of secularism and the emergence of religious fundamentalism both as a value and culture of discrimination. The apathy of the intellectual class mostly drawn from the same milieu kept reticent on violence against the disadvantaged based on the birth of a person.

Against this background, the 2012 report has implications for India. It is reported that the merchandise trade of the world has declined from 5.5 per cent in 2011 to 3.5 per cent in 2012. The growth rate has declined sharply from 4.1 per cent in 2010 to 2.7 per cent in 2012, mostly due to the growth rates of developing countries and China (developed countries confined to less than 2.5%). Financial frauds and low demand in developed countries have lowered exports from developing countries, including India. Except gold, all mineral exports have declined during the period. The report has analysed the so-called Kuznets curve indicating that in the beginning inequalities increase and after some time, with increase in productivity, disparities decline, which seems to have failed. On the contrary, Dani Rodrik and Alesina[13] have proved that inequalities in primary income would hamper growth. It is supported by historical data that the share of wages in the national income of the UK, the USA and Japan was around 60 per cent for a long period to sustain growth.

This went against the rhetoric that liberalization of labour laws to reduce wage rigidities in the Third World would affect development. After a review of the theories, the report has come to the conclusion that,

> these alternative views, by challenging the conventional wisdom that rising inequality is the normal result of development within market economies, may contribute to a new understanding of the functioning of a market economy, and can lead to a paradigm shift towards a pattern of economic development that is both more equitable and more efficient.[14]

The report has noted that the trade between the advanced and the developing countries has caused inequalities in the latter. The estimates of proportion of top quintile share of income to the bottom quintile show that inequalities are higher in developing countries than in developed countries, such as the UK. It is supported by the Gini ratios (measure of inequality) ranging from 35 per cent in the USA to 50 per cent in Malaysia, and India coming in between with 32.5 per cent.

India's trade with the developed and developing counties has a huge component of micro small and medium enterprises (MSME) products. The annual report of the ministry of company affairs shows that around 65 per cent of the overseas trade products of MSME are drawn from OBC, SC and ST. However, they remain only as vendors and the trade is organized by the Gujarati Banias, Marwari and Parsi business houses.

## Caste and Economic Inequalities Reinforce

One wonders how the iniquitous structure in India could be maintained so long without any change. There were, however, some revolts in the form of Sramana traditions (Ajivaka, Buddhist, Jain and so on) that altered social positions in the middle for some period. But they were restored and the hegemony of the *Dvija* continued. (It is said that since the time of Adi Shankaracharya when counter-revolution was initiated in the 8th century AD, there is a continuous stability in the social order as per B. R. Ambedkar.) Scholars, including Imtiaz Ahmad,[15] Reny Delage,[16] Kenneth Ballhatchet,[17] have noted that caste distinctions prevail even among Muslims and Christians in India.

The economic status and the social position of a caste in India broadly correspond to each other's. There are several studies on the inequalities among different castes in relations to education,[18] economic opportunities,[19] wealth[20] and poverty.[21] K. S. Chalam in his studies has empirically proved the gap between SC, ST, OBC and others with the coefficient of inequality in education. The economic opportunities for the socially marginalized castes have been denied in terms of the allocation of funds under special component plan and so on. Comparing

> 'the population share of a given caste group in a given wealth decile, its share in population, Bharati found that forward caste is relatively more represented in top 10 per cent and middle 10 per cent of the population where almost 90 per cent of the wealth is concentrated. SC, ST and Muslims are relatively more represented in the bottom 50 per cent. This is true in the case of land worship, education and other parameters of property. Baroah and others empirically proved that compared to high caste households, households for others groups (OBC Hindus, SC, ST, Muslim and high caste Muslim) were not as well endowed with assets, but even when they did have comparable assets these were rewarded at lower rate than that obtained by HC households'.

Measured by head count ratio (HCR) with their shares in the total number of households, the ST households made a disproportionately large contribution to rural poverty (24% versus 11%) and SC, mostly BC and high-caste Muslims, made a disproportionately large contribution to urban poverty. On the other hand, high-caste Hindus and others groups made a disproportionately small contribution to rural and urban poverty.[22] In other words, low-caste Hindus or the converts to Islam and other faiths have been denied the economic opportunities even under capitalist model of development that was introduced in the name of liberalization in 1991. An Oxfam study on widening gaps[23] in India has produced empirical evidence, such as Gini coefficients of income, percentage share of wealth by decile group, status of education and health and so on, which found that the migrated groups are disadvantaged in the access to wealth and basic services resulting in widening gap between lower castes and others. Presenting the data on percentage share of wealth by decile groups during 1991 and 2012, the report concluded that top 10 per cent held more than 50 per cent of the wealth during the period. Citing Forbes 2012 report, it is noted that top 1 per cent of the population of the country had ₹96.2 lakh cores. The net worth of 68 billionaires was 5.7 lakh corers and the wealth held by 100 billionaires increased from $49 billion in 2004 to $479 billion in 2017, increased almost by 10 times. None of the above billionaires are drawn from SC, ST or OBC (or serially marginalized Dalits, Adivasis and service castes). We do not need more than this to substantiate that the primordial social groups in India are reinforced in the process of accumulation of wealth by the few. However, some experts are shy of accepting this reality, which may be due to want of a theoretical framework or social inhibition (some prejudice).

The concept of patrimonial capital introduced by Thomas Piketty,[24] which is inherited by a generation through parental bequeath in the West is almost similar to our caste system that perpetuates inequalities by birth. He has also noted the role of crony capitalism in the West in perpetuating economic inequalities. In fact, Marx has mentioned about the fictitious capital in his Capital Vol III, which was elaborated by Cedric Durand how it is engulfing the international economy to its brim.[25] The concept of crony capitalism gained currency after the 2008 American financial crisis was captured by the Economist a year before to translate the phenomenon into numbers with assistance from Morgan Stanley, Ruchir Sharma[26] and others. They have listed 10 rent-thick sectors, such as (a) casinos, (b) coal, palm oil and timber, (c) defence, (d) deposit-taking banking and investment banking, (e) infrastructure and pipelines, (f) oil, gas, chemical and other energy, (f) ports, airports, (g) real estate, construction, (h) steel and other metals, (i) mining and commodities, and (j) utilities and telecom services, to estimate the size of the wealth beyond these sectors as obtained by cronies as a proportion of GDP. It is reported that India had a rank of 6 in 2007 and 9 in 2014 and the same is maintained in the year 2018 among 25 countries listed. Though the concept is not accepted universally as a phenomenon, some called it only a crisis in capitalism, such as Jack Farmer and Chiranjibi Sen, claiming that it is not pro-business but only an emerging phenomenon[27] in India.

The crony capitalism is caste capitalism in India. In exception, there may be one or two individuals as agents of the big cronies, but no one from the socially marginalized castes has emerged as a crony capitalist or a rent seeker in India. We have noted in the previous sections about the conditions of cronyism in India and found that they are not conducive for lower sections to enter the club as they do not have the following characters.

1. Collusion
2. Involvement in Public policy
3. Caste cartels

4. Tax evasion
5. Smuggling the results of state-funded research
6. Control over banking and financial instillations
7. Diverting the attention of the people through parochialism, jingoism and so on
8. Getting bureaucratic cronies in plum posts
9. Media and mafia patronage

## Strengthening Existing Socio-economic Formation

The base superstructure imagery in the Marxist domain to describe caste as noted by Murzban Jal in Chapter 6 is a unique character in India. Some of them put forward sophisticated arguments that caste is a superstructure that would disappear once the economic base is removed.[28] And the counter arguments by Dalit groups and others that discrimination prevails even after obtaining economic status.[29] The fact that communist parties split on caste question is a testimony of the failure of the theory of class analysis relevant to socio-economic formation in India. It is strange that Dalits and non-Dalits within the ideological spectrum of Marxism are divided accusing each other for not recognizing their point of view. This is once again a dichotomy that prevailed in the left and radical movements in India, while the cadres from lower castes (except pockets of forest dwellers) almost left the Left and created void. This is a serious problem of academic challenge to study, analyse and resolve the clash. It appears that the problem arises due to our failure to recognize the structure of socio-economic formation in India that is different from the West though the components of MOP might remain to be the same. It may also be due to the failure to recognize the caste groups on the top and bottom, which correspond to the exploiter and the exploited, while some in the middle groups are petty bourgeois in India. In fact, there are very few studies to analyse and explain what castes constitute what classes. In the West, Poulantzas's type of study on classes in contemporary capitalism was outlined while it is hardly attempted in India. The recurrence of Janus-faced socio-economic formation time and again is the crux of the problem. It appears that accepting the lower and the *Dvija* castes as the two countervailing groups in place of classes or parallels might solve some of the riddles in MOP debate. It is not accidental or strange to find the same socio-economic formation in 2020 in the form of crony capitalism helping the *Dvija* and draining the Dalit. The so-called middle castes are not monolithic as some castes are included in SCs while some castes such as Arzal Muslim and Dalit Christian, are included as OBC converts in different states of India, which is a problem to be resolved.

Crony capitalism in India has facilitated the capitalist class to grow in leaps and bounds not by the efficiency of the market mechanism or the innovations that they brought in, but by sheer manipulation of the economic operations restricted to a select group. The cronies are investing in political parties and some individuals act as their proxies once they are in power and accumulate wealth in the form of contracts, licenses and permits, all in the name of democratic decision-making. Majority of the judgements of the courts, as they are superstructure institutions of the system, are helping to legitimize such activities of the state as public policy. This is not rent-seeking behaviour of the public servants as noted by few bourgeois economists, since the capitalists are directly involved in the political process and converting it as a business model, a model of the 21st-century capitalism under the direction of the World Bank, WTO, IMF and so on. As mentioned above, the socially and economically deprived lower classes have remained poor, while the rich and few corporates or business houses, all coming from the higher castes or *Dvija* group with neo-feudal relations, are thriving under crony capitalism, which is only an extension of capitalist exploitation and nothing more or less.

## Notes

1. Musthaq Khan and Jomo K. S., eds., *Rents, Rent-seeking and Economic Development: Theory and Evidence in Asia* (Cambridge, UK: Cambridge Press, 2000).
2. David C. Kang, *Crony Capitalism: Corruption and Development in Korea and Philippines* (New York: Cambridge University Press, 2009).
3. David C. Kang, *Transaction Costs and Crony Capitalism in East Asia*, Working paper 02-11 (Dartmouth: Tuck School of Business, May 2002).
4. Lews Hunter, *Crony Capitalism in America* (Edinburg: AC² Books, 2013).
5. Paranjoy Guha Thakurta, *Gas Wars: Crony Capitalism and the Ambanis*, 2014, sold by Asia Pacific-Amazon.
6. Edward Avelling, *Student's Marx with Introduction by K. S. Chalam* (Delhi: People's Publishing House, 2018).
7. John A. Hobsen, *Imperialism: A Study* (New York: James Pott and Company, 1902).
8. Ibid.
9. Government of India, Hazari Committee on Industrial Planning and Licencing, 1968.
10. Government of India, Mahalnobis Committee on Economic Power, 1964.
11. Government of India, Subimal Dutt Committee on Monopolies Enquiry, 1967.
12. UNCTAD, *Trade and Development Report 2012: Policies for Inclusive and Balanced growth* (Geneva, New York: UNDP, 2012).
13. Alberto Alesina and Dani Rodrik, 'Distributive Policies and Economic Growth', *The Quarterly Journal of Economics* 109, no. 2 (1994): 465–490.
14. Ibid.
15. Imtiaz Ahmad, ed., *Caste and Social Stratification among Muslims* (Delhi: Manohar, 1973).
16. Remy Delage, 'Muslim Castes in India'. www.booksandideas.net/Muslim-Castes-in-India.html
17. Kenneth Ballahat Chatt, *Caste, Class and Catholicism in India 1789–1914* (London: Curizon Press, 1998).
18. Chalam, *Education and Weaker Sections*.

19. Chalam, *Economic Reforms*.
20. Nitin Kumar Bharti, *Wealth Inequality, Class and Caste in India 1961–2012* (France: Paris School of Economics, 2018).
21. Vani Barooah, Dilip Diwakar, Vinod Kumar Mishra, Ajaya Kumar Naik, and Nidhi S. Sabharwal, *Caste Inequality and Poverty in India: A Reassessment* (Delhi: Indian Institute of Dalit Studies, 2016).
22. Ibid.
23. Oxfam, *India Inequality Report* (Delhi: Oxfam India, 2018).
24. Thomas Piketty, *Capital in the Twenty-First Century* (Cambridge: Harvard University Press, 2014).
25. A. Cedric Durand, *Fictitious Capital: How Finance is Appropriating Our Future* (London: Verso, 2017); 'Our Crony Capitalism Index', *The Economist*, 15 March 2014.
26. 'Our Crony Capitalism', *The Economist*.
27. Jack Farmer, 'The Myth of Crony Capitalism', *Socialist Review*, February 2012; Chiranjeebi Sen, *Curbing Crony Capitalism in India*, Azim Premji University, April 2017 Working Paper.
28. *The Caste Question and Its Resolution: A Marxist Perspective* (Chandigarh: Advanced Institution of Marxist Studies, 2013).
29. Sukhadeo Thorat, Anuradha Banerji, Vinod K. Mishra, and Firdaus Rizvi, 'Urban Rental Housing Market', *Economic and Political Weekly* 27 (2015): 47–53.

# 8

# Judiciary and Deprivation of Social Justice

Modern judiciary as a law enforcement agency in India began with the advent of East India Company rule. It began with the mayor's courts under the Royal Charter of 1661 and the Supreme Court of Fort Williams in Calcutta in 1774 to usher in Anglo-Saxon jurisprudence. Macaulay and James Stephen codified law. James Mill wrote that India's traditional legal systems had to disappear in order to service the needs of modern society based on competitiveness and protection of individual rights and freedoms.[1] Earlier, *dharmashastras* and caste codes were used as per the whims of the kings and priest class based on religious prescriptions. In other words, the major function of the codes appeared to be to maintain *varnadharma* and graded inequality. Though the Anglo-Saxon legal system brought uniformity among different regions of the country, the judiciary and the structure of the courts has remained problematic. Judiciary as a part of superstructure of a bourgeois society as formulated by Marxist scholars is supposed to protect the interests of the ruling classes (castes) in a modern society. Gramsci on the conception of law noted that, 'if every state tends to create and maintain a certain type of civilization and citizen (and hence of collective life and of individual relations) and to eliminate certain customs and attitudes to disseminate others, then the law will be its instrument for this purpose'.[2] This is, in fact, what Mao Tse-Tung was also emphasizing about the role of superstructure that includes judiciary, education, culture and so on. He wrote

> in the development of history as a whole it is the material things and social distance that determines social consciousness at the same time. We also recognize and must recognize the reaction of social consciousness on social existence and the reaction of superstructure on the economic foundation.... When superstructure (politics, culture and so on) hinders the development of economic foundation, political and cultural reforms become the principal and decisive factors.[3]

We are examining the role of judiciary within the broad framework of MOP approach here as an academic exercise. We have respect for Indian judiciary and the apex court that gave landmark judgements, and the analysis is in no way intended to lessen the esteem of judiciary.

The structure and the process of delivery of justice in India have not undergone any change in terms of caste bias and privileges enjoyed by the upper caste ever in the era of globalization. This strengthen the argument that judiciary by and large has remained as a superstructure to protect the existing socio-economic structure in India despite constitutional provisions. This may be due to the weak academic and intellectual background of some of the judges and the advocates who are alleged to be in collision with the bench in some cases belonging to some social background. Kiruba Munusamy argued that there is rampant corruption and caste discrimination in the

Indian judiciary.[4] In fact, an analytical study by Marc Galanter and Nick Robinsen[5] about the kind of nexus between judges and advocates and the phenomenon of 'different judges deciding the same point of law as part of differently constituted benches reaching different results' exist in India. Listing the top 'grand advocates' and their annual incomes, Galanter and Robinsen noted that,

> the powerful role of social networks in acquiring clients and setting up a practice helps perpetuate the disproportionate presence of certain ethnic and religious groups in the profession. For example, in Madras Brahmins dominate the upper ranks of bar because of their tight networks and long-standing proficiency in English.... Despite repeated enquiries, we could not identify any scheduled caste, scheduled tribes or other background class advocates who were regarded as part of the elite structure of lawyers.[6]

The same is reflected in the bench and naturally in the orders that they pass, as we see below in some cases. The discrimination did not end up here. Judges who are promoted to the higher judiciary from the socially marginalized groups, such as Justice Dinakaran, are alleged to be victimized and hounded both by the judiciary and the more socially badmouthed media in India. Even judges of the Supreme Court, including the chief justices, were accused as corrupt. Prasanth Bhushan echoed by Shanti Bhushan categorically stated that out of 16 to 17 chief justices, half have been corrupt as of 2009.[7] Out of the three constitutional structures, such as Union Public Service Commission (UPSC) and Election Commission of India, it is the higher judiciary that is being perceived as corrupt, discriminatory, incapable of coming to grip with the changing times to shed its social bias. It is in this context we need to look at the changes brought in by the legislature through amendments to Constitution and the outcome.

## Amendments to the Constitution

The Constitution of India was amended 124 times so far. The Constitution was amended three times within five years of its adoption. Therefore, B. R. Ambedkar in his parliamentary debates in the Rajya Sabha on 15 September 1954 has said that,

> I do not know of any constitution in the world which has been amended so rapidly and if, I may say so rashly, by the government in office.... Is the constitution not different in any sense from an ordinary law? Is it merely a scrap paper to be amended at whim of anybody? I have been noticing the great contempt or the low regard or respect which the government has for the constitution.[8]

Thus, the chairman of the drafting committee himself was disillusioned with the attitude of the elected governments towards the Constitution. But, the sad part of the storey is that not only the legislative wing of the government, but even the judiciary seems to have the same attitude towards the provisions of the Constitution, particularly with reference to the economic and social clauses. Therefore, one need not wonder that the onslaught on the Constitution will remain perpetual and eternal. Let us look at the history of the process of erosion of the constitutional morality and the context in order to understand the reasons for the amendments.

## Concept of Private Property

It is necessary to take into consideration the growing needs of the modern state in its attempt to amend a written constitution. But, that does not mean that the state can rush for a constitutional amendment without exhausting first the available alternative means to achieve an economic or social objective. In fact, it is alleged by scholars that the elected governments are slowly becoming agents of interest groups or representatives of class interests rather than demonstrating the vision of an enlightened society. The contradictions were present even during the framing of the Constitution particularly with reference to the right to property. Before Article 31 was dumped in 1978 through the 44th amendment, there was great debate in the Constituent Assembly. Ambedkar noted that there were three groups within the congress party supporting the use of article to their advantage. It was Jawaharlal Nehru who was against compensation. But Mr Pant was interested in the zamindari abolition and Sardar Patel was arguing for full compensation. Therefore, Ambedkar himself was interested in the first amendment to the Constitution to facilitate land reforms. But, the landed interests seem to have entered the mindset of the judiciary and created problems for the effective implementation of economic programmes that led the Mrs Gandhi government to amend the Constitution to bring Article 300 A and drop Article 31. This was necessitated due to the needs of the emerging society. In fact, Ambedkar has agreed with the idea of an evolving nation of Thomas Jefferson and quoted him in his parliamentary debates. It is said that 'each generation as a distinct nation, with a right, by the will of the majority to bind themselves ... each generation has a right to determine the law under which it lives'.[9] Here one must underline the difference between the will of the majority and the whimsies of the major lobbies that in general came from the propertied classes.

In this context, we may find how Ambedkar as a visionary realized the limitations of constitutional provisions and anticipated the contradictions in our social and economic life. Therefore, he gave a social and economic agenda in his 'States and Ministries' as he thought that some of his ideas could not be brought under the Constitution due to the competing groups in the Constituent Assembly. He wanted that agricultural land be nationalized and the commanding heights of the economy be placed under the control of the public sector. Perhaps, he was expecting that some of his dreams would be realized through the implementation of the provisions of the Constitution. But, the executive and judiciary, two important pillars of Indian democracy, which are delegated with the responsibility of translating the provisions of the Constitution into reality seem to have failed. It is a well-known fact that the special bench of the Supreme Court in the case of Bank nationalization Act 1969 struck down the Act on the grounds that it did not meet certain principles of adequate compensation. It is not only in the case of bank nationalization but even in the area of other economic issues; the Supreme Court seems to have remained always with the property classes. It is strange that neither the courts nor the intelligentsia have ever looked at the concept of private property in India. They have simply adopted the principles as observed in the Anglo-Saxon countries, particularly the USA, where the conditions are different. India never had the concept of private property before the permanent settlement. The laws in the USA are alien to India as they were framed by the settlers to get legal sanction of grabbing property of the natives without the moral authority. The NIs who were basically the Adivasis and Dalits kept outside the purview of land settlement during the British regime both in the princely states and the British India government. Even the land held by these sections obtained through the alienation proceedings are now being taken away by the government using the principles of 'eminent domain'. The compensation paid to the displaced people is based on the colonial Land Acquisition Act 1894. Even in the calculation of valuation of compensation to the owner of the property, the economic principles of law of diminishing marginal utility is not considered and the value of the property of a zamindar, a rich peasant or a small farmer are considered as similar. This is a great flaw in the Indian legal system. Further, the value of the property is now converted into liquid form in stocks and shares. The intensity of this kind of conversion and their transfer to other countries has increased several-fold after 1991. The judiciary seems to have not commented much on these issues and, in fact, allowed privatization of public properties much against the spirit of the Constitution and Directive Principles of State Policy.

The story of private property in India is a fairy tale. We are concerned here how the judiciary is responsible in creating the titles and the legislative wing in reconstituting new dimension to right to property with interpretations by the apex court. It is always the ruling castes or classes that are benefitted by such interpretations starting from the Kesavananda Bharathi case and concept of basic structure of the Constitution. Rakesh Shukla[10] has analysed how the right of the poor are overlooked and the interests of *mathadpathis* and Foreign Exchange Regulation Act (FERA) violators protected. Citing former law minister Shivasankar, who had remarked that 'Mathadi Pathis like Kesavananda Bharathi and Zamindars like Golaknath evoked a sympathetic cord nowhere in the country except in the supreme court of India', Jaivir Singh[11] has elaborately discussed how the right to property is dropped and a new provision is made in the Constitution and the role of the judiciary in protecting the rights to property at the time of bank nationalization and in the process of interpreting 1894 Land Acquisition Act. As Jaivir is trained in economics, he has brought in the theory of Coase (the Nobel laureate) and other economists in understanding the role of transaction costs as the costs establishing and maintaining properly rights. But very few judges sitting on judgement have expertise in economic and social issues and, therefore, rely on linguistic facility to arrive at a conclusion unlike the American and European judges who are now well grounded in these disciplines. (The problem seems to have been addressed after the five-year integrated law course was designed.)

The mineral rich areas of the country are located in the Eastern and Western Ghats and in tribal areas. The Right to Fair Compensation and Transparency in Land Acquisition and Rehabilitation Act 2013 and the Scheduled Tribes and Other Traditional Forest Dwellers (Recognition of Forest Rights) Act 2006 are two important legislations that made the life of the tribes, SCs as victims due to excess litigation. It is reported that there are around 1,200 laws relating to land in the country as it comes under state list.[12] About two-thirds of the total litigations in the Supreme Court relate to landed property (including the infamous Ayodhya dispute 2019). All these laws did not come to the rescue of the victims, mostly the socially marginalized and displaced, but help the upper caste litigants to escape. There are several rights, such as right to education and right to food, which are observed in breach rather than in operation due to litigation and over-indulgence of judiciary in the matters. The privatization of higher education was protected by the judiciary and some of the judges became targets of corruption charges due to medical admissions involving crores of rupees, which speaks about the status of judiciary. However, there are brilliant judges and judgements under the category of public interest litigation (PIL) that keep the esteem of judiciary in haven.

The issue of compensation and right to life are becoming serious issues in the process of rapid economic development. The state is increasingly considered as an agency of a class or caste as articulated by activist scholars, which would be seized of limited vision about the future victims with new paradigm of governance. The Dalits and Adivasis are now left with limited opportunities in a growing private sector and their displacement from the existing sources of livelihood, such as land, traditional skills and other sources (with an agenda of capitalist expansion), will be double marginalized. It is in this context, the provisions of the Constitution need to be ingeniously and effectively interpreted by the judiciary to protect the common man in general and the Dalits and Adivasis in particular. In an era of judge-made law replacing constitutional wisdom, the ingenuity and enlightened outlook of the judiciary is the last resort for the victims. Otherwise, the dominant groups and the propertied classes who are increasingly getting into the legislature will make and unmake constitutional amendments to suit their self or class interests. This may be kept in mind by the judiciary in pronouncing judgements on constitutional issues so as to restrict the vested interests not to mend or amend constitutional wisdom.

## Social Justice and Indian Constitution

Social justice is generally understood as equality and the absence of injustice. Amartya Sen[13] in his book *The Idea of Justice* has identified three components of a theory of justice.

1. A theory of justice must include ways of judging how to reduce injustice and advance justice rather than aiming only at characterization of perfectly just societies.
2. There is a need for a reasoned argument with oneself and with others in dealing with conflicting claims.
3. The presence of remedial injustice may well be connected with actual lives rather than with institutional shortcomings.

Though Sen was evaluating the relevance of John Rawls'[14] theory of 'justice as fairness', in the book, he was at the same time indicating the Indian concepts of justice. He was very clear in not mentioning social justice here, because he knew that the concept of social justice was alien to Indians. However, he noted the early Indian jurisprudence of 'Niti' and 'Nyaya'. Niti is related to organizational propriety as well as behavioural correctness. 'Nyaya' is concerned with what emerges and how, and in particular the lives that people are actually able to lead. Quoting from Mahabharata, and Gita, 'Niti' according to Sen is consequent-independent, while 'Nyaya' is reasoning in an ethical or political evaluation of human lives. Sen has not fully explained the context and the text of Bhagavad Gita in his book on the dialogue between Krishna and Arjuna on 'Niti' and Nyaya. Krishna was asking Arjuna here to perform his duty as a Kshatriya which was independent of any consequence. Interestingly, it is here in Bhagavad Gita (Chapter 18, Sloka. 41–44) that the duties and functions of the *varnas* are explained as inborn qualities, which Sen has omitted conspicuously to avoid controversy. Because it is common knowledge of every Indian that 'niti' is related to 'Jati' and 'Nyaya' is related to 'dharma'. The common man understanding of Niti–Nyaya seems to be a little different from the academic elucidation of Sen. Here *dharma* is or to be implied as *varnashrama dharma* and it is not based on reason. Therefore, the concepts are of limited help to clarify social justice from the tradition of Indian jurisprudence?

We may examine here John Rawls' 'Theory of Justice' that has revolutionized liberal thinking about equality. Rawls theory can help us to solve the age-old dichotomies of social justice. Rawls original position is an imagined situation of primordial equality when the parties involved have no knowledge of their personal identities. It is in the state of 'veil of ignorance' the principles of justice are chosen unanimously. The following principles of justice will emerge in the original position.

1. Each person has an equal right to a fully adequate scheme of equal basic liberties which is compatible with a similar scheme of liberties for all.
2. Social and economic inequalities are to satisfy two conditions. First, they must be attached to offices and positions open to all under conditions of fair equality of opportunity, and second, they must be to the greatest benefit of the least advantaged members of society.

Thus, the principles of social justice enunciated by Rawls make sure that public opportunities are open to all, without anyone being excluded or handicapped on grounds of say, race or ethnicity or caste or religion. The second part is concerned with distributive justice as well as overall efficiency, and it takes the form of making the worst-off members of the society as well off as possible. These principles can be used to argue for the distribution of opportunities in higher education among different social groups in India. However, our intellectuals and activists can still argue that by admitting reserved category students in higher education, they are denied fair opportunity. I think the argument here can be little extended by saying that in matters of social opportunity, we cannot compare two human beings in India as the same in terms of flesh and blood. They are two individuals as members of a social group called 'caste' within the boundaries of a state. Each one is representative of a history, social norms, characteristics and other factors that are not the same between the two. Therefore, it is not related to two human beings, but two individuals representing two social groups or castes with different endowments and they are to be treated differently. In fact, the problems of distribution of resources or spaces arise due to limited resources and unlimited demand for them. This is purely an economic problem. It can be solved in such a way that the scarce resources are to be allocated to those individuals from whom the society gets the highest marginal returns to maximize the total benefit.

### Elusive Social Justice in Apex Court

The socially and educationally deprived sections of the society have reposed greatest confidence in the Constitution with the belief that it will come to their rescue in times of impingement. Therefore, the evaluation of the process of constitutional support to the poor and underprivileged and socially and historically marginalized groups can be attempted in terms of the judicial activism in social laws. It is in this context, the Supreme Court judgement pronounced by Chief Justice Y. K. Sabharwal and four other Hon'ble judges evoked wide publicity and discussion in the media.[15] However, some of the observers and intellectuals have been saying that once the State has accepted and executed the lopsided judgement delivered in the case of Mandal Commission (*Indira Sawhney* case 1993), it is inevitable to expect a judgement of this kind for SC and STs also. Some scholars of social jurisprudence have commented that our judiciary has remained by and large a Hindu feudal Institution and there is no surprise if they adhere to those values. It is said that the same is abundantly reflected in the majority of cases where upper caste orthodox Hindus deliver the controversial judgements on social issues. The Supreme Court has so far not represented the people of India or the democratic principles for which the Constitution stands for, and in its shadow, it survives. It is irony that none of the judgements relating to social jurisprudence contain an element of basic principles of justice nor a reference is made about the developments that are taking place in the world of knowledge in legal profession. Most of the time they represent simply a few statements devoid of any intellectual vision generally expected in a subject of this kind.

It is generally expected that a constitutional bench sitting on a judgement will shape the destiny of millions of people and will be guided by principles of justice. The basic tenet of justice is 'fairness'. It is also true that the learned judges cannot take shelter under 'the veil of ignorance'. They are all learned and experienced judges and they know the dynamics of Indian society. They are also aware of the fact that scholars, such as John Rawls who has maintained that the background 'conditions of justice' need to be taken into consideration while making an analysis of a case. But, unfortunately, in most of the cases, including the recent judgement on creamy layer, there is no profound scrutiny of the issues involved or any intellectual inputs are put in coming to terms with the reality of the Indian society. It is very strange that the learned judges have often not seriously read the provisions of the Constitution and are guided by the popular opinion of the educated elite who constitute a minority in the Indian society and the opinions are sometimes reflected through the bar. It is clear from the judgement, which speaks of constitutional requirements as backwardness, inadequacy of representation and overall administrative efficiency in Article 16 of the Constitution. However, Article 16, including Articles 16(4A) and 16(4B), is an unconditional provision to provide equality of opportunity to majority of the population of the country who have been denied opportunities because of the operation of the *dharmashastras* (which were upheld by traditional priesthood). It is found that the learned judges in the Mandal Commission judgement and also in some landmark judgements, such as Golaknath, have been protecting the *dharmadhipatis* and their traditional roles. They have created precedents. They are all judge-made legal provisions, but they have never gone through the scrutiny of the democratic legislative process. Like many traditional religious institutions, the Supreme Court is upholding those precedents as tenets of law, as they are convenient both to the judiciary and to the ruling classes.

The flaw in the legal process of the apex court is inherent as the Supreme Court is considered as above board and is not publicly accountable. In most of the cases, it is alleged that the learned judges are not even accountable to their conscience as some of their pronouncements are deliberately done without reference to the facts of the cases and actual constitutional position. It is clear from the Indira Sawhney case that a deliberate quantitative restriction of 50 per cent reservation is imposed while Article 335 speaks about the maintenance of efficiency of administration while considering the claims of members of SCs and STs who constitute 22 per cent of the population. And how can a 50 per cent ceiling be imposed on the reservation for the 22 per cent population? Article 335 is not related to the reservation of OBCs. The case of backward classes arises at a separate Article only after the appointment of a commission to investigate the conditions of backward classes under Article 340. Therefore, the Mandal judgement appears to be a misreading or one can allege that it is a deliberate attempt to distort the constitutional provisions relating to caste-based reservations.

In the judgement relating to the creamy layer, the Hon'ble Chief Justice and the other members of the bench, it is alleged, have been citing their own judgements as set of guidelines of law to substantiate their arguments. This is definitely a bad tradition devoid of any ethical or theoretical substance. It seems there is a growing literature relating to precedents and their limitations.

The founding fathers of the Constitution knew the background conditions of social justice in India while making Articles 15 and 16. These two Articles are fundamental in protecting the interest of the socially and educationally backward classes of citizens and or SCs and STs. One must see the historical conditions under which the first amendment to the Constitution was made to incorporate Article 15(4). This article mentioned about two distinct groups of backward classes of citizens. It is elementary knowledge that we cannot read Articles 14 and 15 together. Article 14 relates to any person and this person can be a citizen or a non-citizen, a child or anyone, whereas Articles 15 and 16 speak about citizens in a group. Therefore, the learned judges should have considered the distinction between an independent person and a citizen in a group. The rights of a person are individual in nature, whereas the special provisions conferred on a citizen under Article 15 and Article 16 relate to the entire group. If, one is inclined to read more in Article 15(4), it is clear that it is an open-ended category as far as backward classes of citizens are concerned. It is the duty of the National Commission for Backward Classes to study, scrutinize and classify any person in a group as backward classes. There is no restriction. That is the reason why in certain states Brahmins and so-called upper castes are also classified as backward classes, based on the yardsticks used to classify them as backward classes. But in the case of SCs and STs, it is a closed-ended category as the classifications of SCs and STs were made before the Constitution came into existence. There is a long history about the classification of the SCs and STs. There is one single test which is very significant in classifying SCs as a separate category, that is, untouchability. Apart from other 10 classifying tests, none of them is applicable for other social categories like backward classes. SCs are only a unique category. Similarly, STs both in the schedule V and VI areas are those who are isolated from the mainstream society. They cannot be grouped with any other category. It is strange that the learned judges have not considered this unique nature of constitutional categories of people as separate entities and put them together as one erroneously to arrive at a 50 per cent quantitative limitation for reservations. There is no legal or theoretical justification in lumping SC, ST and OBC together. Even if one considers 50 per cent as a quantitative restriction to ensure efficiency, it is possible to argue that the efficiency levels of open category candidates, which ranges above 50 per cent efficiency will be more than the efficiency levels of the below 50 per cent reserved category. In other words, if the total efficiency levels of all the open category candidates are aggregated, there will still be enough places for the below category candidates to extend it to even 70 per cent as the elite believe that the open category of 10 per cent are so efficient. This will take care of the efficiency of administration. In fact, the reverse is happening in administration as the reserved categories are carrying the brunt of work while the open category officers boss over. Further, the creamy layer is applied only to the disadvantaged groups and similar creamy layer is not applied to open category candidates in employment that creates a blatant discrimination against them. This is nothing but *varnadharma* of feudal era which the learned judges of the apex court appear to uphold. This was not the intention of the founding fathers of the Constitution.

It is instructive to find from the legal history of advanced societies that when judgements on social issues are pronounced, a lot of discussion, thinking and expert advice is taken as it has far-reaching implications for the society at large. It is the intellectual competence and the willingness of the learned judges that makes them to be broad based and visionary in outlook to foresee the future of a country. It is the incapable way to use the language of the Constitution and incapacity of a judge to see the large implications of the constitutional provisions that make the judgement trivial. It is always found in the legal literature that the legal luminaries have been dynamic in their pronouncements to make the society progress by providing enough scope and opportunities for the majority of the oppressed to advance, even by creatively interpreting some of the static provisions of a written constitution. Unfortunately, in most of the judgements, particularly during the last two decades, the judgements delivered by learned judges of the Supreme Court of India appear to be narrow and backward, bending to uphold the traditional feudal values. The 124th amendment to the Constitution on 12 January 2019, providing 10 per cent reservations to upper castes with less than ₹8 lakhs annual income, did not evoke any dissent though poverty among others is less than 5 per cent in most of the states and the economic criterion is only used as an alibi (it is also true in the case of some Marxists who supported the argument without empirical evidence that attracted the rebuke of lower castes).[16] This is a blemished trend as the prestigious institution owes its existence to the majority will of the people and if the majority of the people do not repose confidence in the institution, the institution will collapse, but not the Constitution. As the Constitution is a gift of the democratic process and a social contract, it shall always prevail. But the contemporary history of judiciary speaks differently.

## Precedent, Plagiarism and Some Flawed Orders

It is boasted that the doctrine of separation of powers, which is a theoretical model based on Roman, British and the American traditions, was adopted for India. However, the allegation that the legal minds and fraternity who contributed in the drafting of the Constitution were a little inclined to provide supremacy to judiciary stands. It can be noticed in the form of exhaustive clauses and articles relating to judiciary, including the salary and perks along with the third schedule describing its details, while such advantage is deprived of other constitutional authorities. They are meticulous. In fact, the provisions in the Constitution in terms of number of articles formulated by founding fathers are almost the same for the parliament and judiciary (Articles 43 and 41, respecively). This is anticipated as the learned judges under whose shoulders the providence of the underprivileged, the deprived and the marginalized is placed are expected to entail them with their wisdom. Yet, by default or design the framers did not infuse democratic spirit into the processes of judicial decisions that might have triggered the present crisis. In fact, the first generation of legal minds after independence due to their commitment to fair play have collectively lived up to the expectations until the 1970s.

The judgement in the case of Criminal Appeal No. 416 of 2018 delivered on 20 March 2018 by honourable judges of the apex court can be taken for an academic detour. The guiding spirit or principle of Indian Constitution is justice—social, economic and political. Notwithstanding the 42nd amendment to the Constitution, Sri Shivasankar's interpretation and action as Minister for Law and Justice, the judiciary is made fragile by the learned judges themselves through their interpretations and personal opinions expressed as judgements with least regard for the so-called constitutional morality or spirit, particularly with respect to justice as fairness. As noted above, John Rawls and Amartya Sen have elaborated on the theory and idea of justice, such as with reference to caste-based iniquitous society. It seems the Niti–Nyaya dichotomy and its application to India has not touched the conscience of our learned judges. There is a general feeling among the academic fraternity of legal education and governance that the amount of time and resources used by some learned judges on important issues, such as privatization of public sector units, caste-based reservations and SC/ST atrocity cases, that affect large sections of society are inadequate. It is often seen that the popular beliefs of the elite of the society (to use a popular phrase of the court 'creamy layer' of minority) are carried into the courtrooms rather than reflecting on the efficacy, prudence and the needs of an evolving society with empathy. Sometimes, they are cold-hearted and as a matter of fact orders disposing of the cases with impunity. Let us look at the case of Sri Bhaskar Karbhari Gaidwad, an employee of the College of Pharmacy, Karad, Maharashtra, the respondent No. 2 of case on Prevention of Atrocities (POA) Act 1989 and how it is interpreted in the above order of learned judges.

The above judgement contains 89 pages consisting of 2,401 lines, out of which 1,620 lines are citations as precedents from 65 cases. It means nearly 68 per cent of the judgement is lifted or borrowed from previous proceedings. If the wisdom of the amicus and other mentions are also included, it comes to three-fourths of the written order, leave alone their relevance and verisimilitude. The conclusion part of it includes the warning in Para 83 that, 'any violation of direction (iii) and (iv) will be actionable by way of disciplinary action as well as contempt'. Direction III above is about arrest of public servant with the approval of appointing authority, and IV is preliminary enquiry to be conducted by a deputy superintendent of police (DSP) to find allegations are not frivolous or motivated under Atrocities Act. As the Constitution under Article 141 conferred that law declared by the Supreme Court to be binding on all courts, it becomes operational with prospective affect making the essence of 1989 POA Act infructuous. The SCs of North India who have been subjected to several heinous crimes intensely and continuously for the last few years found the judgement adding fuel to fire. It is common knowledge of every literate person how the atrocities on the Dalits are perpetuated near Delhi, but unfortunately it did not reach the portals of the Supreme Court which otherwise is very proactive. The interesting part of the judgement is that the learned judges cited Article 21 to substantiate their reasoning.

> In the present context, to balance the right of liberty of the accused guaranteed under Article 21, which could be taken away only by just fair and reasonable procedure and to check abuse of power by police and injustice to a citizen, exercise

of right of arrest was required to be suitably regulated by way of guidelines by this Court under Article 32 read with Article 141 of the Constitution. Some filters were required to be incorporated to meet the mandate of Articles 14 and 21 to strengthen the rule of law.

It is further noted that, 'thus, unless this Court laid down appropriate guidelines, there will be no protection available against arbitrary arrests or false implications in violation of Article 21 of the Constitution.' We have checked the sentence twice before citing it here, as we knew about Article 22 that deals with, 'protection against arrest and detention in certain cases' and not necessarily Article 21 'protection of life and liberty' that requires procedure established by law. In this case Article 22 seems to be relevant and not that of 21. In fact, Article 21 should have been used to protect the Dalit victims. In fact, the learned Judges have totally ignored Article 17, abolition of untouchability, the basis on which POA has evolved over a period of time. We may give benefit of doubt to learned judges as they were under moral pressure to protect an ignorant officer Dr Mahajan, the appellant a non-SC person who refused permission to file charge sheet against two non-SC officers who were alleged to be responsible for committing the atrocity on Sri B. K. Gaidwad the complainant. This case appears to be simple but trivial. In the whole judgement of 89 pages, there appears to be over-dependency on the submissions of the deponent and his counsel along with the amicus's comparative table of the provisions of the Act and their application here. The amicus is supposed to be an expert in the area of the subject given to him, but the analytical aspects in relation to the constitutional morality and its impact on the future of the society are solely that of the judges who pass the orders.

It is noticed in some of the judgements that the honourable judges, may be due to heavy work and pressure, rely on the so-called precedents and cite passages from different sources verbatim to fill not less than 100 pages in each case. The conclusion and the operation part contain few sentences, and sometimes there appears to be lot of confusion as to which part is analysis and which part is direction. In a lighter vein, we can say that, without which there will be less business for the legal professionals. However, we need to understand that the scrutiny of facts and material on record considered by a judge to deliver the judgement should contain reasonable, just and rational account that correspond to the details of the case based on submissions made. It should not appear to be a prejudged dispute more so when it is a constitutional matter. The learned Judge of our apex court is not a technocrat to achieve Pareto optimality, where 'goods are allocated in such a way that it is impossible to redistribute them so that at least one person is better off and nobody is worse off'. Even the fallacy of this theorem that is cited quite often by a section of the elite who argue for efficiency was exposed by Nobel Laureate Amartya Sen. He revealed that,

> a society in which some people lead lives of great luxury while others live in acute misery can still be Pareto optimal if the agony of the deprived cannot be reduced without cutting into the ecstasy of the affluent. He adds that a state can be Pareto optimal and still be sickeningly iniquitous.

It is cited here in the context of a section of the judiciary defending the clause of equality before law in a structurally iniquitous society and tries to preserve social division on grounds of technical efficiency, even if it is against the basic spirit of the Constitution. There can be some legal matters where software can be used to decide the matter purely on the facts of the case. However, here is a constitutional matter with enormous social implications that essentially involves the competence, capacity and candour of the person who delivers the judgement.

Para 41 of the above judgement speaks about law spreading casteism and cited not only Articles 14–16 but also referred to B. R. Ambedkar to substantiate their reasoning, which may be a false or coarse logic to ignore Articles 17 and 22 and rely on their chosen precedents and articles. In paragraph 72, the learned judges asserted that 'harassment of an innocent citizen, irrespective of caste or religion, is against the guarantee of the Constitution. This Court must enforce such a guarantee. Law should not result in caste hatred'. There is no dispute with this ideal. But the way in which data are interpreted and situations cited to illustrate an erroneous point is perhaps bad in Law. It is noted in several publications of legal luminaries that 'precedent' or principle of *stare decisis* needs to be used cautiously and infrequently to achieve the objectives of predictability, stability, fairness and efficiency and not to avoid the challenge of delivery of justice. The distinction between two categories of horizontal and vertical precedents, the former adhering to its own precedent and the latter derived from a higher court, is hardly observed in some of the judgements. The citation of case law and the mushrooming of legal consulting firms and professionals made the job of a judge easier compared to her predecessors who did not get the support of computer-assisted documentation. Yet, the present generation of judges have problems of plagiarism as the legal support system, if incapable and dubious, might throw him into a cauldron of copying ideas and paragraphs that might end up in a condition of fallaciously reasoned, inadequately considered and badly argued judgement. That is not good either for the judiciary or for the clients and even for a progressive nation. In the academic world, authors and scholars were penalized for copying others' studies either inadvertently or intentionally without giving credits to the original author in a thesis or research paper. They are dubbed as plagiarists and frauds due to the rules of the game. We hardly come across such issues in the judiciary where similarly placed judges cite each other. If an analysis is made to correlate the socio-economic and ideological background of each judge and the content of judgements passed following a linear path resulting in regression in society, what does it signify?

Marxists simply dismiss judiciary, as a part of superstructure protecting the ruling class may not help us to understand the process of class suppression even in seats of justice delivery?

In fact, the powers and functions prescribed for the Supreme Court are not absolute, as it is repeatedly noted 'unless parliament by law otherwise provides'. There seem to be no headway in the present SC/ST atrocity judgement like all other previous cases relating to the socially and educationally marginalized.[17] Why should the parliament go to sessions every time and bring an amendment to suit the whims of select judges? It is necessary to understand to what extent the judgements are advisory and orders are binding? The whole exercise has unfortunately exposed the system when the same court recalled the directions in October 2019. The Indian judiciary is not democratized while enjoying all the benefits of parliamentary democracy and not even remotely mentioning about Article 312 and made the parliament lick its wounds in the appointment of judges.

How is it possible? There may be an implicit agreement between the benches of the judiciary and benches of parliament on all important issues relating to the economic and social development of the country to subvert the ideals of the founding fathers of the nation while pretending to do justice. Are the birds of the same feather flocking together or upholding the *varna dharma* need to be reflected?

## Notes

1. David Skuy, 'Macaulay and the Indian Penal Code of 1862: The Myth of the Inherent Superiority and Modernity of the English Legal System Compared to India's Legal System in the Nineteenth Century', *Modern Asian Studies* 32, no. 3 (1998): 513–557.
2. Gramsci, *Selections*, 246.
3. Mao Tse-Tung, 'On Contradiction', in *Collected Works I*, 326.
4. Kiruba Munisamy, 'The Nauseating Nepotism and Caste-Based Discrimination That Exists in Indian Judiciary', *The Print*, 11 April 2018.

5. Marc Gallanter and Mick Robinson, 'India's Grand Advocates: A Legal Elite Flourishing in the Era of Globalisation', *Harvard Law School Research Papers* 2013-No 15, November 2013.
6. Ibid., 16.
7. Prashanth Bhashan, 'My Honest and Bona Fide Perception', *Outlook* 9 December 2009.
8. Government of India, *Parliamentary Debates (Rajya Sabha)*, Vol. I 7B (New Delhi: GOI, 1954).
9. Ibid.
10. Rakesh Sukla, 'Rights of the Poor: An Overview of Supreme Court', *Economic and Political Weekly* 55, no. 10 (2006): 3755–3759.
11. Jaivir Singh, *Unconstituting Property: The Deconstruction of Right to Property in India* (New Delhi: Centre for the Study of Law and Government, JNU, 2004).
12. 'Court Battles Underline Completing of India's Myriad Land Laws', *Business Time*, 10 July 2019.
13. Amartya Sen, *The Idea of Justice* (Cambridge, MA: Harvard University Press, 2011).
14. Rawls John, *A Theory of Justice* (Cambridge, MA: Harvard University Press, 1994 revised).
15. Case No. Writ Petition 61 of 2002 delivered on 19 October 2006, popularly known as the *Nagaraju* case.
16. Ajaj Ashraf, '"The Supreme Court Has Erred": Former Madras HC Judge K Chandru on EWS and Maratha Reservations', *Caravan*, 20 July 2019.
17. The Hindu 'A Sound View: On Supreme Court recalling its verdict diluting SC/ST anti-atrocities law', (Editorial), The Hindu, 3 October 2019.

# Social Barriers as Impediments of Information Flow

K. E. Boulding once remarked that, 'it is certainly tempting to think of knowledge as a capital stock of information, knowledge being to information what capital is to income'.[1] Thus, the economic value of information and knowledge has been a source of great debate in economics of education for the last several decades. Sociologists have also been emphasizing on the need to improve social communication for development. The advent of electronic media and the monopoly of these sources by MNCs has created a hiatus between information haves and information have-nots. While the issue of digital divide is attracting the attention of social scientists at the global level, the traditional division between the untouchables and others in India during the 21st century seems to have attracted very little attention. Technocrats and policymakers who are trained in the modern methods of intervention and management, care little for the flow of information from groups like Dalits. Communication seems to be very important in decision-making process of development planning and the information flows are the life blood of communication. However, in traditional societies, such as India, the barriers to free flow of information is not only limited by technical rigidities, but even the social institutions, such as caste, gender and others, limit the communication. It is the responsibility of the decision-maker and the information expert to understand these rigidities in order to democratize communication. An attempt is made in this chapter to examine to what extent simple and known government social programmes are communicated to the target groups. As the Dalits are an alienated community and the social intercourse between Dalits and others appear to be limited in public sphere, it is assumed that the free flow of information is limited by social taboo.

The data for the study is culled out from a study undertaken by the author for District Primary Education Programme (DPEP), government of Andhra Pradesh. The sample study is undertaken in 19 rural districts covering 1,520 samples. All the sample households belong to SC category.

## Reasons for Educational Backwardness

The educational backwardness of SCs is examined here on the basis of primary data collected from the household survey. It is generally held that several incentives and schemes are thrown open to Dalits to improve their educational opportunities. It is also believed that despite all these schemes, Dalits have remained backward in literacy and educational development. But, the fact of the matter is that many of the schemes are not known to them. The communication channels and the democratic institutions in the rural areas, including the recent Village Education Committee (VECs), are found to be ineffective. The conclusions based on primary data are supported by the qualitative information obtained from the focus group discussions. Some of the details are given here.

## Incentives Known to Dalits

School education up to the age of 14 is compulsory according to the directive principles of the Constitution and now right to education. The Government of India and the state governments have been providing different categories of incentives to promote elementary education. As the item of school education comes under state list, the state government has also taken interest in the development of school education. The socially and educationally disadvantaged groups, such as SCs, are provided with hostel or residential facility, clothes, books and so on free of cost. The impact of these items of incentives varies from region to region and from caste to caste. Here, we have presented information as to what extent these incentives are known to the target groups. We have collected data relating to the respondent's knowledge about different categories of incentives, adequacy of the item of incentive, the quality of the item and its timely supply to the target group. The data are provided in the Table 9.1.

It is found that only 23 per cent of the respondents are aware of the scheme of scholarships for SCs. However, 55.3 per cent of the total respondents are aware of the supply of rice as an incentive for sending children to school. But, only 12.5 per cent are satisfied with the adequate supply of rice and its quality is found to be good among 25 per cent of the respondents. Not even 21 per cent of the respondents consider that rice is supplied on time. In total, 41 per cent of the respondent's know about the supply of free textbooks, but only 18 per cent are satisfied with the supply and 90 per cent complained that they are not supplied on time. Many people (around 90%) are not aware of schemes, such as mid-day meals, free stationery and free clothes. It is very interesting to find that 95 per cent of the SCs who are sending their children to school are not aware of the existence of hostels for SC children. The data suggest that the government schemes are not reaching the target groups, and therefore the expected results

**TABLE 9.1** Respondents' Knowledge about the Incentives (in Percentage)

| Sl. No. | Name of Incentive | Knowledge | | Quantity | | Quality | | Supply | |
|---|---|---|---|---|---|---|---|---|---|
| | | Yes | No | Sufficient | Insufficient | Good | Not Good | Timely | Delay |
| 1. | Scholarships | 23.7 | 76.4 | 2.6 | 97.4 | 6.4 | 93.6 | 4.2 | 95.8 |
| 2. | Mid-day meals | 6.3 | 93.7 | 2.3 | 97.9 | 2.6 | 97.4 | 1.6 | 98.4 |
| 3. | Free clothes | 16.3 | 83.7 | 5.1 | 94.9 | 4.9 | 95.1 | 3.1 | 96.9 |
| 4. | Free textbooks | 41.2 | 58.8 | 18.5 | 81.5 | 16.7 | 83.3 | 11.2 | 88.8 |
| 5. | Free stationery | 9.4 | 90.6 | 3.3 | 96.7 | 2.5 | 97.5 | 1.4 | 98.6 |
| 6. | Rice | 55.3 | 44.7 | 12.5 | 87.5 | 25.1 | 74.9 | 21.0 | 79.0 |
| 7. | Hostel facility | 6.2 | 93.8 | 1.7 | 98.3 | 1.4 | 98.6 | 0.7 | 99.3 |

*Source*: Author (estimates based on BSE data sources).

are not realized as the schemes are not known to the people. Even if schemes, such as rice and free text books, are known, they are considered to be poor in quality and are not reaching the target groups on time for motivating them to send their children to school.

### Communication Channels

The Dalits or SCs are an isolated community. Though they live in the same village, they are always kept on the outskirts of the village for generations. They do not have established channels of communication with the mainstream society except when they are required for their labour power and the upper castes come to the *basti* to order them to work. Therefore, the general development of education and literacy in the rural areas has very little impact on the development process of the Dalits. In a modern society, community development means that one can move up the ladder or get to know about the subsidies, government projects, and so on. Even the existence of a school and the need to send their children to school requires communication; otherwise, the Dalits hesitate to send their children to school, as they are treated as untouchables.

We have collected information both from school-going and non-school-going respondents about the communication channels that they use in general and in education sector in particular. We have identified 18 modern channels of communication and the data are presented in Table 9.2. It is found that the traditional channel of 'dandora' is still the most prominent channel both among the school-going and non-school-going respondents. Television (TV) and radio are being used by less than 10 per cent of the respondents. However, the non-school-going respondents are more favourable to radio and TV than the school-going respondents. The village officers, including the teacher, constitute less than 10 per cent of the means through which the SCs receive information. It is interesting to find that 11.7 per cent among school-going and 10.5 per cent

### TABLE 9.2  Communication Channels

| Sl. No. | Source of Communication | School-going Respondent | Non-school-going Respondent |
|---|---|---|---|
| 1. | Villagers/neighbours | 11.7 | 10.5 |
| 2. | Village president | 6.4 | 5.1 |
| 3. | Local caste leaders | 4.5 | 5.9 |
| 4. | Gram panchayat members | 1.7 | 3.6 |
| 5. | Village officials | 1.2 | 6.2 |
| 6. | School teacher | 6.4 | 2.5 |
| 7. | MRO/MDO/RI | 5.3 | 5.7 |
| 8. | Print media (newspapers, etc.) | 4.1 | 3.0 |
| 9. | Radio | 5.3 | 9.3 |
| 10. | Television | 6.6 | 13.6 |
| 11. | Posters | 0.4 | 0.1 |
| 12. | Dandora | 14.0 | 10.4 |
| 13. | TV, poster, dandora | 11.0 | 2.2 |
| 14. | TV and radio | 5.5 | 4.3 |
| 15. | Radio, newspaper | 0.7 | 0.8 |
| 16. | Radio, neighbour | 1.3 | 0.4 |
| 17. | TV, radio, villagers | 0.1 | 0.1 |
| 18. | Radio, officials | 0.1 | 0.1 |
| 19. | Others | 11.4 | 16.2 |
| Total | | 100.0 | 100.0 |

*Source:* Author (estimates based on BSE data sources).

*Note:* The overlapping is due to the design of the schedule and each source is independent of the other.

among non-school-going respondents still receive communication through villagers and neighbours. It is observed that the mainstream leaders and the development functionaries are still guided by social barriers in communicating with Dalits about development programmes. This shows the isolation of the Dalit community from the mainstream society, which may be one of the reasons why majority of Dalits still remain illiterate.

*Role Perception of Respondents about VEC*

Village Education Committee (VEC) as a method of decentralization of school administration was conceived as a cost-effective method by the World Bank experts. In a democratic set up, the functioning of the grassroots level committees need to be emphasized. Keeping this in mind, the Government of India adopted the 73rd and 74th constitutional amendments to enable the gram panchayat and local body institutions to participate both in developmental and welfare activities. The government of Andhra Pradesh is one of the earliest to make use of these to develop school education. The Ramakrishna Rao Committee was appointed to recommend the establishment of VECs for the better management of schools. The government of Andhra Pradesh has passed an Act to implement these recommendations and the VECs were formed to look after certain functions of the school. It is assumed that these committees will be able to generate funds, resources and support the development of education in the villages. It was also thought that the involvement of the SCs in the VEC would help in strengthening not only the effective management of the school, but also the effective participation of the students in the schools. Therefore, one member in the VEC is reserved for SCs and STs. It is, however, very disturbing to find from the survey that only 36 per cent of the respondents of parents of school-going children are aware of the existence of VEC, while the number is much lower in the case of non-school-going respondents (with only 25 per cent knowing about it). It is quite clear that the respondents whose children are going to school are well aware of the committee than the non-school-going respondents. Keeping this in mind, we have analysed the role perception of the respondents about VEC. The data are presented in Table 9.3.

**TABLE 9.3** *Role Perception of Respondents about VEC (in Percentage)*

| Sl. No. | Role of VEC | School Going | Non-School Going |
|---|---|---|---|
| 1. | Collection of funds | 7.5 | 6.1 |
| 2. | Giving donation | 3.3 | 4.6 |
| 3. | Discussion with govt on school | 11.8 | 11.0 |
| 4. | Donating land | 2.2 | 2.0 |
| 5. | Protecting school | 7.0 | 5.2 |
| 6. | Repairing school buildings | 5.5 | 7.5 |
| 7. | Supervision of mid-day meals | 5.0 | 6.6 |
| 8. | Appointment of voluntary teacher | 4.5 | 4.6 |
| 9. | Supervision of school administration | 7.5 | 5.8 |
| 10. | Ensuring regularity of teacher | 13.5 | 16.5 |
| 11. | Ensuring good teaching | 15.5 | 14.7 |

*Source:* Author (estimates based on BSE data sources).

In the table, information relating to the respondents who are aware of the VEC is analysed. The table also shows the responsibilities of VEC as perceived by the respondents. Among the school-going respondents, less than 10 per cent consider the role of the VEC in only to get resources for the development of the school. It is interesting that around 30 to 35 per cent of the respondents consider that the role of the VEC is to supervise the teacher and school administration. Strangely, the same proportion of respondents even among non-school-going respondents considers the same as important. It appears that there is a misconception about the role of VEC among the respondents. At the same time, there are some people who are willing to give funds, resources and time for the development of school in the village.

### Decision-makers in the Family

It is generally considered that the decision to send the child to school, work or attend to siblings is decided by the head of the family who is normally the eldest male member of the family. As the SCs are still in a matriarchal family set up, the decisions are still taken in consultation with other members of the family, including women. The data relating to the decision-makers with reference to different activities are presented in Table 9.4.

It is found that the role of the grandparents in the family is almost wiped out in taking decisions on important issues relating to the family, except the marriage of the granddaughters. As far as the school-going respondents are concerned, the father in 38 per cent of cases takes decisions about the admission of the girls' enrolment, and the same is the case with the admission of male child. However, father plays an active role in the sense that around 45 per cent of the fathers among the respondents take decision as to the engagement of the child as a labourer. Even in the case of attending meetings and taking loans, the male member in the family takes the decision. It is also true in the case of non-school-going respondents.

As far as the role of the mother in the family is concerned, in 20 to 30 per cent of the cases, mother takes the decision for keeping children at home to assist her. In all other cases, the role is limited. Interestingly in 30 to 50 per cent of the cases, both the parents (including mother) are collectively involved in taking decisions even in the case of admission or withdrawal or putting children in jobs, including marriage of the daughters. It shows that remnants of matriarchal forms of family organization among the SCs still persist. Therefore, it is necessary that both the male and female members among the SC are to be motivated in sending their children to school.

## Conclusion

The above analysis of knowledge, communication and decision-making process among the Dalit families regarding schooling of their children is really amazing. Contrary to the popular

**TABLE 9.4** Decision-Makers in the Family (in Percentage)

| S. No. | | Father | | Mother | | Parents | | Grand Parents | | Children | | Others | | Total | |
|---|---|---|---|---|---|---|---|---|---|---|---|---|---|---|---|
| | | SG | NSG | SG | NSG | SG | NSG | SG | NSG | SG | NSG | SG | NSG | SG | NSG |
| 1 | Girl child enrolment | 37.9 | 35.8 | 5.8 | 10.0 | 44.2 | 0.3 | 0.4 | 0.1 | 0.1 | 0.1 | 8.9 | 9.5 | 100 | 100 |
| 2 | Male child enrolment | 35.7 | 36.6 | 10.3 | 11.8 | 43.4 | 0.4 | 0.3 | 0.1 | 0.1 | 0.0 | 7.6 | 7.9 | 100 | 100 |
| 3 | Withdrawing child from school | 34.7 | 36.7 | 7.6 | 8.6 | 38.2 | 0.8 | 0.5 | 4.6 | 4.6 | 4.1 | 15.1 | 12.0 | 100 | 100 |
| 4 | For assisting mother | 32.5 | 31.3 | 27.3 | 26.6 | 21.6 | 1.1 | 1.1 | 0.5 | 0.5 | 0.1 | 20.9 | 19.3 | 100 | 100 |
| 5 | Engaging in farm labour | 43.6 | 43.8 | 7.1 | 10.4 | 27.1 | 0.1 | 0.3 | 0.3 | 0.3 | 0.3 | 21.5 | 19.5 | 100 | 100 |
| 6 | Wage labour | 42.8 | 43.4 | 5.5 | 6.1 | 29.5 | 0.9 | 0.9 | 0.3 | 0.3 | 0.1 | 20.9 | 2.7 | 100 | 100 |
| 7 | Daughter marriage | 33.0 | 32.1 | 6.4 | 6.8 | 33.7 | 7.9 | 6.7 | 0.1 | 0.1 | 0.1 | 18.7 | 17.9 | 100 | 100 |
| 8 | Attending meetings | 53.4 | 52.8 | 5.5 | 5.8 | 23.2 | 0.8 | 0.3 | 0.4 | 0.4 | 0.5 | 16.6 | 18.3 | 100 | 100 |
| 9 | Others | 48.0 | 45.8 | 5.7 | 7.1 | 29.9 | 0.4 | 0.3 | 0.1 | 0.1 | 0.0 | 15.9 | 17.6 | 100 | 100 |

*Source*: Author (estimates based on BSE data sources).

*Note*: SG—school going children's family; NSG—non-school going children's family.

opinion about the knowledge of the government incentives among the Dalits, the study revealed that the information is not within the reach of the Dalits. The Dalits as an ex-untouchable social category is still found to be away from the social communication network. The social barrier or taboo in speaking to them and sharing the necessary information on development programmes appears to be in operation. The data have clearly shown that very few functionaries, including the village officers, are communicating with the Dalits about government programmes. This calls for a review of the existing sources of information and the institutions of communication of development programmes. It appears that the use of technology in breaking this barrier through effective implementation of media in the rural areas, in general, and inaccessible habitations of Dalits, in particular, is essential to reap the results of modernization. Though the study was undertaken a decade ago, the broad inferences that arise from this sample study is that information flow has a social barrier, one more condition to facilitate CMOP.

## Note

1. K. E. Boulding, 'The Economics of Knowledge and the Knowledge of Economics', *American Economic Review* 56, no. 2 (1966): 1–13.

# 10

# Physical Alienation
## Offences and Atrocities against Scheduled Castes

SCs are the most vulnerable social group in the Indian society. They are vulnerable both as an economically and socially deprived segment and also as a physically and psychologically dispossessed category to be despised by the non-SCs. It is not only the so-called *Dvijas* who abhor them as untouchables, even the *Shudras*, OBCs and sometimes those who have migrated to other faiths and creeds from this category treat them with contempt. The Hindu ethos and to a large extent the Indian ethos makes a person to look for someone who is seen as inferior to him to establish his relative position in the society. Perhaps, it is because of this phenomenon that the iniquitous caste system is perpetuated. Interestingly, one cannot establish one's caste absolutely without reference to others. It is to demonstrate the fact that one belongs to a particular caste; each individual practices certain customs, norms and mores that are said to be the exclusive property of the caste. Some castes and individuals use physical symbols, such as *tilak* or marks or dress code, to distinguish themselves from others. But in a majority of cases, caste is exhibited only in terms of certain practices, such as untouchability. In fact, untouchability is not a typical attribute of the Dalits alone.[1] But the practice of untouchability is essential condition for the existence of Hindu caste system and without which it is difficult to maintain the social order. That is why all the authors of *dharmashastras* and *grihya sutras*, such as Apastamba, Manu, and Gautama, who have codified Hindu *dharma* had attributed different values to different castes. Naturally, caste system demands that these values are to be imbibed by the beholder. As caste system is an intangible social practice, its presence can be seen when it is practised. Untouchability is one very important physical attribute that is being naturalized by every Hindu much less the Indian.

The nature of untouchability and caste atrocities against SCs in India is not confined to rural areas. Its presence is very much appalling in metros, such as Bangalore. It was reported in November 2018 in Deccan Herald that as many as 207 cases were filed in Bangalore Urban and 9 in rural Bangalore in 2017. The city stands second in SC/ST atrocities.[21] The distressing part of the news is that only 42 are reported as convicted cases out of 1,108 cases. The case is cited here to indicate that offences against Dalits are not a bygone phenomenon. It is kicking every day, as a crime is committed against Dalits every 15 minutes; three women raped and two murdered as of 2017. Then, why are these atrocities committed? As noted in Chapter 1, CMOP prevails under the conditions of 'shock and awe' and alienate them from mainstream. This is a technique being perpetuated to link Hindutva with corporate capitalism.[3] In order to provide an empirical reality of the atrocity at the grassroots, we have given below a study conducted by the author based on the data provided by Justice Punnayya during 2001[4] in Andhra Pradesh. This is the first report that generated data at district level.

## Offences versus Atrocities

The SCs or Dalits are subjected to various kinds of humiliations, ill treatment and physical abuse by the non-SC community. They have been doing it as a matter of right and social sanction for ages. Therefore, these acts are never considered as legally punishable offences in the Hindu code. It is only on the advent of a democratic and civil society that these offences were recognized as crimes by the mainstream society. Several leaders of the Dalits must have fought against them, but they were neither recognized nor recorded in the past. In the 1850s, the British for the first time banned the inhuman practice of untouchability. Once it is banned, anyone who is found to be practising it is said to be an offender. The legal lexicon defines an offence 'as an act or omission punishable by law'. Thus, the British has for the first time introduced the concept of offence for acts of inhuman treatment meted out to untouchables or Dalits. The Indian Constitution under Article 17 prohibited the practice of untouchability. Later the government passed the Protection of Civil Rights (PCR) Act 1955 and it was further amended in 1976. The PCR rules were passed on 15 September 1977. The chronology of events relating to this Act shows how the government sluggishly acted towards the implementation of PCR Act 1955. Even after the passing of the rules, the implementation of the Act was very lukewarm and the provisions of the Act were related only to petty issues belonging to untouchability. But the number of Dalits who were persecuted, raped, humiliated, looted and killed by the non-SCs had increased during the 1970s and 1980s in the country. Major incidents, such as Kilvenmani, Kanchikacherla, Karamchedu, and several other ghastly incidents took place in the country and the PCR Act was found to be very inadequate to deal with such cases. The culprits were booked under Indian Penal Code (IPC) only. Therefore, the government has passed the SCs and STs (POA) Act 1989 on 11 September 1989. The major purpose of the Act was to prevent the commission of offences of atrocities against the members of SCs and STs to provide for special courts for the trial of such offences and for the relief and rehabilitation of the victims of such offences. A new term is added to the legal lexicon, 'atrocity'. The offences against Dalits that come under PCR Act 1955 were different from the offences that are booked under this Act. The Act has defined atrocity as one committed by whoever, not being a member of SC or ST, causing any of 15 kinds of damages (both physical and psychological) to the SCs and STs. It has further identified 7 categories of legal implications that cause injury to Dalits and also come under atrocity. The rules for the POA Act, including the schedule of punishment and relief to victims, were passed on 31 March 1995. Thus, the crimes against SCs and STs are broadly categorized under two groups.

Under the IPC

1. Murder
2. Hurt
3. Rape
4. Kidnapping and abduction
5. Dacoity
6. Robbery
7. Arson
8. Others (other classified IPC crimes)

Under Special Laws

1. PCR Act 1955
2. The SCs and STs (Prevention of Atrocities) Act 1989

The incidence of above crimes was booked under different sections by the police. They were finally consolidated by the Ministry of Home Affairs, Government of India, and the same data are being supplied to various agencies that prepare reports on the status of Dalits in India. Therefore, the concept of atrocities with reference to SCs is of recent origin. This may be kept in mind while analysing the data on atrocities.

There are different government and non-government organizations that publish data on atrocities or crimes or offences on Dalits. But the source of information for all these is the same. The crime bureau records of Ministry of Home Affairs, Government of India is the source of information on crime, including various categories of crime on Dalits. The Ministry of Welfare (now Social Justice and Empowerment), Government of India has been publishing the following reports that contain data and information on Dalits.

1. Annual Reports of the Ministry
2. Annual Report on PCR Act
3. Report of National Commission for Scheduled Castes and Scheduled Tribes (earlier Commission for SCs, and STs)

and chapters on crime against weaker sections in 'Crime in India', and reports of the ministry of Home Affairs, Government of India. Some NGOs who are working in the area of human rights do also publish occasional reports on atrocities on Dalits.

The above reports provide data on an all India basis with reference to individual states. Thus, we can have secondary data on atrocities on Dalits on Andhra Pradesh. But, the data relating to each district in the state can be obtained only from the records of the Department of Home Affairs of the state.

## Approach of the Study

As the study is basically concerned about the atrocities of Dalits in Andhra Pradesh, the data relating to various crimes against them as recorded in the crime bureau are obtained. We have found a lot of discrepancy in the data. Though the source of information is the same, the presentation of data in terms of the concepts of PCR Act and POA Act are found to be different. Therefore, we have approached the problem through alternative sources of information. The government of Andhra Pradesh has appointed a commission on untouchability under the chairmanship of Justice K. Punnayya. The committee has visited all the districts in the state and collected a lot of information. The committee has produced a report of three volumes containing rich information on offences and atrocities. So far, no one has attempted to use the information for a statistical analysis to test the validity of data presented in the reports of the Government of India. We have culled out the data from these reports and employed simple statistical tools not only to establish the validity of data, but also to examine the source of the significant determinants of crime against Dalits.

### Crimes against Dalits in Andhra versus India

The relative position of Andhra Pradesh vis-à-vis other States and the all India status of crimes against Dalits is examined here. We have examined the atrocities relating to SCs only and it does not include STs. The main offences committed against SCs in the country, including atrocities registered under various sections of PCR and POA, are included in the data in Table 10.1. The data are for a period of three decades from 1979 to 2016. It can be seen that the offences and atrocities against SCs have increased from 13,975 in 1979 to 33,908 in 1994 and 42,212 in 2016, which are an increase of 20 times in a period of four decades. The number of people murdered has increased from 388 in 1979 to 546 in 1994 and has declined to 505 in 1999 and again increased to 799 in 2016. There is no decline in the number of cases of rapes against SC women. They are continuously increasing from 430 in 1979 to 992 in 1994, 1,000 in 1999 and 2,693 in 2016. Some data relating to murders during the period 1966 to 1970 are available and not presented in Table 10.1. The annual average of these years is found to be 370. The total crimes, including offences against SCs, in the period are estimated to be 847 per year. Perhaps no civilized society

**TABLE 10.1** *Main Offences Committed against Scheduled Castes in India during 1979–2016*

| Crime Category | 1979 | 1983 | 1993 | 1994 | 1995 | 2016 |
|---|---|---|---|---|---|---|
| Murder | 388 | 525 | 510 | 546 | 571 | 799 |
| Grievous hurt | 1,441 | 1,362 | NA | 4,542 | 4,544 | 1,149 |
| Rape | 430 | 641 | 798 | 992 | 873 | 2,693 |
| Arson and rioting | 1,013 | 982 | 369 | 533 | 500 | 1,957 |
| Other offences | 10,703 | 11,324 | 23,296 | 27,295 | 26,509 | 34,853 |
| Total | 13,975 | 14,834 | 24,973 | 33,908 | 32,997 | 42,212 |

*Source:* Ministry of Social Welfare, Government of India and National Crime Records Bureau, New Delhi, Ministry of Home Affairs.

in modern period has witnessed such a raze of crime against a particular social group merely on the basis of the birth of a person in a community.

The relative position of Andhra Pradesh can also be found in terms of the number of crimes reported per lakh of the SC population. It is not proper to report and analyse the absolute number of crimes against SCs in each state as the presence of the SC population in each of the state in India is not uniform. Therefore, the incidence of atrocities can be expressed in terms of the cases per lakh of the SC population. The National Commission for SCs and STs in its fifth report presented such data.[5] In absolute terms, Uttar Pradesh has recorded the highest number of 10,492 cases in 2016 followed by Bihar with 5,944 cases, Rajasthan with 5,134 cases, Madhya Pradesh with 4,922 cases, Andhra Pradesh with 2,424 cases, Gujarat with 1,494 cases and so on. But if we express the cases in terms of a lakh of population, the first rank goes to Rajasthan with 755 cases per lakh of population, second rank to Madhya Pradesh with 683 cases and Andhra Pradesh comes as sixth in the list in 2016. Interestingly, the cases pending trial from the previous year in 2016 are reported as 18,131 out of 38,670 in 2015. It means almost 50 per cent of cases remain on files, and the conviction data are reported to be around 15 per cent.

The data relating to the offences and atrocities committed against SCs in Andhra Pradesh are presented in Table 10.2. It is observed that there is a substantial rise in the number of crimes in the state during the period 1982 to 2016. The number of

**TABLE 10.2** *Offences and Atrocities Committed against Scheduled Castes in Andhra Pradesh during 1982–2016*

| Category | 1982 | 1983 | 1993 | 1994 | 1995 | 2016 |
|---|---|---|---|---|---|---|
| Murder | 16 | 11 | 29 | 16 | 25 | 25 |
| Hurt | 8 | 26 | – | 307 | 516 | 10 |
| Rape | 17 | 25 | 38 | 36 | 64 | 90 |
| Kidnapping and abdication | – | – | 7 | 10 | 22 | 12 |
| Assault on women* | – | – | 0 | 0 | 0 | 303 |
| Robbery | – | – | 1 | 1 | 3 | 1 |
| Arson | 13 | 5 | 1 | 5 | 12 | 11 |
| PCR Act cases | – | – | 277 | 238 | 265 | 446 |
| SC&ST (POA) Act cases | – | – | – | 307 | 519 | 1,371 |
| Other offences | 159 | 114 | 325 | 282 | 338 | 155 |
| Total | 213 | 181 | 678 | 1,202 | 1,764 | 2,424 |

*Source:* Department of Social Welfare, Government of India and NCRB, Ministry of Home Affairs Notes:

*Note:* *Added in 2016.

cases of murder has increased from 16 in 1982 to 25 in 2016. The number of cases booked under PCR Act was not shown separately in 1982 and we have data separately for PCR and POA from 1994. The data show a lot of inconsistencies. Though the number of total cases has increased from 213 in 1982 to 1,880 in 1997 and 2,424 in 2016; there is no uniformity in other cases under PCR and POA. It is only to examine the consistency in these cases that we have approached alternative sources of information on crimes against Dalits.

### Reliability of Data

We found that the data presented by government agencies are not reliable, as these cases are booked by the police on the basis of complaints from victims. In majority of the cases, FIRs or cases are not recorded. Therefore, the number of cases reported either in the National Commission or crime against Dalits presented by government sources is found to be under reported. Some attempts have been made by some NGOs, such as the Kula Vivaksha Vyathireka Porata Committee (committee to fight against caste discrimination) and A.P. Human Rights Watch. But the data of these agencies are secondary in nature as they cull out this information from newspaper clippings, occasional surveys and so on. They do not have data on all the districts of Andhra Pradesh[6] and do not possess any official significance.

The government of Andhra Pradesh has appointed Justice K. Punnayya to enquire into the problems and incidence of untouchability in Andhra Pradesh in 2000. This is an official committee and has visited all the districts in the state and received representations and complaints from the Dalits. The cases have been narrated and reported as appendices to the report. Therefore, we have culled out the data from the report and presented them in quantitative figures. Before taking up the analysis of this data, we have tested the validity of the data of the districts. We have calculated the Chi-square as 0.91 between the total villages in each district and the data

**TABLE 10.3** *Number of Villages Represented in the Commission in Andhra Pradesh*

| Sl. No. | District | Total No. of Villages | No. of Represented Village to the Commission | Total Number of Petitions Presented to the Commission |
|---|---|---|---|---|
| 1. | Adilabad | 1,750 | 32 | 105 |
| 2. | Anantapur | 965 | 312 | 316 |
| 3. | Chittoor | 1,550 | 531 | 663 |
| 4. | Cuddapah | 980 | 93 | 313 |
| 5. | East Godavari | 1,412 | 81 | 227 |
| 6. | Guntur | 733 | 505 | 625 |
| 7. | Karimnagar | 1,103 | 49 | 110 |
| 8. | Khammam | 1,241 | 233 | 850 |
| 9. | Krishna | 1,005 | 68 | 243 |
| 10. | Kurnool | 990 | 357 | 316 |
| 11. | Mahbubnagar | 1,557 | 908 | 694 |
| 12. | Medak | 1,265 | 139 | 121 |
| 13. | Nalgonda | 1,158 | 193 | 256 |
| 14. | Nellore | 1,207 | 125 | 373 |
| 15. | Nizamabad | 921 | 45 | 173 |
| 16. | Prakasam | 1,103 | 297 | 324 |
| 17. | Ranga Reddy | 1,055 | 224 | 297 |
| 18. | Srikakulam | 2,088 | 232 | 318 |
| 19. | Visakhapatnam | 4,273* | 221 | 521 |
| 20. | Vizianagaram | 1,551 | 275 | 218 |
| 21. | Warangal | 1,998 | 147 | 467 |
| 22. | West Godavari | 908 | 109 | 409 |
| | Total | 30,813 | 5,176 | 7,939 |

*Source:* Justice Punnayya Committee Report, Government of Andhra Pradesh, Hyderabad.

*Note:* *Most of the villages are tribal villages with 5–10 habitations.

on offences reported by Dalits from the villages and found it statistically significant. Then we have considered the data on various issues of atrocities reported in the report as valid. In Table 10.3, the data are presented to show the volume of cases reported to the commission in relation to the number of villages in a district and the villages that are represented to the commission in each district. It is found that out of 30,813 villages, 5,176 villages or 6 per cent of the total villages in the state are represented. We consider this as a significant sample of the population of SCs in the state. It can also be seen that the number of petitions submitted by Dalits to the commission in each district is in relation to the size of villages in the district. Therefore, it is taken as a representative sample of cases of Dalits in the state. After confirming that the data are reliable and scientific, we have culled out the cases that come under PCR and reported in Table 10.4. We have collected data relating to 4 important cases of untouchability and discrimination reported in the years 2000–2001. We have taken the cases of (a) restriction of temple entry, (b) two glasses system, (c) restriction of *dhobi*/barber and (d) restriction of wells for drinking water. If we compare the data of this report to the data presented by the Ministry of Home Affairs through their crime records, we will find that they are totally under-reported. If the data of Table 10.4 are compared with the data in Table 10.2 relating to the year 1999 on PCR cases, it is found that the records of police show that there are only 266 cases.[7] In the case of the Punnayya Commission, it is reported as 6,605 cases. This does not include cases which are not reported due to lack of information, inaccessibility and so on. We can take this to even out the cases that are over-reported or repeated from the previous years. The data show the atrocious nature of under-reporting of cases of discrimination and untouchability. Though we have data on crimes, such as murder and rape, from the same report, we have not considered them here due to the legal issues involved. We have reported in Table 10.6, the data on crimes as per the records of the police.

**TABLE 10.4** *Discrimination against Scheduled Castes in Andhra Pradesh (PCR), 2000–2001*

| Sl. No. | District | Temple Entry Restricted | Two Glasses System | Dhobi/Barber Restricted | Wells/Pumps Restricted | Total |
|---|---|---|---|---|---|---|
| 1. | Adilabad | NR | NR | NR | NR | NR |
| 2. | Anantapur | 222 | 222 | 222 | 222 | 222 |
| 3. | Chittoor | 233 | 233 | 233 | 233 | 233 |
| 4. | Cuddapah | 24 | 24 | 24 | 24 | 24 |
| 5. | East Godavari | 25 | 25 | 25 | 25 | 25 |
| 6. | Guntur | 181 | 181 | 181 | 181 | 181 |
| 7. | Karimnagar | 9 | 9 | 9 | 9 | 9 |
| 8. | Khammam | 77 | 77 | 77 | 77 | 77 |
| 9. | Krishna | 6 | 6 | 6 | 6 | 6 |
| 10. | Kurnool | 335 | 335 | 335 | 335 | 335 |
| 11. | Mahbubnagar | 836 | 836 | 836 | 836 | 836 |

| | | | | | | | |
|---|---|---|---|---|---|---|---|
| 12. | Medak | 80 | 80 | 80 | 80 | 80 | 80 |
| 13. | Nalgonda | 187 | 187 | 187 | 187 | 187 | 187 |
| 14. | Nellore | 50 | 50 | 50 | 50 | 50 | 50 |
| 15. | Nizamabad | 18 | 18 | 18 | 18 | 18 | 18 |
| 16. | Prakasam | 75 | 75 | 75 | 75 | 75 | 75 |
| 17. | Ranga Reddy | 260 | 260 | 260 | 260 | 260 | 260 |
| 18. | Srikakulam | 53 | 53 | 53 | 53 | 53 | 53 |
| 19. | Visakhapatnam | 40 | 40 | 40 | 40 | 40 | 40 |
| 20. | Vizianagaram | 51 | 51 | 51 | 51 | 51 | 51 |
| 21. | Warangal | 51 | 51 | 51 | 51 | 51 | 51 |
| 22. | West Godavari | 16 | 16 | 16 | 16 | 16 | 16 |

*Source:* Justice Punnayya Committee Report, Government of Andhra Pradesh, Hyderabad.

*Note:* NR—not reported.

The data on the practice of untouchability, which attracts PCR Act, as reported to the Punnayya Commission by the SCs in Andhra Pradesh show the nature and magnitude of the problem. It is clear that out of 6,605 cases only around 260 are reported in official records. In other words, the under-reporting of untouchability cases is around 96 per cent in Andhra Pradesh or we can say that only 4 per cent of the cases of incidence of untouchability are booked. We do not have the data to show how many of the guilty among them are ultimately convicted.

### Composite Index of Caste Discrimination

Caste system in India ascribes different values to different castes. This can be found across all castes. Some castes are discriminated in private sphere, some are in public life and Dalits are discriminated everywhere. This is because of the low value attributed to the life of a Dalit. This discrimination is practised in several ways. But in a civilized society, certain minimum human relations are expected to be exchanged between individuals who are equal in physical terms. But this is found to be not valid in India. The Dalits[8] are discriminated even in simple human gestures, such as giving drinking water and treating all human beings as equal before God. In order to find out how the Dalits are discriminated on the basis of their birth, a statistical estimate is made on the basis of the data culled out from Punnayya Commission Report. As the number of cases in each item of discrimination is not uniform and the severity of injury varies from one incidence of discrimination to another, we thought of estimating a composite index of discrimination. Out of the 4 events of discrimination reported in Table 10.4, we have taken two important events, temple entry and two glasses to represent discrimination across districts. These two events are reported in all the districts in the state. We have assigned two-thirds weight to temple entry and one-third weight to two-glass system to estimate the composite index. The indices are presented in Table 10.5 along with the illiteracy rates and incidence of general poverty and agriculture labourers among Dalits in each district. The value of composite index shows the magnitude of discrimination. It is found that the composite

**TABLE 10.5** *Composite Index of Caste Discrimination*

| Sl. No. | District | Composite Index of Discrimination | SC Illiterate (%) | General Poverty (%) | SC Ag. Lab (%) |
|---|---|---|---|---|---|
| 1 | Adilabad | 11.33 | 75.74 | 77 | 23.51 |
| 2 | Anantapur | 211.33 | 74.32 | 62 | 35.43 |
| 3 | Chittoor | 209.33 | 64.72 | 62.4 | 35.97 |
| 4 | Cuddapah | 23.33 | 67.65 | 54 | 37.87 |
| 5 | East Godavari | 23.67 | 60.11 | 51 | 35.44 |
| 6 | Guntur | 143.33 | 62.51 | 56.6 | 42.14 |
| 7 | Karimnagar | 6.33 | 75.1 | 53 | 36.17 |
| 8 | Khammam | 66.33 | 68.39 | 58 | 35.47 |
| 9 | Krishna | 5 | 59.84 | 47 | 40.43 |
| 10 | Kurnool | 290.67 | 71.92 | 50.5 | 37.23 |
| 11 | Mahbubnagar | 754 | 85.49 | 65 | 47.97 |
| 12 | Medak | 74.33 | 82.73 | 58 | 25.72 |
| 13 | Nalgonda | 165 | 75.4 | 58.5 | 37.65 |
| 14 | Nellore | 43 | 64.94 | 48 | 37.54 |
| 15 | Nizamabad | 15.67 | 80.46 | 42 | 32.98 |
| 16 | Prakasam | 81.33 | 68.61 | 53 | 43.36 |
| 17 | Ranga Reddy | 244.67 | 69.94 | 58 | 26.01 |
| 18 | Srikakulam | 65.33 | 68.99 | 60 | 34.85 |
| 19 | Visakhapatnam | 61 | 55.27 | 58.8 | 19.37 |
| 20 | Vizianagaram | 61.33 | 71.46 | 55 | 31.81 |
| 21 | Warangal | 41 | 72.74 | 48.5 | 25.85 |
| 22 | West Godavari | 15.33 | 59.26 | 46.9 | 42.57 |

*Source:* Author (estimates based on BSE data sources).

index is not uniform across the districts. It may be related to the economic status of the people represented by their poverty and economic calling. Therefore, we have run the following regression to test the determinants of discrimination.

The determinants of discrimination

$$CID = \beta_0 + \beta_1 \text{ ill} + \beta_2 \text{ Pov} + \beta_3 \text{ Aglab}$$

where CID = Composite index of caste discrimination
Ilt. = Rate of illiteracy among SCs
Pov = Percentage of population below poverty line
Aglab = Percentage of agriculture labour among SCs
$\beta_1, \beta_2, \beta_3$ are coefficients to be estimated.

We have obtained the following results.

$$CID = \beta_0 + 0.331\ \beta_1 + 0.440\ \beta_2 + 0.445\ \beta_3 \qquad R^{-2} = 0.45$$
(1.82)   (2.14)           (2.46)

Figures in brackets are $t$ values. They are statistically found significant.

The above results show that the model is statistically significant as it is explaining 45 per cent of the variations. Out of the three variables, poverty among the people and incidence of agricultural labourers among Dalits are found to explain strongly the prevalence of caste discrimination than illiteracy. They are also found to be statistically significant. It is interesting to observe from these results that economic factors are still contributing for the prevalence of caste discrimination in Andhra Pradesh. We have also estimated correlation coefficients between CID and the percentage of the Christian population as a stimulant for discrimination. We found that there is no relation between the two. The correlation coefficient between CID and the percentage of the SC population in a district is found to be 0.52. Therefore, we are of the opinion that the above model of regression is valid in explaining the determinants of caste discrimination.

## The Most Affected Districts in Andhra Pradesh

Andhra Pradesh is touted as a highly sophisticated and modernized state in India. But the conditions in the districts particularly in the four regions of the state are in bad shape and are not uniform. We have therefore obtained data on incidence of cognizable crimes (IPC) against SCs in Andhra Pradesh for the period 1998–2001 for each district to find out which district is the worst hit in terms of crime against Dalits. The data are presented in Table 10.6. In order to even out the high and low incidence across the events, we have calculated the four-year average for each incident. On the basis of the four-year average of two important crimes, murder and rape, we have identified eight districts whose average is found to be more than four. They are Adilabad, Chittoor, Guntur, Kurnool, Mahaboobnagar, Medak, Nellore and Warangal. In order to arrive at the actual districts that observe untouchability and discrimination, we have looked at the index of discrimination presented earlier. We found that Anantapur, Nalgonda and Ranga Reddy are the worst affected districts in caste discrimination. Finally, the following districts are found both in crime and caste discrimination as the worst-affected districts.

1. Chittoor
2. Guntur
3. Kurnool
4. Mahaboobnagar

Interestingly, two of the above districts are from Rayalaseema region, while the other two districts represent one each in coastal Andhra and Telangana. There is not even a single district in any of the crimes from north coastal Andhra Pradesh in the dubious distinction where the average crime is found to be less than 1.

The statistical analysis clearly demonstrates that the data reported by the government agencies is totally

**TABLE 10.6** Incidence of Cognizable Crimes (IPC) against Scheduled Castes in Andhra Pradesh during 2000

| Sl. No. | District | Murder | Rape | Hurt | Arson | Other IPC | Total |
|---|---|---|---|---|---|---|---|
| 1. | Adilabad | 1 | 10 | 14 | 0 | 40 | 65 |
| 2. | Anantapur | 0 | 0 | 36 | 0 | 30 | 66 |
| 3. | Chittoor | 2 | 4 | 7 | 0 | 26 | 39 |
| 4. | Cuddapah | 1 | 1 | 27 | 1 | 45 | 75 |
| 5. | East Godavari | 2 | 3 | 4 | 0 | 3 | 12 |
| 6. | Guntur | 3 | 4 | 48 | 4 | 63 | 122 |
| 7. | Karimnagar | 0 | 3 | 6 | 0 | 2 | 11 |
| 8. | Khammam | 2 | 2 | 5 | 0 | 12 | 21 |
| 9. | Krishna | 2 | 6 | 7 | 0 | 18 | 33 |
| 10. | Kurnool | 6 | 2 | 59 | 1 | 53 | 121 |

|  |  |  |  |  |  |  |
|---|---|---|---|---|---|---|
| 11. | Mahaboobnagar | 5 | 5 | 8 | 1 | 15 | 34 |
| 12. | Medak | 1 | 4 | 4 | 0 | 2 | 11 |
| 13. | Nalgonda | 2 | 3 | 4 | 0 | 8 | 17 |
| 14. | Nellore | 0 | 1 | 6 | 0 | 21 | 28 |
| 15. | Nizamabad | 0 | 2 | 6 | 0 | 23 | 31 |
| 16. | Prakasham | 0 | 2 | 17 | 2 | 28 | 49 |
| 17. | Ranga Reddy | 1 | 2 | 1 | 0 | 13 | 17 |
| 18. | Srikakulam | 0 | 1 | 11 | 1 | 9 | 22 |
| 19. | Visakhapatnam | 0 | 1 | 5 | 0 | 12 | 18 |
| 20. | Vizianagaram | 0 | 3 | 0 | 1 | 3 | 7 |
| 21. | Warangal | 3 | 6 | 15 | 0 | 43 | 67 |
| 22. | West Godavari | 1 | 6 | 7 | 1 | 20 | 35 |
| Total |  | 33 | 72 | 298 | 12 | 491 | 901 |

*Source:* Author (estimates based on BSE data sources).

under-represented both in the data on atrocities and also on offences against Dalits. The regression results indicate that economic factors are still found to be major determinants of crime against Dalits. There seems to be no respite in the number of cases of atrocities, including mob lynching of Dalits, after NDA II came to power at the centre, which substantiates our above empirical results from a report of a southern state supposed to be a progressive state.

## Conclusion

Caste discrimination and crime against Dalits is an age-old practice in the Indian society. Attempts have been made by government through acts of law to fulfil the constitutional obligation of providing protection to Dalits and to abolish untouchability. There are several studies that highlighted the kind of caste problems that prevail in India. It appears that there are very few attempts to test the significance of these incidents in terms of empirical evidence. This study is a modest attempt to fill the gap though we realize some of its weaknesses. It is found that the cases reported by the government and the SC and ST commissions are absolutely under-reported, as they may be providing reports on the basis of 5 per cent of the cases booked. The incidence of caste discrimination is found to be related to the economic deprivations of Dalits in the distribution of land and other assets. It may be considered that these factors might provide self-respect and self-esteem to reduce the prevalence of crime and discrimination against Dalits in India, in general, and Andhra Pradesh, in particular.

The empirical study is presented here to show that the practice of untouchability and crime against the marginalized community prevails even in the 21st century to make them physically alienated from the mainstream and at the same time supply labour at lower wages. The data from the National Crime Records Bureau (NCRB) as revealed in the PCR Act cases noted above speak about the offences and also reflect the transactions in rural economy.

## Notes

1. R. Rakshita, 'Bengaluru City Stands Second in SC/STs Atrocities', *Deccan Herald*, 13 November 2018.
2. Ibid.
3. Patnaik, 'Decoding the Corporate Hindutva'.
4. Government of Andhra Pradesh, *Report of the Single Member Commission of Enquiry to Enquire into the Practice of Untouchability against, Scheduled Castes and Tribes (Punnaiah Commission)*, Vols. I–III (Government of Andhra Pradesh, 2001).
5. National Commission for Scheduled Castes and Scheduled Tribes, Government of India, 1994, p. 155.
6. We have consulted the conveners of the NGOs who have collected the data and found that they have certain gaps in data.
7. We do not have data on PCR cases for the year 2000 and therefore we have considered the 1999 data. This is not an extreme year as seen from Table 10.2, the number has never crossed 280. Whenever we use the term Dalit in this paper, it may be taken as Scheduled Castes.
8. We have consulted the conveners of the NGOs who have collected the data and found that they have certain gaps in data.

# 11

# The Fragmented Assertion
*Divide and Rule*

Political economy of caste looks at how the class formation takes place over a period of time and the social antagonisms that restrict the process to transform groups (castes) into classes. In this context, caste ideology perpetuated by reactionary forces seriously do dent the process of 'class in itself' or 'class for itself' of the oppressed class due to segmentation in society.

The division of society based on one's *Karma* and *guna* (Chapter 4 sloka 13) as enunciated in Bhagavad Gita and elaborated by generations of Hindu pundits time and again has reminded a classical myth in India. It is now devoid of any practical use and the graded inequalities have been used by the *Dvija* political class to perpetuate privileges for themselves. No entry for those from non-*Dvija* who satisfy the myth to enter the privileged position is allowed. It has been used as a convenient structure to divide the major chunk of *Shudras* and Dalits and unite the *Dvija* to rule. There are around 2,100 castes among OBCs and 1,284 among SC categories, while the *Dvija* got restricted to the broad three sub-divisions within. This has to a large extent facilitated the CMOP. Therefore, wherever an attempt is made to get the exploited sections united, God descend on earth to restore the caste order as avatar (Gita 4.6). You can see this happening today with million *karyakartas* working to protect the *dharma*. It was dismissed by some as imagination, but it is reported to be happening everyday even today.

The massacre of *mahars* in Bombay on the desecration incident and the death of two *malas* in a lathi charge in Hyderabad in 2013 indicate the growing fury against an emerging Dalit assertion. The situation in the southern districts of Tamil Nadu pose a much serious threat to the formation of a cohesive social force to fight against historical injustices perpetuated among the lower castes in India. It is an irony that the backward classes who claim allegiance to Periyar EVR, the legendary figure of social revolution in southeast Asia did not allow the legitimate constitutional right of Dalits to assemble in Chennai. A Dalit was elected as the president of the country as a part of the golden jubilee celebrations of independent India signifying a symbolic achievement, which appears to be elusive due to the sporadic incidents of suppression of Dalits, simultaneously. These incidents do also convey the false and fragmented consciousness among the Dalits. It is not an outburst of a sudden upheaval. It is a logical outcome of a policy pursued by successive governments in different parts of the country that lead to the breach of caste solidarity among the SCs and STs. The social tensions created among lower castes and between castes and minorities in the recent past are a serious concern for those who wish to look at the class formation and social revolt. This phenomenon indicates a malady that still haunts Indian ethos. Unless it is checked and corrected, the future of India in the era of liberalization appears to be bleak, particularly for those who wish to see sustainable development. An attempt is made here to examine some of the internal challenges of the emerging Dalit assertion.

The British officials have coined the term 'Scheduled Castes' during the early part of this century particularly in the

Government of India order 1936. All the untouchable castes were referred to as depressed castes even by B. R. Ambedkar and have been identified and noted as SCs from 1931 census onwards. The Government of India notified for the first time the list of SCs under the Constitution order 1950. The list of castes notified in 1950 have since been amended and new castes have been added from time to time. It appears that the government has not modified substantially the criteria used by the British in identifying the depressed castes (SC and OBC) in 1931. The same criteria of untouchability, distance from the Brahmins, illiteracy and so on, numbering around 10 factors have been used to identify a caste and bring it under the schedule of the Constitution to give the constitutional safeguards. A number of castes have been deleted and some are reorganized in each census. The data are generally presented in the social and cultural tables of the census of Government of India. So far, the data relating to these aspects for 1991 are not available. However, we are making the analysis on the basis of the census data of 1981 and other secondary sources. As we have information on the characters of each sub-caste from 1981 census, the analysis is restricted to 1981 and assume that it remains valid for other years.

## Increase in the Population of SCs

The number of SCs and their absolute population has been increasing over a period of time. It is found that there are 1,081 castes under the list of SCs entered in the schedule of the Constitution in various states and Union Territories of India in 1991. The proportion of the SC population to the total population has also increased from 15.75 per cent in 1981 to 16.48 per cent in 1991 and to 16.63 per cent in 2011. Similarly, the number of STs listed in the schedule of the Constitution amounts to 545, and their population is estimated at 8.08 per cent of the total population in 1991 and stands at 8.63 per cent in 2011. The data presented in Table 11.1 show the state-wise details.

**TABLE 11.1** Total Number of Existing Castes and Their Percentage to Total Population in India 1991

| Sl. No | Name of the State/UT | No. of Castes in SC Category | SC Pop. to Total Pop. (%) 1991 | SC Pop. to Total Pop. (%) 2011 | No. of Tribes in ST Category | ST Pop. to Total Pop. (%) 1991 | ST Pop. to Total Pop. (%) 2011 |
|---|---|---|---|---|---|---|---|
| 1. | Andhra Pradesh | 59 | 15.93 | 16.41 | 33 | 6.31 | 7 |
| 2. | Arunachal Pradesh | 16 | 0.47 | 0.4 | 12 | 63.66 | 68.79 |
| 3. | Assam | 16 | 7.4 | 7.15 | 14 (Kukees 36) | 12.82 | 12.45 |
| 4. | Bihar | 22 | 14.55 | 15.99 | 30 | 7.66 | 1.28 |
| 5. | Chhattisgarh | 94 | – | 12.82 | – | – | 30.62 |
| 6. | Goa | 5 | 2.08 | 1.74 | 5 | 0.03 | 10.23 |
| 7. | Gujarat | 30 | 7.41 | 6.74 | 29 | 14.92 | 14.75 |
| 8. | Haryana | 37 | 19.75 | 20.17 | – | – | – |
| 9. | Himachal Pradesh | 56 | 25.34 | 25.19 | 8 | 4.22 | 5.71 |
| 10. | Karnataka | 101 | 16.38 | 17.15 | 49 | 4.26 | 6.95 |
| 11. | Kerala | 68 | 9.92 | 9.1 | 39 | 1.1 | 1.45 |
| 12. | Madhya Pradesh | 47 | 14.55 | 15.62 | 46 | 23.27 | 21.09 |
| 13. | Maharashtra | 59 | 11.09 | 11.81 | 47 | 9.27 | 9.35 |

*(Continued)*

**TABLE 11.1** Continued

| Sl. No | Name of the State/UT | No. of Castes in SC Category | SC Pop. to Total Pop. (%) 1991 | SC Pop. to Total Pop. (%) 2011 | No. of Tribes in ST Category | ST Pop. to Total Pop. (%) 1991 | ST Pop. to Total Pop. (%) 2011 |
|---|---|---|---|---|---|---|---|
| 14. | Manipur | 7 | 2.02 | 3.41 | 33 | 34.41 | 40.88 |
| 15. | Meghalaya | 16 | 0.51 | 0.58 | 14 | 85.53 | 86.15 |
| 16. | Mizoram | 16 | 0.1 | 0.11 | 14 | 94.75 | 94.43 |
| 17. | Nagaland | – | – | – | 5 | 87.7 | 86.48 |
| 18. | Orissa | 93 | 16.2 | 17.13 | 56 | 22.21 | 22.85 |
| 19. | Punjab | 37 | 28.31 | 31.94 | +– | – | – |
| 20. | Rajasthan | 59 | 17.29 | 17.83 | 12 | 12.44 | 13.48 |
| 21. | Sikkim | 4 | 5.93 | 4.63 | 2 | 22.36 | 33.8 |
| 22. | Tamil Nadu | 76 | 19.18 | 20.01 | 36 | 1.03 | 1.1 |
| 23. | Tripura | 32 | 16.36 | 17.83 | 19 | 30.95 | 31.76 |
| 24. | Uttar Pradesh | 66 | 21.05 | 20.7 | 5 | 0.21 | 0.57 |
| 25. | West Bengal | 59 | 23.62 | 23.51 | 38 | 5.59 | 5.8 |
| 26. | India | 1,284 | 16.2 | 16.63 | 645 | 8.2 | 8.63 |

*Source*: Author (estimates based on BSE data sources).

*Note*: Same castes might appear in different states.

It is noted that Karnataka has the largest number of 101 castes followed by Orissa with 93 castes. Goa and Dadra Nagar Haveli have fewer than 10 castes each. Punjab with 31.94 per cent has the largest proportion of the SC population to the total population in the state in the country followed by Himachal Pradesh with 25.19 per cent and West Bengal with 23.51 per cent in 2011. These data do not indicate the socio-economic status of each caste within the SC population in a state. Therefore, we have identified castes, which are dominant in each state in terms of their population. It is found that each state has the predominance of one or two castes in terms of number. Therefore, castes which account for more than 10 lakhs of population are identified and listed in Table 11.2. The data relating to these castes are available from the 2011 census. As per the 2011 census, the proportion of the SC population in the rural areas has marginally declined from 79.6 per cent in 2001 to 76.4 per cent in 2011. In other words, Dalits are predominantly rural based and agrarian in character.

### The Dominant Castes among SCs

The data show that there are 22 dominant castes in the country, which have accounted for about 56 per cent of the total SCs as per 2011 census. There are, however, more than 1,000 other small castes, which account for the remaining 44 per cent. The problem is also similar among the STs. The socio-economic and educational development of these 22 castes has been discussed in a cursory manner by various social scientists and even by Dalit leaders during the last five to six decades.

The problem today, however, is that some kind of differentiation is taking place not only among the 22 dominant SCs vis-à-vis dominant and small castes. This can be attributed largely to the ruling classes in the country who have been systematically co-opting the dominant castes in each state through identifying and encouraging leaders only among the dominant SC castes for

**TABLE 11.2** *Numerically Large Caste Groups, 2011*

| % of Pop. Each Caste to Total SC in the States, 2011 | State | SC 2011 in Lakhs |
|---|---|---|
| Pod | West Bengal | 24.5 |
| Namasudra | West Bengal | 35.04 |
| Dusadh | Bihar | 49.45 |
| Adi Dravid | Tamil Nadu | 72.42 |
| Chamar | Punjab | 20.7 |
| Chamar | Bihar | 49 |
| Mahyavanshi | Gujarat | 16.08 |
| Musahar | Bihar | 27.25 |
| Chamar | Madhya Pradesh | 53.68 |
| Chamar | Haryana | 24.29 |
| Mahar | Maharashtra | 80.06 |
| Badgi | West Bengal | 30.58 |
| Rajbanshi | West Bengal | 38.01 |
| Mazhab | Punjab | 26.33 |
| Adikarnataka | Karnataka | 29.2 |
| Meghaval | Rajasthan | 30.6 |
| Mala | Andhra Pradesh | 55.7 |
| Chamar | Uttar Pradesh | 224.9 |
| Dhobi | Uttar Pradesh | 24.32 |
| Madiga | Andhra Pradesh | 67.02 |
| Pasi | Uttar Pradesh | 65.22 |
| Kori | Uttar Pradesh | 22.93 |

*Source:* Author (estimates based on BSE data sources).

the benefit of electoral politics. They have done this deliberately through various government welfare programmes, such as private social welfare hostels, 1RDP scholarships and other kinds of subsidies. These programmes have benefitted mostly the cluster of families of the leader of the dominant caste in the region. For instance, Jagjivan Ram for *chamars* in the North and Sanjeevaiah for *malas* in the South can be cited as examples (some people allege the same for *mahars* in relation to Ambedkar). Though the leadership among the dominant Dalit castes has helped in articulating the problems of the Dalits in general, they have not been able to bring out the problems of the small and minority castes among the Dalits. They have also failed to develop a strategy of development suitable to other sub-castes among the SCs. This does not mean that they have neglected the interests of the Dalits in general. As the leadership of the Dalits during the post-Ambedkar period was under transition, they had no opportunity to study, analyse and understand the problems of the 1,000 and odd castes in India. Therefore, in all the development policies for SCs, a uniform and identical national strategy has been followed without reference to the specific problems of each caste in a region and the regional dimensions of the caste.

In fact, there are several castes in the country, which are peculiar to a region and similar castes are not found outside the region. Therefore, the general policies pursued by the government never addressed the specific requirements of the small castes. The rural–urban disparity index presented for each dominant caste by Y. K. Agrawal and Sarika Sibu[1] in their study on SCs have shown that there are variations among the 22 numerically dominant caste. However, the proportion kept on changing from census to census due to the change of category of castes. For instance, in Uttar Pradesh and Bihar, the governments have shifted some castes from BC list to SC list.[2] This disparity is, however, declining marginally over a period of time.

Even the benefits drawn by castes in each state is not uniform. It is found that the SCs in a state who have a historical advantage over other states have been found more advanced compared to the latter. In Table 11.3, we have presented the number of post-matric scholarships drawn by each state in the country during 1993–1994 (we have access to data for this

**TABLE 11.3** *Post-matric Scholarship for SCs during 1993–1994 (Provisional)*

| Sl. No. | State and UT | No. of Beneficiaries | % to Total | % of SC Population to Total India |
|---|---|---|---|---|
| 1. | Andhra Pradesh | 132,380 | 9.89 | 7.6 |
| 2. | Assam | 41,453 | 3.09 | – |
| 3. | Bihar | 120,611 | 9.01 | 9.7 |
| 4. | Goa | 130 | 0.01 | 0.02 |
| 5. | Gujarat | 66,871 | 4.99 | Feb-30 |
| 6. | Haryana | 13,313 | 0.99 | 2.3 |
| 7. | Himachal Pradesh | 2,678 | 0.22 | 1 |
| 8. | J&K | 1,965 | 0.15 | 0.5 |
| 9. | Karnataka | 106,333 | 7.94 | 5.3 |
| 10. | Kerala | 45,090 | 3.36 | 2.4 |
| 11. | Madhya Pradesh | 77,097 | 5.76 | 7 |
| 12. | Maharashtra | 187,708 | 14.02 | 4.3 |
| 13. | Manipur | 755 | 0.05 | 0.02 |
| 14. | Meghalaya | 124 | 0.01 | 0.01 |
| 15. | Orissa | 24.972 | 1.86 | 3.7 |
| 16. | Punjab | 19,916 | 1.48 | 4.3 |
| 17. | Rajasthan | 32,744 | 2.44 | 5.6 |
| 18. | Tamil Nadu | 118,250 | 8.83 | 8.4 |
| 19. | Tripura | 3174 | 0.38 | 0.3 |
| 20. | Uttar Pradesh | 243,826 | 18.21 | 22.4 |
| 21. | West Bengal | 85,610 | 6.39 | 11.5 |
| 22. | Daman and Diu | 130 | 0.01 | – |
| 23. | Dadra and Nagar Haveli | 50 | 0.01 | – |
| 24. | Delhi | 9,648 | 0.72 | 1 |
| 25. | Pondicherry | 1,466 | 0.11 | – |
| | Total | 1,311,347 | 100 | 100 |

*Source:* Annual Report of the Ministry of Social Welfare.

year only and is being used here to highlight the point). The post-matric scholarships are considered here as an indicator of social and educational advancement of Dalits as it helps to promote them to enter into the elite and also makes a Dalit to participate in the modern sectors of development, including bureaucracy, political power and so on. It is found that states, such as Andhra Pradesh (9.89%), Gujarat (4.99%), Karnataka (7.94%), Kerala (3.36%), Maharashtra (14.02%), are cornering most of the post-matric scholarships, which are in excess of their proportion in the SC population of the country, namely, Andhra Pradesh (7.6%), Gujarat (2.3%), Karnataka (5.3%) and Maharashtra (4.3%), respectively. States, such as West Bengal, Uttar Pradesh, Rajasthan, Punjab, Orissa and Bihar where the largest concentration of SCs are present are not in a position to fully avail the benefits. This shows that there are regional inequalities which accentuate the inequities among the different castes of SCs further. These differences indicate the inequity in the distribution of benefits among the SCs living in different states. This also brings to light that the SCs living in backward states, such as Bihar and Orissa are further marginalized by being inhabitants of a backward state. If we go further deep into the problem, it will be clear to us that among the fifth sub-castes, the rate of growth of social and economic mobility is very fast among some castes and is much slower among the marginalized sub-castes. For instance, in Andhra Pradesh, the *madigas* are relatively backward compared to *malas* of Costal Andhra Pradesh and Telangana. In fact, some kind of patronage has been developed by the few advanced groups among their families. This has given the upward mobility to few groups or cluster of families in a caste. Nandu Ram[3] has pointed out in one of his studies that the upward mobility among the SCs has created educated middle class elite. But, they are suffering with 'status anxiety' for not being accepted by their peers in forward community, while their unfortunate brethren among the Dalits are still languishing to enter into a civilized mainstream.

## Intra-caste Differentiation as an Emerging Phenomenon

The location of a caste in a region within a state has both advantages and disadvantages. The castes that are placed in historically advanced states, such as Maharashtra where Babasaheb Ambedkar started the social revolution had an advantage over states, such as Bihar and Orissa where the Buddhist revolution is now almost a matter of history.

Therefore, people inhabited in Bihar or Orissa are relatively at a disadvantage compared to Kerala, Maharashtra or Gujarat. The SCs, particularly the numerically small castes located in the backward states, are double marginalized. This kind of double marginalization is also possible within a state in different regions. People living in high fertile and irrigated areas will have continuous sources of income and employment compared to people living in dry and high land areas. The SCs who are spread in different regions of a state do also acquire the same qualities. The backwash effects of the development of certain dominant SCs result in the underdevelopment of several small and marginalized castes within the region. The sub-castes among the SCs who have obtained the benefits of the welfare programmes and education are able to utilize the advantages of modem technology in becoming more advanced. This will further strengthen the gap between the less developed and the socially and economically advanced dominant castes. But the disparity between the dominant and the marginalized castes is more pronounced than the gaps among the advanced. There are very few studies at the sub-caste level to substantiate this point. But, a case study of a state, such as Andhra Pradesh might throw some light on this problem to recognize the internal contradictions among the castes that has resulted in the differentiation among the sub-castes over a period of time. These indicators are to be presented and studied for each sub-caste to avoid homomorphic policy. The recent developments in the economy through liberalization and market orientation will further widen the gap and alienate the disadvantaged among the backwards creating a gulf that might result in the creation of another world within the 4th world. Even the missionaries that have worked among the Dalits could not bring them together; rather, they have succumbed to intra-caste rivalries by promoting each denomination in a particular caste (for instance Baptists among *madigas* of Andhra).

## Deficiencies in the Emergence of Dalit and *Bahujan* Formation

Though the ruling classes have been pursuing a policy of preferential treatment among the Dalit castes favouring those who have been helping them, the emergence of intra-caste differentiation is not entirely due to their machinations. They have utilized the internal contradictions and iniquitous nature of the caste system for their advantage. The problem of intra-caste differences approach to have been existing from the time of Ambedkar. It seems that Ambedkar started his social movement as a leader of *mahars* and slowly realized the deficiency of his movement when *mangs* started alienating from him. He changed his strategy and adopted a universal approach of inclusiveness that attracted *jatavs* of North India and *namasudras* of Bengal. But the differentiation among the Dalit castes at that time was not as much pronounced as it is today. It is due to the iniquitous distribution of benefits among the sub-castes and regions and also due to the constant promotion of a particular caste by the ruling classes. The emergence of a preferred layer consisting of extended families and people from developed regions is also responsible for shrinking opportunities for other marginalized groups. The role of the left parties in the promotion of Dalit and Adivasi development within welfare state programmes is subjected to criticism in terms of weakness in their theory and practice in Bengal and Kerala. The role of SCs in educational development and their representation in educational institutions in both the states is a subject of Dalit bashing.

However, the elite among the Dalits have started articulating the problems of the Dalits as a whole in recent times. The issues of the Dalits have been surfaced and are being discussed continuously at various levels due to the constant efforts of these elite. Interestingly, the interest groups among the Dalits are using Ambedkar and Jagjivan Ram as symbols of mobilization. But, mobilization never crossed the boundaries of sub-caste and region. The mobilization of the Dalit forces across the country became more pronounced cutting across the language, region and sub-castes during the Mandal agitation. This was made possible because of the support from the other backwards who also used Ambedkar as a symbol of revolt. The Mandal agitation provided opportunities for the ruling classes, particularly the enemies of the Dalits, to identify the strong and weak points in the movement. They have identified that the *Bahujan* formation of the Dalit masses and the backwards is not uniform and universal. There are internal differences and dissensions that could be used to alienate one from the other based on emotional appeals as seen in Andhra Pradesh, Uttar Pradesh and Bihar before elections.[4] The issue of sub-caste division is against the spirit of the Constitution that considers SC is a single caste under Article 341, which was upheld by Supreme Court.

The socio-economic and cultural ethos of different castes is not uniform. No attempt seems to have been made to study the diversities and uniqueness of each caste in participating in the *Bahujan* formation. It appears that no intellectual section has emerged even in the Bahujan Samaj Party (except that of a few bureaucrats) to analyse and articulate these problems on a continuous basis.[5] The slogan of capturing power by the brute majority of the number is spread across the country without considering the specific requirements of each caste and also tribe. Politics may be a number game but social reform and amalgamation of different castes as a mass is not equal to the sum that aggregates the parts. It is something more than that as all the parts are not equal in size and quality. This has been realized by the ruling classes who are now trying to encourage one sub-caste against another by applying the same traditional tactics of calculated disparities and slogans. It appears that the castes that are now in the saddle of power will break the solidarity of the SCs, which was built on the emotional issues of untouchability and exploitation using the same language and methodology. The Dalits have started fighting with each other. Sometimes, it is orchestrated by the ruling classes who ultimately wanted to prove that each sub-caste among the Dalits is also a minority and may not be equivalent to that of any *Dvija* caste. Therefore, the slogan of minority ruling the majority according to them does not arise, as Indian democracy today is an oligarchy of castes.

The above distorted social formation needs to be corrected. The Ambedkar's slogan of political democracy in principle can be translated as social democracy[6] put into practice at all stages. In a country, such as India, social democracy should provide opportunities for each caste small and big to equally participate in the decision-making process. This is possible when the leadership learns from history and also from social reformers, such as Kabir, Phooley, Ambedkar and Periyar, first in bringing people, that is, castes together. The strategy to develop a *mala* sale cannot be the same as for a *madiga* as their existential problems are different. It is also necessary to change the uniform policy of the government in providing the same kind of prescriptions for different problems of the Dalits. A rational criterion, such as the disparity index and regional inequalities, needs to be considered for each caste among the SCs in dispensing state aid. A political upsurge without a social reform movement shall remain as a lacklustre crusade. Therefore, a mass movement first among the Dalits to bring the feeling of brotherhood and solidarity through inter-marriage, inter-dinning and more than that recognizing the existence of each sub-caste as a unique cultural entity needs to be built into their ethos to thwart the attempts of ruling classes to bring a counter-revolution much before the beginning of a social revolution of *bahujans* in India. If the counter-revolution succeeds as it happened in the past, it will totally usurp the inalienable rights of the Dalits.

## Notes

1. Agrwal Yash and Sarika Sibu, *Educating Scheduled Cases* (New Delhi: NIEPA, 1994).
2. 'U.P. Government Gives Assent to Include 17 Other Backward Castes in S.C. List', *The Times of India*, 22 December 2016.
3. Nandu Ram, *The Mobile Scheduled Castes: Rise of New Middle Class* (Delhi: Hindusthan Publishing, 1985).
4. 'U.P. Government Gives', *The Times of India*.
5. Rajashekhar Vundru, 'Mayavathi: The Woman Inside', *South India Journal of Social Sciences* (June 200): 3–10.
6. B. R. Ambedkar, *Babasheb Ambedkar Writings and Speeches*, Vol 3, ed. Vasant Moon (New Delhi: Ambedkar Foundation, 2010).

# 12

# Globalization and the Future of Dalits and Adivasis

*No one is born hating another person because of the colour of his skin, or his background, or his religion. People must learn to hate and if they can learn to hate, they can be taught to love, for love comes more naturally to the human heart than its opposite. Man's goodness is a flame that can be hidden but never extinguished.'*
—Nelson Mandela

Globalization as a method of economic integration is as old as colonialism. It has been used in different meanings and contexts. Several scholars are counter-posing globalism to imperialism. Globalization is generally referred to as cross-national flow of goods, investment, production and technology. It relies heavily on technological innovations in the area of information technology. In fact, the idea of global market became operational with the advent of satellite channels and Internet. However, this globalization is not entirely different from the concept of imperialism. As imperialism is a phase of the capitalist expansion on a global scale, some scholars are not willing to use the term and rather prefer to use globalization.

But globalization as defined above needs to be linked with the historical concepts of colonialism, neo-colonialism and imperialism. They are all interrelated. Colonialism emerged as a part of imperialism in the 19th century through territorial division of labour. It is established through violence, exploitation of labour and unequal exchange. Several dependency theorists have conceptualized centre-periphery imagery on the basis of the concept of imperialism. There was a great debate on the origin and development of imperialism as a part of capitalist development in economics literature. But the debate is now reopened after the popularization of the concept of globalization. It is argued that globalization is not an independent phenomenon and it is to be understood as a part of imperialism.

The British India government wanted to introduce gold exchange standard in trade as the leading authorities of that time including J. M. Keynes were supportive of this. Ambedkar had critically examined this theory, including Keynes proposal on the ground that lower exchange rate increase export and boosts internal.[1] This will benefit the trading classes and harm the poor. If this is reinterpreted along with his proposals in 'state and minorities' today, Ambedkar[2] would have argued for protection and against globalization.

Imperialism has three phases of development. The first phase was organized around the conquest of the Americas in the framework of mercantilist system of Atlantic Europe. 'The net result was the destruction of the Indian civilization and their Hispanicization–Christianization or simply the total genocide on which the USA was built.[3]

The second phase of imperialist devastation was based on the industrial revolution and manifested itself in the colonial subjection of Asia and Africa in the name of opening of the markets. The capitalist civilization from 1500 to 1950 with breaches here and there developed first-class technological potential and military traditions for capitalist accumulation.

The third phase of devastation of the world by imperialist expansion, encouraged by the collapse of the soviet system and the regimes of popularist nationalism in the third world, is contemporary in nature. It is founded on 'duty to intervene', 'rights of peoples' and 'humanitarianism' to exploit the labour reserves in the periphery. The objectives of dominant capital are still the same. It is superficially called as globalization. But the quality of imperialism is enriched with ideas, such as economic reform, liberalization, privatization and transnational corporations.

There seems to be a difference between the first two phases of imperialism and the globalization process of imperialism. In the first two phases, there were no international institutions to guide and control the operations. But with the advent of Bretton Woods institutions and, particularly, after the establishment of WTO in 1995, imperialism is coordinated and supervised through these institutions. The invisible hand, which was supposed to be operating for the international division of labour in the first two phases, has been taken over by the Keynesian interventionist institutions to restore what is called distortions in global market? Further, the discovery of corporation as a form of business organization with semi-democratic principles reduced the negative image of capitalism in the popular discourse.

'According to most advocates of the globalization theory, we are entering a new epoch of interdependency in which stateless corporations transcend national frontiers, spurred by a third technological revolution and facilitated by new information systems ... the nation state is an anachronism, movements of capital are unstoppable and inevitable, and the world market is the determinant of the macro- and micro-political economy'.[4]

Thus, the transnational corporation has emerged as a new tool unlike the East India Company which was confined to the shareholders within the boundaries of a nation state.

The emergence of transnational corporation has facilitated the 'global approach' of finance capital. 'Globalization represented freedom for the corporation to set itself wherever it wanted for as long as it wanted, to produce whatever it wanted, buying and selling with least possible number of restrictions as far as labour laws and social conventions were concerned'. This globalization is understood by many in the context of the expansion of corporate capitalism. Even corporate capitalism is overwhelmed by finance capital. It is on the basis of the experience of these corporations, the American business schools coined the term 'globalization' to indicate the global approach of these corporations. Majority of these corporations offer a variety of financial services and enter into exchange markets even if majority of their operations continue to be in industry. It was estimated that more than $1,400 billion changed hands everyday on currency markets in 1996. As a result, the corporations have become the policeman, judge and jury of the world economy, which is very worrying given their tendency to see events and policies through the distorting prism of fear and greed (Financial Times, 30 September 1994). The over-accumulation of capital has been accompanied by a real potential of production of commodities in terms of excessive productive capacity. As a result, much of the capital accumulated from new super-profits is not invested productively. This capital flows into real estate and stock markets for speculation and for merger and take over-operations. It is said that this phenomenon is responsible for the financial crisis in the South East Asia in 1997.

It is found that 70 per cent of international trade and 75 per cent of FDI are controlled by MNCs. According to a UNCTAD report in 1995, 37,000 MNCs and their 2 lakh subsidiaries have assets worth $5,000 billion. Of which, 200 biggest MNCs have a total turnover equivalent to more than a quarter of the sum of the entire world's GDP. The turnover of General Motors ($132.4 billion) is higher than the GDP of Indonesia ($126.4 billion) or Denmark ($123.5 billion). The five biggest MNCs had a turnover of double the size (526.1 billion) of the GDP of South Asia ($297.4 billion) in 1995. James Tobin has shown that every day more than 90 per cent of international financial transactions are purely speculative and, therefore, called for a proportional tax on all international currency transactions to spend the amount on projects of social justice. It is estimated that a 0.5 per cent Tobin tax would bring $1800 billion in the year 1995. These figures are quoted here to indicate the potential of corporate capitalism in the 20th century. Further, these corporations are unevenly distributed across the continents. It is found that out of the 500 biggest corporations of the world, 244 originate in the USA, 46 in Japan, 173 in Europe and the rest in other countries.[5] By early 2018, global debt stocks had risen to nearly $250 trillion, three times global income from $142 trillion a decade earlier.[6] It is noted

> the digital revolution has the misfortune of unfolding in a neo-liberal era over the last four decades; a mixture of financial chicanery, unrestrained corporate power and economic austerity has shredded the social contract that emerged after second world war and replaced it with different set of rules, norms and policies at the national, regional and international levels. This has enabled capital to escape from the regulatory oversight expand into new areas of profit making and restrict the influence of policymakers.[7]

It is necessary to identify the tools through which globalization or imperialism is able to operate. Most of these tools are acquired by the system during the 20th century, particularly after the information revolution. It is observed that the following are important tools of imperialism.

1. Media (both print and visual)
2. Capital (both finance and investment)
3. Military power (ever-expanding defence budgets)
4. World Bank and IMF (the voting pattern favourable to the USA)
5. WTO [Trade-Related Aspects of Intellectual Property Rights (TRIPS) and Trade-Related Investment Measures (TRIMS)]
6. The structural reform package consisting of (a) trade liberalization, (b) liberalization of banking system, (c) privatization of public sector, (d) tax reform (VAT), (e) land privatization, (f) labour market reforms, (g) trade unions, (h) pensions, (i) social safety nets to alleviate poverty and (j) good governance.

The above tools of imperialism, Samar Amin has said, have helped to develop five important monopolies in the imperialist centres (Samir Amin, 2001). They are as follows:

1. The monopoly of technology with the support of the state, especially of military spending
2. The monopoly of the control of global financial flows
3. The monopoly of access to the natural resources of the planet
4. The monopoly in the field of communication and media, homogenizing world culture and opening up of new means of political manipulation
5. The monopoly of weapons of mass destruction

Globalization or imperialism in the third phase is three decades old now. It has been implemented in about 100 less developed countries of various sizes and dimensions. The impact of the implementation of the package of structural adjustment seems to be non-uniform. Depending upon the context, the nature of the society, economy and polity, the costs and benefits of globalization vary. There are several studies undertaken by international agencies, such as UNCTAD, UNDP, World

Bank and individual scholars assessing the impact of these policies pursued during the last two decades. In some of the Latin American countries, such as Brazil, Chile, Argentina and Indonesia, harsh military dictatorships were pursued to sustain the reforms. Somalia a pastoral economy was self-sufficient in food until the 1970s and introduced the reforms package in 1980. The civil society was subjected to a breakdown and the US military got involved in 1993. Today Somalia languishes as one of the poorest countries in the world. The story of Asian tigers, including (the American and Japanese market centre) Singapore, is quite interesting. The countries are now slowly recovering from the 1997 currency crisis. The crisis in the civil society due to the failure of reforms in Argentina is still fresh in our minds. The success of Chinese version of reforms and further fragmentation of East European countries after the implementation of the reforms need to be studied afresh. The experience of India with the second phase of reforms with a regime with religious fundamentalism as its background is undergoing convulsions.

The political and social fallout of the economic globalization is responsible for the shrinking role of the state and the social consequences of it. The privatization of public sector is essentially a political act with no additional gain in terms of creation of new jobs, high rates of savings or investment or the development of new productive forces. Privatization of the existing public sector units through outright sale, disinvestments and transfer to private individuals, corporations and MNCs has deep-rooted maladies. The process of privatization has involved corruption and transfer of properties worth billions of dollars at throwaway price without proper legislative sanction and public auction. Several workers lost their jobs due to voluntary retirement scheme (VRS), pushing them to a new class of urban poor or low-paid informal workers. The increased prices of services, electricity, transport and so on accompanying privatization have decreased living standards for wage and salary workers, while increasing profits for the private monopolies that have taken over the public ones.[8] The public sector units were established in countries, such as India, to build infrastructure and occupy commanding heights of the economy. This was made possible because of the sacrifices of the poor who have postponed their current needs to a future date by foregoing their education, health and welfare. The same public sector units are now being transferred to the rich and possessed creating intergenerational transfers of a different kind. This has deprived the poor in general and Dalits in particular.

Globalization seems to have not increased the competitive edge of developing countries as 78.5 per cent of the world income is held by Organisation for Economic Co-operation and Development (OECD) countries and the remaining got distributed among the less-developed junior partners in trade. How can a less-developed country of the periphery with low capital base and high interest rates will be able to compete with an imperialist centre and gain out of the trade. It may benefit few individuals in the periphery through a collaborating elite. Commenting on the links between centre and periphery Karl Deutsch[9] has said that

> the centre of the centre of course, gets all the advantages. The periphery of the centre gets less than the centre, but ... it gets a rake-off .... In the periphery countries, the middle class will become somewhat reactionary. According to the Galtung theory, they are likely to be bought by the imperial system and to make up its bridgehead in their native countries. The middle classes of Buenos Aires, Rio de Janeiro and Santiago de Chile, who completely accept the West European and North American standards of consumption ... live about as well as, or better than middle class persons who live in the advanced countries. But the poor of Brazil, Argentina and Chile are poor by the grim standards of the poor Latin America.[10]

The inequalities among world's people and within countries among different groups of people are found to be increasing during the third phase of imperialism or globalization. Citing from a recent study of Milonovic, the Human Development Report 2001 mentioned that

> in 1993 the poorest 10% of the world's people had only 1.6% of the income of the richest 10%. The richest 1% of the world's people received as much income as the poorest 57%. The richest 10% of the US population (around 25 million people) had a combined income greater than that of the poorest 43% of the world's people (around 2 billion people).

Similarly, the ratio of the income of the richest 20 per cent to that of the poorest 20 per cent grew from 34 to 1 in 1970 to 70 to 1 in 1997. Technology, the hallmark of globalization, has not been used effectively to reduce these inequalities. Further, it has intensified the digital divide. The Human Development Report 2001 has introduced a new Technology Achievement Index (TAI) to identify the inequalities among countries in the area of creation of technology, diffusion of recent innovations, diffusion of old innovations and human skills. It is said that

> many countries are using the latest technology competitively in manufacturing industries as shown by their success with high-tech exports. Of the 30 top exporters, 11 are in the developing world, including Korea, Malaysia and Mexico. But in sub-Saharan Africa, the Arab states and South Asia high-tech exports still account for less than 5 per cent of the total.[11]

Interestingly, India's place in this ranking is found at 63 out of the 72 countries ranked in 2001 and it stands at 130 with a value of 0.638 out of 189 countries in 2019.

Now, we can turn our attention to the developed metropolis to examine the impact of globalization among different social groups within. It is estimated that in the USA, the difference in the life expectancy between a White male and Black male was

8 years in 1970 (White 68 years and Black 60 years) and the difference is increased to 10 years in 2000.[12] Similarly, the infant mortality was 10.9 for Whites and 22.2 for Blacks in 1980. There is a slight decline in the disparity in 1994 with the infant mortality of Whites remaining at 6.6 and Blacks at 15.8. The inequality in the educational attainment of Whites, Blacks and Hispanics is found to be much higher at the collegiate level, though it is declining over a period of time. It is reported that 10.3 per cent of White males had four years or more of collegiate education in 1960 and the percentage has increased to 26.9 per cent in 1996. Only 2.8 per cent of the Blacks had similar education in 1960. The percentage has increased to 12.4 in 1996. Among Hispanics, 7.8 per cent population had four years of collegiate education in 1970 and it is found at 10.3 in 1996. Though there is a difference in the rate of growth in the educational attainment between Blacks and Whites, the gap remains. In the area of money income and unemployment rates, the disparity remains much wider. The percentage of Black families earning between $10,000 and $49,000 has dropped, while the percentage of those with earnings of $50,000 and above has increased.

> The difference in family median income among Whites, Blacks and Hispanics is still in the double digits. One of the most encouraging developments in recent years has been the steady decline in unemployment rates for Blacks and Women.... By the end of 1998, the US department of labour reported the unemployment rate for African Americans reached an all-time low of 7.9 per cent. A combination of factors has contributed to this: overall expanding economy, greater job skills and educational training of Blacks, and enforcement of anti-discrimination laws on employment and voluntary implementation of fair employment practices by private industries and public agencies.[13]

The situation in Brazil, one of the earliest to enter globalization in the periphery appears to be different. It is said that Brazil in 1999 ranked after only Sierra Leone with the second most unjust income distribution in the world; income concentration consistently increased over time. Racial groups do exist in Brazil and people are discriminated on the basis of their colour. It is observed that in the income hierarchy, race is the first determining factor and then gender. White women in Brazil have privileged position compared to Black men and Afro-Brazilian women

> 'Income disparities among racial groups exist regionally ... the north and north east, where African Brazilians are the large majority, have the lowest income and economic activity levels in the country and the highest inequality rates (Gini index) ... average family income by region confirms that the regions with majority Afro-Brazilian populations are by far the poorest – Blacks generally earn less than half as much as Whites. White men earn almost four times as much as Afro-Brazilian women, who earn less than half the value of White women's average income. About 26 percent of Blacks, compared to 16 percent Whites, earn less than the minimum wage, while one percent of Blacks as opposed to four percent of Whites earned more than 10 times the minimum wage. Educated African Brazilians earn less than Whites with same education, and in higher income brackets Whites receive about 5.6 times more income than Blacks.[14]

On the positive side, the network age promoted by globalization has contributed greatly to the acceleration of human progress. It has given tremendous resilience to capitalism. In 1975–1999, per capita average income quadrupled in East Asia and the pacific, growing 6 per cent a year. The growth rate in South Africa exceeded 2 per cent. India and China with one-third of the world population are growing at 8 per cent and 3.2 per cent a year, respectively. OECD countries are growing at 2 per cent a year raising already high incomes to an average of more than $22,000 (PPP). The average incomes in developing countries during 1975–1998 have almost doubled from $1,300 to $2,500 (PPP).

## Contrast Between Centre and Periphery Imagery

The above two contrasting experiences of different racial groups in the metropolis and in the periphery have provided evidence to draw a strategy of empowerment of the poor. It is in this background the position of Dalits in the contemporary society is to be examined. The Dalits of India for the first time in Indian history had an opportunity to share their experiences of discrimination and affirmative action at the Durban world conference against racism in September 2001. The Dalit representatives have aptly listened to the agonizing and enlightening episodes of representatives of similar people elsewhere in the world. The Durban Conference has also made it possible to the world civil society to discern the pathetic conditions of 250 million Dalits in the world. In the process of exchange of ideas, experiences and agonies, the Dalits have gathered some evidence as to the sincerity and honesty in implementing programmes of emancipation of the marginalized groups in different societies. Naturally, they are struck by the innovative ideas as no scholar or activist of repute belonging to non-Dalit categories has ever discussed about those experiments in India. This intellectual vacuum has resulted in the enthusiastic overtures in India when some of those who attended the Durban Conference[15] have returned back home. The Bhopal Conference was one such occasion where intellectuals and activists of different hues met and exchanged ideas for an agenda of Dalit emancipation. This is only a first step in a long march. However, this has attracted unprecedented response both from the left- and right-wing intellectuals and activists. But in none of the writings, any innovative and creative idea came up for discussion except repeating the traditional Marxist polemics. Even these writers did not crave for reading and learning about the latest developments in their ideological positions at the international level. However, the debate is interesting and historical since it has reopened the vexed issues of Dalit emancipation in an era of globalization.

It is necessary at this stage to assess the historical legacy of the Dalit movement in order to understand their future. The socio-political situation during the first quarter of the 20th century was charged with revolutionary upsurge that promoted egalitarian ideology and democratic values. The principles of liberal democracy, the gift of the English utilitarian to Indian masses, had influenced several leaders, including Ambedkar. The success story of Bolshevik revolution had promoted the ideology of socialism. At the same time, a section of the conservative Brahminical Hindu minority started a movement to recreate *puranic* India.

The adherents of the egalitarian principles used to express sympathy with the issues raised by Ambedkar along with the British bureaucracy who were trained by the utilitarian scholars in the UK. This has helped Ambedkar to push his agenda of Dalit emancipation. In this process, he has succeeded in creating constitutional safeguards for caste-based reservations.

The programme of reservations in public sector employment has resulted in the creation of a section of Dalit job holders who have been able to enter the civil society. If the Ambedkar project of Dalit emancipation and total liberation of Dalits from social and economic oppression is alive today, it is because of the work undertaken by some of these educated Dalits. Therefore, one must remember here that there are two categories of intellectuals among the Dalits. The organic intellectuals, the Gramsci's category of intellectuals who are committed and have been working among the Dalits for their emancipation, are different from the lumpen intellectuals who act as the agents of the mainstream social order with short-term and immediate gains and perks. There is also an elite category which is a part of the mainstream elite formation. There is hope today only in the organic intellectuals and their creative work for the emancipation of Dalits.

The Dalits are today interested in working with these organic intellectuals. They are now searching for alternatives and projects to work with for the overall development of the community. A critical evaluation of the work and progress made during the 20th century should enable us to understand the weaknesses of the movement. Religious reform movements and their contribution to Dalit emancipation can be mentioned here. But, the basic aim of all religious reform movements of the previous centuries appeared to be developing a Dalit person who was equal before God along with others. Therefore, some of these movements tried to bring the alienated untouchables nearer to the mainstream society at least in theological terms within the Hindu fold. The two central Asian religions, Islam and Christianity, tried to emancipate the Dalit by developing him as an independent self-sustained individual. These movements have enabled the Dalit to develop his self-consciousness but failed to bring social consciousness. The social reform was not an important issue on the agenda of the independence movement, though Gandhi and few others have tried to make it a point in their social agenda (after the threat of Ambedkar as a leader of the Dalit masses). The last phase of Ambedkar's movement in religious conversion as a project of cultural identity brought some change and development in some pockets of Maharashtra, and it never became an all India programme after his death. The recent developments in Buddhism as a religious emancipatory project of some Dalit activists need to be evaluated to what extent it has alienated or assimilated the Dalit with the mainstream society. Ironically, there is a total absence of any kind of 'social reform movement' after independence. The progress achieved by Dalits as a part of the radical left movement and the enormous human sacrifices made by the Dalit community need to be assessed separately.

The Dalits of India are not a homogeneous community (see previous chapter). There is also no pattern in the distribution of the population among different states (see previous chapter). Half of the Dalit population live in Uttar Pradesh (3 crores), West Bengal (2 crores), Bihar (1.5 crores), Tamil Nadu (1.10 crores) and Andhra Pradesh (1.5 crores). But, the Ambedkar movement and Dalit consciousness is much stronger in states, such as Maharashtra (11%), Karnataka and Andhra Pradesh, where the Dalits constitute less than 20 per cent of the population. Interestingly, Dalits constitute around one-third of the population in Punjab (28.3%) and one-fourth in Himachal Pradesh (25.4%). It appears that the future success of Dalit movement depends upon the consciousness of the Dalits in larger states where it is now weak.

The little progress made so far by the Dalits in the post-independence period was confined to one or two dominant castes in each state. It is identified that around 25 castes out of 1,091 castes in the country have cornered majority of the assistance declared by the government.[16] There are inequalities within each caste as some families among the beneficiaries have formed into a lobby and diverted some of these benefits to their members. This has created problems of intra-caste differences that led to separatists' struggles within the Dalit community in states, such as Andhra Pradesh, Haryana, and Karnataka.

One of the weaknesses of the Dalit movement appears to be its adherence to the popularization of Ambedkar as a personality and emancipator without explaining his emancipatory project. The issue of Adivasis is discrete as left extremism is found in some pockets of the fifth schedule areas and inter-tribal hostilities do exist in several others. The Ambedkar movement and its petty leadership failed to digest his ideology and never translated it into an action programme. (We have limitations of comprehending this at all India level. This is based on some experiences of Andhra Pradesh.) Therefore, we have in every village, Ambedkar Associations but no Dalit organizations. There are limitations for Ambedkar associations to take up the issues of the Dalits in totality. There is also the failure of Dalit intellectuals to assess the development process of Ambedkar movement and have failed to provide a concrete programme of action to the activists. They have also remained as members of the same bandwagon. No attempt seems to have been made by some of the Ambedkarite organizations at the state or centre level to give directions to the activists. The SC and ST employees associations are confined only for the implementation of reservations within each establishment and never emerged as a body to provide guidance to the activist. No attempt seems to have been made to develop a self-respect or social reform movement among the Dalits. The Dalits are never constituted an organic whole. Each subcaste has its own social and cultural identity. The only common identity that has emerged during the last half a century is developed around Ambedkar, as an emancipator. This is to be further strengthened with innovative interpretations for practical work. It is also necessary to develop the Dalit epistemology which is deep rooted in 'Tantra', the original scientific approach to life by the natives. This has been destroyed by the British during the colonial period and a major chunk of it was appropriated by the Brahminical Hinduism and Buddhism. The culture of poverty that existed among the Dalits for ages has strengthened certain traits and behaviour patterns, which are inimical for the development of Dalit emancipation. There are several factors contributing to these decadent drift in the Dalit movement.

The Brahminical preparation to encounter modernization and the Dalit emancipatory movements started from almost the same year from Maharashtra in the year 1925. Now the Sangh Parivar is in the saddle of power to dictate terms to the majority and continue to enjoy the hegemony. The Dalit parivar has remained today what they were in 1925, still daliting for equality of opportunity. There are several non-Dalit castes which have mobilized their caste resources and fought against the Brahminical forces and have recorded as upper castes without any support from outside and government. The emergence of Nadars in Tamil Nadu as a ruling class from that of a low social status in modern India is only one example.[17] The upward mobility of some Sudra castes, such as Kamma, Reddy, Vakkaliga and Yadav, of the south need to be studied and emulated by Dalits as these groups are influenced by the Dravidian movement.

It is irony that the Dravidian movement so assiduously built by the non-Brahmin stalwarts is ultimately rested under the tutelage of its enemy for a long time to change the discourse in Tamil Nadu.[18] It is here that one needs to ponder over the weaknesses of the whole Dravidian movement because the weaknesses have also been reflected in the Dalit movements in the formative years. The upper castes or the so-called Srinivasan category of 'dominant castes' in South India carved the Justice Party to fight against the hegemony of Brahmins in the South, particularly in the Madras presidency (which became divided and formed parts of the four South Indian states). The dominant castes are said to be dominant in a region 'when it preponderates numerically over other castes, and when it also wields preponderant economic and political power'. Some of the dominant castes have started upward mobility and continued to have their sway in political front until the *Dvija* rule under the Bharatiya Janata Party (BJP) came to occupy Delhi. The fundamental flaw in the formation of the anti-Brahmin Dravidian ensemble consisting of not only the South Indian states in geographical terms, but also the OBC, Muslim, SC and ST categories in cultural terms have been reduced to that of communal category without positioning itself just against the pan-Aryan *Dvija* identity. It is this flaw that weakened the whole reform project, including the Dalit emancipation as a part of the whole movement.

The erosion of Dravidian identity started during the time of Periyar EVR when the Dalits and small depressed BCs alienated from the DK. Perhaps Periyar realized this and seems to have expressed his agony with his closest followers. But, the DK and the DMK were later hijacked by the emerging dominant castes in Tamil Nadu and reduced the Dravidian movement to that of a conduit for political power. In the north, the anti-Brahmin movement started within the *Dvija* castes. Ram Manohar Lohia and some of his contemporaries, such as P. S. Deshmukh, R. L. Chandrapuri, and Karpoori Thakur, initiated the BCs movement as a parallel to the Dravidian movement in south. Though, the North Indian BCs movement established contacts with the South Indian movement and even invited Periyar to visit Bihar, no systematic attempt was made to integrate the North Indian anti-Brahmin struggles with the Dravidian movement. It was only after the Mandal Commission and the post-Mandal situation, the non-Brahmin leadership realized the need for a united and all-India character for the anti-Brahmin struggles.[19] The socialist–BCs movement, which was projected for some time as an anti-Brahmin movement was not homogeneous. There were two streams within it. The upper caste socialist stream who wanted to achieve equality without caste reservations and the BC socialists with an agenda to achieve socialism through caste reservations. Interestingly, the upper caste non-Brahmins have achieved upward mobility both in economic and social sphere and, therefore, in political front through a protracted fight against Brahmanism. They have displaced Brahmins from positions of political power at the regional level. This has also provided them with opportunities to consolidate the regional aspirations. The emergence of regional parities signifies these developments. It was these regional parties that played a significant role in the short-lived United Front. Most of these regional parties represented the interests of the dominant castes of the region, such as Vanniyar, Vokkaliga, Kamma, Yadava, Jat and similar castes. These dominant castes have formed into an oligarchy with the common minimum program as an agenda for governance. Similar to the 18th-century Whig oligarchy of Great Britain, the dominant caste oligarchy of India constituted of unprivileged feudal and middle classes with backing from aristocracy. It was during the leadership of Walpole, the British Whigs wanted to increase the base of the party. It was later appropriated by the Tories and the Whig oligarchy came to an end. It is exactly the same way the dominant caste oligarchy at the centre collapsed when the Hindutva nationalism (pan-Aryan) appropriated the dominant castes. However, the reasons for the dominant castes to surrender to the Hindutva are said to be historical and diverse in nature.[20] The Dalits with a national character have failed to join in any of the regional outfits and the so-called all India Bahujan Samaj Party is reduced to that of a regional party. Unlike that of the regional dominant castes, the Dalits do not have an oligarchy to fall back.

The development of the elite class from among the *Dvijas* and more particularly among the Brahmins took place during the 1960s. In fact, the criteria used by M. N. Srinivas to call a caste dominant are not appropriate to capture all castes in a village or region, because landholdings are no more an important base for economic mobility. It is subsidized higher education, access to banks and credit institutions, contracts, public sector sales outlets and so on that make a caste dominant. The opportunities created by the public sector of the Nehruvian era were systematically seized by the educated Brahmins. That is why Periyar called the bank nationalization at that time as bank Brahminization. There is nothing wrong in it, because Brahmins were the only group that was eminently qualified at that time to enter into public sector. Several Indian doctors, engineers, scientists and technocrats have migrated to the USA, the UK and other industrialized countries. Most of them got absorbed in the multinational companies and developed close contacts. Some of them have also occupied important positions in fund-bank institutions. In other words, a separate caste, a universal dominant caste crossing across the narrow geographical boundaries of state emerged, such as that of Zionism. A pundit of Kashmir, a Shastry of Tamil Nadu and a Sharma of Uttar Pradesh carved out a pan-Indian collectivity. They have started learning Hindi, Sanskrit and revived the Vedic rituals in New York, Delhi, London and elsewhere 'to share common culture and way of life'. First time in the history of India, Brahmins as a group started entering into economic sphere and have been using the bureaucracy for the accumulation of capital, human and physical. The tycoons of public sector have started ploughing the money into private coffers. They have used their positions for contacts with multinationals to establish units in India either in their name or with a *binami* to start with. Once the blood of the public sector unit is totally sucked, they leave it. Most of the media houses are owned and operated by the Bania–Brahmin combine. Several of the neo-rich industrialists of the pre- and post-liberalization period belongs to this genre.[21] They are supported by non-resident Indians (NRIs). The formation of this internationalized elite has been taking place without isolation from the nationalist pan-Aryan or Vedic revivalism in India and abroad. In fact, one should not forget the fact that more amount of money and bricks were said to be poured into India from the USA and other developed countries. This could not have been possible without a systematic networking. The so-called pseudo-religious secularists (*sarva dharma samabhava* type) in Congress, including some United Front constituents and others, did not take this trend very seriously. It was this universal dominant caste with pan-Aryan identity who wanted the country to be liberal. It was this group who wanted the economy to be opened up for global opportunities. It was ultimately they who appropriated the opportunities created in the economy. The small conglomerations of regional entities have started their own political outfits to bargain power. The power is ultimately used to get economic opportunities in the post-liberalization period. In the whole process of the so-called globalization of Indian economy, Dalits remained as untouchables once again.

Dalits are now concentrated mostly in the agriculture sector and a few in urban informal sector. Both the sectors are not remunerative. Further, the proportion of income from the agriculture sector to the total GDP is declining over a period of time. Yet, a greater number of Dalits depend on it. This implies that a greater number of people are distributing lesser amounts of income. They are caught in a vicious circle of low productivity, high concentration and declining income. Even the Bhopal declaration is not clear about the strategies to bring them out of this vicious circle. Unlike the hidden agenda of several caste groups, the Bhopal Dalit agenda is open and clear. This is for the first time after the death of Ambedkar, Dalits have expressed their aspirations and intentions. Interestingly, no political party or group has ever indicated a specific programme for the amelioration of the Dalits until the Dalits themselves did it in January 2002. The broad state-of-the-art radical models of liberation on a global scale do not work now and the Dalits are not sure how long should they wait? The experience of the Dalits in the country during the last 50 years has not provided any evidence of its operation and its successful completion. The operation of the CMOP both in the rural and urban areas is evident. This will not allow any of the models to operate. The CMOP and the capitalist expansion are not contradictory. Both the modes have developed resilience to survive in an era of globalization. In fact, the caste system is the most suitable form of social organization eminently suitable to the operation of mechanics of globalization. The caste system has provided the 'bridge heads' in the form of *Dvija* castes emerging as agents of MNCs and slowly co-opting other dominant castes as partners of MCCs. As the founders of critical school, Horkheimer, Adorno and others have proved that capitalism has improved its 'integrative trend' and dominance over political apparatus for planned capital accumulation. They have shown that there was total inter-dependence between Nazi party and big business. Similarly, the fundamentalist forces in India have absorbed the elements of globalization and strengthened it. There is no evidence that the *Dvija* castes are ever excluded from it, while all the Dalits are now outside its orbit. Do the Dalits afford to remain outside the system forever and allow the *Dvija*s alone to get benefited?

## The Future of Dalits and Adivasis

The future of the Dalits and Adivasis depends upon the way in which they organize themselves. It is a fact that most of the caste-based welfare organizations in the organized sectors are named as SCs and ST welfare associations, which have almost the same issues for redressal. They have also common problems of discrimination, marginalization and displacement in all the development projects. The typical Indian social system made the Dalits and Adivasis ostracized and socially excluded from the mainstream civil society. Now the trend appears that they have already been alienated from the economic sphere. Therefore, the Dalits will remain as one of the most vulnerable group in the world to bear the brunt of globalization. This will subject the Dalits to 'soft genocide' the harsher version of which the Indians had experienced during the first phase of imperialism in the Americas. What are the lessons the Blacks, Hispanics and others have learnt to survive in such hostile conditions? Do the Dalits have any parallels here?

It appears that the Dalits have not developed any strategies of their own for the survival and development of the community in the 21st century. The Blacks in America and some lower castes in India have proved that through the mobilization of the community resources, it is possible to break the social and economic barriers. One must be very clear here that the people of America and their experiences are different from the American government. If someone emulates the models of the Blacks or Hispanics, it does not mean that he/she is following the American government. In this context, the success story of black-owned business in America is cited as an example in recent discussions. The emergence of black-owned business is not a state-sponsored or capitalist charity. It is purely a community-based long-drawn struggle that made it possible for the blacks to emerge as an important economic group during 1980–2000. It is observed that the black-owned business increased by 7.3 per cent and their employment capacity grew by 11 per cent annually during the above period. 'Assuming the current growth rate can be sustained through the first decade or next century, black-business, will number well over 2 million'.[22] This impressive growth in business is not due to (as some people in India think) the opportunities created by the benevolent white government. It is purely on the basis of the community mobilization and the leadership qualities of the first black mayor, Maynard Jackson, who got elected to the city of Atlanta in 1973.

> In 1975, Atlanta established the country's first minority business affirmative action plan at the local level. Its significance resided in the fact that it was not tied to a federal mandate and its goals greatly exceeded those proposed at the federal level. Over a quarter of a century later, the Atlanta metropolitan area has the nation's faster growing black-most successful cadres of black business owners.[23]

Today blacks occupy around six important sectors, including transport, construction, and services, as a formidable force. Perhaps, the federal government has supported it later with diversity provisions. However, these affirmative actions were not left free without challenging them in the courts and the blacks are now continuing their legal battle without losing ground in business. Do we have any such accounts in India? A mere mention of it attracts onslaught by several people as if it is an illegitimate and anti-caste activity. People still think (perhaps unconsciously) that how could a Dalit do business and enter secular positions other than their caste-based occupations? Will the Dalit business operators emerge as black bourgeoisie, such as that of the red bourgeoisie? We are not sure. But Brahmins and some non-Vaisyas have made use of opportunities created by liberal economic policy and have emerged as the new capitalists.[24] The euphoria created by a group of Dalit entrepreneurs after the union government declared a vendor policy of accommodating 4 per cent reservation in public sector procurement has not yet produced one billionaire. But one thing appears to be clear. If the Dalits, including Adivasis, fail to mobilize their caste resources and organize themselves effectively to get their share in all economic activities, soon they will be reduced to that of the original 'panchama' category of the *varnashrama dharma* and be permanently excluded from the mainstream society under the CMOP. Will they allow it to happen or fight against it depends upon their ingenuity and creative work of the leaders of the oppressed in the years to come.

## Notes

1. S. Ambirajan, *Dr. Ambedkar's Contribution to the Indian Economics* (Chennai: Dr. Ambedkar Centre for Economic Studies, University of Madras, March 1999).
2. Ambedkar, *Babasaheb Writings and Speeches*, Vol. I.
3. Samir Amin, 'Imperialism and Globalisation', *Monthly Review*, June 2001.
4. James Petras and Henry Veltmeyer, *Globalization Unmasked: Imperialism in the 21st Century* (Delhi: Madhyam Books, 2001).
5. Michel Chossudovksy, *The Globalization of Poverty* (Goa: Other India Press, 1997).
6. UNCTAD, *Trade and Development Report 2018* (Geneva: UNCTAD, 2018).
7. Ibid., I.
8. Petras and Veltmeyer, *Globalization Unmasked.*
9. Karl Deutsch, 'Theories of Imperialism and Neo-colonialism', in *Testing Theories of Economic Imperialism*, eds. Steven J. Rosen and James R. Kurth (Lexington, MA: Lexington Books, 1974).
10. Ibid., 27.
11. UNPD, *Human Development Report* (Delhi: Oxford University Press, 2001), 42.
12. Thomas D. Boston, *Affirmative Action and Black Entrepreneurship* (London: Routledge, 1999).
13. Charles Hamilton, Lyn Huntlay, Antonio Sergio Alfredo Guimaraes, and Neville Alexander, eds., *Beyond Racism: Race Inequality in Brazil, South Africa and the United States* (Dallas: Lynne Reinner-Public Press, 2001).
14. Ibid.
15. Government of Madhya Pradesh, *Charting a New Course for Dalits for the 21st Century* (Bhopal: Government of Madhya Pradesh, January 2002).
16. K. S. Chalam, 'Intercaste and Intracaste Differentiation among Dalits in India', Occasional Paper, SRTRI Pochampally, 1997.

17. Robert L. Hardgrave, *Nadars of Tamilnadu: The Political Culture of a Community in Change* (Mumbai: Oxford University Press, 1969).
18. Aprameya Rao, 'Downhill Goes the Dravidian Movement', *Qrius*, 14 July 2014. https://qrius.com/downhill-goes-dravidian-movement/
19. K. S. Chalam, *Caste-based Reservations and Human Development in India* (New Delhi: SAGE, 2007).
20. K. S. Chalam, *Social Economy of Development in India* (New Delhi: SAGE, 2017).
21. Aakar Patel, 'When Will the Brahmin–Bania Hegemony End?' *Livemint*, 28 August 2009.
22. Boston, *Affirmative Action*.
23. Ibid.
24. Harish Damodaran, *India's New Capitalists: Caste, Business and Industry in Modern Times* (Delhi: Palgrave Macmillan, 2008).

# 13

# Democracy, Dalit Rights and the Paradigm Shift

The caste mode production and the determinants under which it has been operating in India discussed in the previous chapters brought out issues for discussion by scholars. The concept and its application to India along with primitive accumulation, relevance of classes, social relations, the hegemony of the functioning capitalists in the garb of *Dvija* and so on are discussed to give primacy of the caste category as an analytical term to understand the Hindu system of production and its survival even in post-industrial society, which are to be gripped to delve deep into the political economy of caste. The transition debate particularly the one between Maurice Dobb and P. Sweezy[1] seems to be still valid to understand how in India the so-called feudalism did not transform into Western-type capitalism. Instead, the caste-based crony capitalism has emerged that makes the concept of caste of MOP appropriate as its predecessor. Thus, transition from CMOP has resulted in caste crony capitalism and not the Western or classical mode of capitalism to exploit wage labour to generate surplus value.

We may draw the attention of scholars to the development of ideas, such as 'accumulation by dispossession' analysed within the Marxian idea of primitive accumulation.[2] In fact, primitive accumulation is more relevant to a caste-based society, such as India, where the major chunk of the society are excluded or dispossessed from the mainstream production relations through displacement of 'the whole class of people from control over the means of production, at first through legal acts, but ultimately, as in the enclosure legislation in Britain the rough actions of the state'.[3] The sentence from David Harvey study cited here is aptly fit into caste model of production in India.

## Accumulation by Social Exclusion

We have noted in previous chapters how the SCs, STs and service caste are physically and socially excluded from the mainstream production process. One wonders how the economy could survive by excluding the major sections of population. It here lays the magic of CMOP. The excluded castes are brought under the production relations with lower ranks and assigned functions that are ascribed by birth. At any stage of development in India either the *Dvija* group or Dalits or Adivasis constitute a substantial quantity of population that would not have made operations difficult. The institution of untouchability discussed below is like that of the 'enclosure' movement used in Europe to transform agriculture to create surpluses and reinvest to usher in capitalism. However, social exclusion is a permanent non-negotiable enclosure that would not allow the labourers or working class to cross their ranks, lest they might be lynched. The proportion of Dalits and Adivasis in any of the modern sectors of production, particularly the information and communications technology (ICT), technology-based units, financial sector and so on is very low. Further, as Durand[4] noted, 'a situation where profits take place without accumulation through financialization of trade and creation of fictitious capital is in place now.' As we have seen before, the role of the lower castes in these sectors is marginal and the *Dvijas* combine is dominant. David Harvey in his study noted, it is not pre-history of capitalism and is an ongoing process. It can encompass everything, including taking away the rights of these sections' access to land and livelihoods.

The role of the agriculture sector in the Indian economy is still substantial with around 16 per cent contribution to GDP unlike in other countries. Interestingly, the share of the sector in GDP was around 59 per cent in 1950–1951 and has slowly declined. But the proportion of agriculture labourers among the SCs is increasing from around 50 per cent in 1951 to 71 per cent in 2011. The inverse relationship between agriculture sector contributions to GDP and proportion of agriculture labourers among Dalits is the real paradox of social exclusion. In other words, the economic base of SCs is related to primitive accumulation and the social relations of discrimination, untouchability and displacement are, therefore, reproduced even in modern caste-based capitalist production system. This needs to be understood and changed in a modern democratic capitalist economy. It is 'precarious working class' that is found to be the reserve army only among Dalits and Adivasis in agriculture sector. But caste and sub-caste cleavages are a deterrent to form a generalized proletariat as noted by Samir Amin. This is not unique to India as Hymer Stephen noted on the basis of multiplication of proletariat across the countries, 'thus the competitive cleavages between workers often reflect lines of race, creed, color, age, sex and national origin which make working class consciousness more difficult'.[5] It is in this context, Jomil Jonna R. and John Bellamy Foster brought to light the concept of working class 'precariousness' as noted originally by Marx and elaborated by Hymer once again in the 21st century.[6] The industrial reserve army is growing due to casualization, informalization of labour and other techniques used by multinational corporations. This appears to be true in the case of Dalit, Adivasis and service castes in India, particularly the growing reverse army of agriculture labourers, among Dalits noted above.

## Democracy as a Transitional Phase

Though India had ushered in a constitutional form of democracy in 1950, it had already experimented with the election process of selecting representatives of the people through 1935 Act. The constituent assembly has decided to provide representation to SCs and STs to represent the categories in proportion to their population in the state for a period of 10 years under Article 330. However, it has been extended continuously on political and social grounds from time to time. Elections are only one aspect of democratic form of government where decisions are being taken by the elected representatives. The history of the SC and ST political reservations is a mixed bag. The provisions of double member constituencies and the representation of Dalit and Adivasi issues in the legislative started vanishing one after the other.[7] Democracy as Ambedkar noted as 'one value and one vote' became one vote and several values making the Dalits and Adivasis to remain relatively backward and the gap between them and others as noted in the previous chapters continued to widen with *Dvija* rule in its full form implementing *varnashrama dharma*. Therefore, Dalits and Adivasis can consider the present form of capitalist democracy where they are given certain guarantees through fundamental rights along with others in a temporary phase. It is proved beyond doubt that 70 years of independent rule has only made a tiny section of the Dalit and Adivasi class of educated elite realize their democratic rights. But most of the rights are seen in breach rather than in operation in terms of the increasing incidence of atrocities. Therefore, Dalit and Adivasi rights are to be integrated with human rights so that others who are in the same economic deprivation are made to come together to liberate from repression: social and economic.

## Concept of Human Rights

The rights of man basically arise out of the Western moral conviction that every human being is sacred. The secular version of human rights arises out of the experiences of the humanity with the brutality of religious practices and as dialectic of Protestantism and science. The claim that every human being is sacred means that only people who are really human beings and other people, such as women, tribes, Dalits or Muslims, are not truly human. Michael J. Perry in his book on 'The Idea of Human Rights' says that 'this is because, the first part of the idea of human rights—the claim that every human being is sacred—is the claim that every member of the species Homo sapiens is sacred (or at least every born member); it is the claim that the sacredness of a human being (Homo sapiens) does not depend on his or her race, colour, sex, language, religion, political or other opinion national or social origin, property, birth or other status'.[8] This language of the universal declaration of human rights in Article 2 of the Universal Declaration of Human Rights (UDHR) appears to have been influencing the ideology of human rights in several countries. Human rights in India is defined as the right relating to life, liberty, equality and dignity guaranteed by the Constitution.

The idea that some humans are sacred, and others are not, indicates that there are pseudo humans or sub-humans. Caste being the predominant unit of social and political status and therefore connected to economic mobilization need to be given due weightage in the Indian version of class formation. This ideology suits the Indians, particularly the Hindu ethos. In India, the status of an individual is religiously determined by the birth of the person in a caste. Therefore, the ritual status of the individuals is determined by the religious leaders. The moral code, the basis on which human relations are maintained in India appear to be unequal. They are unequal as the ideas of inequality, fraternity and democracy have different meanings in the Indian situation. The basic structure of the society is based on graded inequality, first sanctioned by the religious scriptures and internalized by individuals by practice. It is in this context, the rights of the Dalits play a very significant role in universalizing the human rights. The mere declaration of human rights and the bill of rights comprising of (a) universal declaration of human rights (1948), (b) the international covenant on economic, social and cultural rights (1966) and (c) the international covenant on civil and political rights (1966), may not ensure the rights to Dalits in India. The Dalits are treated as sub-humans and even as non-humans by the mainstream society for a long time in human history. The slaves in the USA and in other European societies were better placed in terms of certain minimum access to civilized life, such as education and training. But in India even those minimum needs of human beings were denied to Dalits. It is in recognition of this discrimination, the Constitution of India restored some of the basic rights through constitutional provisions, such as Article 17 (abolition of untouchability).[9]

## Untouchability as a Form of Intolerance

When we look at human rights from the point of view of universal equality among humans, we come across certain limitations in societies, such as India where untouchability is still practised. The Dalits of India who constitute the major segment of Indian society are also called as untouchables. Untouchability has three dimensions: unseeables, unapproachables and untouchables. It is a practice that keeps a section of the society physically away from the mainstream in all social transactions except in using their labour for production. It is sanctioned by *dharmashastras* and implemented by the society with religious fervour from historical times. However, it is not practised in the same rigour in all the regions of the country. Its intensity is severe in the Aryan mainland and is found to be non-existent in northeast. It was the Europeans who called the indigenous people of this country as Dravidians, *Dasyus*, *Asuras* and untouchables on the basis of the *dharmashastras* and Hindu practices. In the Hindu ritual status, each caste is given a social rank. The highest rank is given to the Brahmin and the Dalit or the SC person is ascribed a zero rank at the bottom. These ranks are ascribed to different castes based on birth and they are permanent. The place of dwellings, the food and their social relations are dictated by the *dharmashastras*. Manu, the law giver of the Hindus whom a section of the ruling elite in India revere with respect even today had codified the conduct. B. R. Ambedkar citing Manu tells us that 'if the Hindu observed untouchability it is because his religion enjoins him to do so'. Manu, the architect of Hindu society said, 'If one who (being a member of the *chandalas* or some other low caste) must not be touched, intentionally defiles by his touch one who (as a member of twice born caste) may be touched (by the other twice born persons only) he shall be put to death' (Manu X 56 cited by Ambedkar, Vol. V, p. 91). One might say that these are only provisions in ancient Hindu order, but may not be relevant now. Ambedkar has cited cases of extreme form of the practice of untouchability during his lifetime and cited court judgements upholding the practice of untouchability during 1950s. Even after independence and the abolition of untouchability in the Constitution and several Acts made to punish the guilty, the practice of untouchability is still prevailing both in rural India as well as in urban India as noted in previous chapter. The British rulers have defined it and recorded it in the census enumeration. It was in 1911 census; they laid the following tests to mark off the untouchables from that of touchables. The untouchables are those who

1. Denied the supremacy of the Brahmins
2. Did not receive the mantra from Brahmin or another recognized Hindu guru
3. Denied the authority of the Vedas

4. Did not worship the great Hindu gods
5. Were not served by good Brahmins
6. Have no Brahmin priests at all
7. Have no access to the interior of the ordinary Hindu temple
8. Cause pollution
9. Bury their dead
10. Eat beef and do not revere the cow.

It is on the basis of the above tests, the census of SCs and STs has been undertaken in India. The proportion of the untouchables to the total population has been increasing in the Indian society from 1911 to 2011 census. One needs to understand why the majority of the Indians still practice untouchability. It is observed not only among the Hindus, but even among the Muslims and Christians and in other faiths. That is the reason why it is prevalent among the communities which are influenced by Hindu India, such as Nepalese, Japanese and Thais. Sociologists have tried to identify the reasons within the ideology of purity and pollution. Based on the concepts of 'Jatidharma' and the practice of 'Jajmani system', sociologists have tried to explain the hierarchy of castes. They have identified the priestly transactions with God as one of the causes of the emergence of the idea of purity. It is also said that any waste product from a human, animal or divine body is impure. This is carried, they said into the dietary practices of the Hindus. Some sociologists who see in Hindu customs a rationale have identified some Vedantic ideas, such as *trigunas—satogun, rajogun* and *tamogun*—as the virtues that helped the Hindu *Dvijas* to practise purity and pollution. Some of them even tried to justify one's rank in the social order on the basis of the kind of food they eat, making Brahmin the superior as he eats *satvik* food and so on. But they have failed to explain why the *Vaisya* who eats the same *satvik* food remains next to a Kshatriya who eats, in fact, food that instils *rajogun*. Interestingly, most of the sociologists, including Dumont, Srinivas, Inden, Marriott, Andre Beitte, et al., who wanted to rationalize the great virtues of Hindu practices of caste discrimination were guided by the 'nonsensical belief' (to use Andre Beitte words) of the superiority of the Aryan practices over the lifestyles of indigenous Indian population. Therefore, one aspect of caste discrimination, the practice of untouchability, itself is a sufficient ground to take up the case of Dalits as a human rights violation. Some OBC castes in the South, such as dhobi, barber and fisher folk, are listed under SCs in several states in the North. Therefore, here Dalit includes some OBCs.

The value of graded inequality as practised by some groups to consider some humans inferior by birth needs to be denounced in modern society and in democratic polity. This is possible with the provision of constitutional guarantee and international support for a human rights movement. Apart from civil and cultural rights that come under the broad framework of human rights, in a country, such as India, human rights are to be emphasized to make the common people understand the significance of being human and the responsibility of state to protect them. There is a need to advance a human rights movement among the Dalits and Adivasis to make them realize their constitutional guarantees.

## The Strong and Weak Aspects of Dalit Movement

The Dalits of India are not a homogeneous community. There is also no pattern in the distribution of population among different states. It is noted that a little more than half of the Dalit population (20.13 crores) lives in Uttar Pradesh (4.13 crores), West Bengal (2.14 crores), Bihar (1.10 crores), Tamil Nadu (1.44 crores) and Andhra Pradesh (1.4 crores) in 2011. But, Dalit consciousness is much stronger in states, such as Maharashtra (11%), Karnataka and Andhra Pradesh where the Dalits constitute less than 20 per cent each of the state population. Interestingly, Dalits constitute around one-third of the population in Punjab (31.90%) and one-fourth in Himachal Pradesh (25.4%) and Bengal. It appears that the future success of the Dalit movement depends upon the consciousness of the Dalits in larger states where it is now weak.

The little progress made so far by the Dalits in the post-independence period was confined to one or two dominant castes in each state. It is identified that around 22 castes out of 1,091 castes in the country have got major share of the assistance declared by the government (see chapter 2). There are inequalities within each caste as some families among the beneficiaries have formed into a lobby and diverted these benefits to their members. This has created problems of intra-caste differences that lead to separatist struggles within the Dalit community in states, such as Andhra Pradesh, Haryana and Karnataka.

One of the weaknesses of the Dalit movement appears to be its adherence to the popularization of personalities, such as Ambedkar, as an emancipator without explaining his emancipatory project. The Ambedkar movement and its petty leadership failed to digest his ideology and never translated it into an action programme. Somewhat jaundiced studies on the Dalit formation by scholars and populist writers did not really capture the reason for internal differentiation that is built into the system.[10] They failed to understand that it not unique to Dalits alone. There are limitations for Ambedkar associations to take up the issues of Dalits in totality. There is also the failure of Dalit intellectuals to assess the development process of Ambedkar movement and have missed to provide a concrete programme of action to the activists. Some of them have also remained; it is alleged as members of the same bandwagon. No attempt seems to have been made by the Ambedkar organizations at the state level to give directions to the activists. Some Dalit activists endure as commodities due to poverty. The SC and ST employee associations are confined only for the implementation of reservations within each establishment and did emerge as a body to provide guidance to the activist. No attempt seems to have been made to develop a self-respect movement among the Dalits as the Dalits never constituted an organic whole. Each sub-caste has its own social and cultural identity. The only common identity that has emerged during the last half a century is developed around Ambedkar, as an emancipator. This is to be further strengthened with innovative interpretations for practical work. The kind of interpretation of the works of Marx and Engels by Lenin and Mao had not taken place in case of Ambedkar and other emancipators. It is also necessary to develop the Dalit epistemology, which is deep rooted in 'Tantra', the original scientific approach to life by the natives. This has been destroyed by the British during the colonial period and a major chunk of it was appropriated by the Brahminical Hinduism and Buddhism. Dalits are now left as disconnected and disengaged group with little empathy to secure their rights as humans. Adivasi areas in some pockets are different due to Maoist campaigns.

### The Culture of Poverty

The culture of poverty that existed among the Dalits for ages has strengthened certain traits and behaviour patterns which are inimical for the development of Dalit rights movement. There are several factors contributing to these. The following are some important factors.

(a) Illiteracy and ignorance, (b) hatred and jealousy towards fellow Dalits, (c) lack of leadership qualities, (d) lack of vision for future, (e) lack of caste consciousness, (f) lack of survival skills, (g) easy prey to upper caste machinations, (h) multifarious leadership, (i) lack of habits of savings, (j) indulgence in panchamakaras (matysa, mamsa, mudra, maithuna and madya), (k) succumb to short-term material benefits, (l) lack of discipline, (m) considering caste reservations as ultimate liberation, (n) lack of unity and (o) in fighting on petty issues.

The Brahminical preparation to encounter modernization and the Dalit emancipatory movements were started in 1925 from Maharashtra. It was also during this period the communist party was activated. Now experts comment that the Sangh Parivar is in the saddle of power to dictate terms to the majority and continue to enjoy the hegemony. The left is in disarray. There are several non-Dalit castes which have mobilized their caste resources and fought against the Brahminical forces and have recorded as upper castes without any support from outside and government. The emergence of Nadars in Tamil Nadu as a ruling class from that of a low social status in modern India is only one example. The upward mobility of some *Shudra* castes such as Kamma, Reddy, Vakkaliga, Jat and Yadav, need to be studied.

### Dalits Rights as Human Rights

The instruments of UN human rights, such as human rights bodies, conventions and protocols, have limited application in India as India did not sign some of the treaties. This calls for an international campaign for the declaration of the rights of Dalits as human rights. This is essential to consider the rights of the Dalits to enforce within the framework of the Constitution through human rights organizations, such as the National Human Rights Commission and the State Human Rights Commission. A special campaign to declare Dalit rights as human rights is necessitated due to the fact that the international community and the UN system of human rights treaties do not recognize problems, such as untouchability, which is unique in the Indian context. The right to land, education, basic health services, drinking water, shelter, right to work and so on is basic for life sustenance. But these basic rights are denied to the Dalits in India because of their alienation from the mainstream. It is in this context, that a charter of Dalit rights has been drafted as human rights by a group of Dalit intellectuals and social activists. They include the following.

1. Dalit rights are human rights.
2. The denial of basic needs of the Dalits is a gross violation of Dalit human rights.
3. There should be inclusion of caste discrimination and untouchability in the international convention on racial discrimination.
4. The perpetrators of untouchability should be severely punished according to the provisions of SC/ST Atrocities Act and rules.
5. Full protection should be provided to Dalits in the Panchayat Raj institutions and other democratic institutions of the country.
6. The land usurped by the state and private bodies, be restored to the Dalits.
7. Reservations to Dalits in all private bodies and organizations.
8. Special measures be taken for the protection of the rights of Dalit women.
9. Dalits, irrespective of their religious faith, be considered as SCs.
10. They should have the right to freedom of thought and expression.
11. A white paper be placed in the parliament on atrocities against Dalits and reservation facilities be actually granted to Dalits from 1947.
12. Dalit's human rights be explicitly and constitutionally guaranteed in the Asian countries where they are domiciled.

Keeping the paradigm of human rights as a transitional phase to educate the socially and economically marginalized to get united under the banner to discard caste inhibition to form a coherent class of exploited, the social proletariat, the following programme of action is indicated.

## The Agenda and the Programme of Action

The past experiences of the Dalit movement and the present socio-economic situation in the country, enable us to prepare an agenda. An agenda is a list of programmes to be implemented during a period of time. But, the strategy to implement such an agenda is more important than the agenda. Therefore, it is necessary now to work out an agenda along with the strategy to implement it.

The programme of action can be broadly divided into short-term and long-term strategies. The short-term programme should concentrate on the organizational issues and mobilization of resources for self-development and community involvement. The long-term strategy should always aim to capture political power and economic development. (The following approach is only an indicative outline.)

## Short Term

*Concentrate on Dalit Formation*

Though people eulogize about the unity of Dalits, there is no apt understanding among the sub-castes and even within a caste about the need to form a Dalit identity. No systematic and concerted effort has been made by any organization to form all the SCs as one identity. *Mahars* and *mangs, malas, madigas, chamars, pasis,* and so on, each sub-caste has its own identity. The democratic process of understanding each other's existence and their requirements needs to be built to form a Dalit society first, may be a *Bahujan Samaj* or reservation of army of proletariat as a continuation of this. A separate Dalit cultural centre needs to be established with the single purpose of bringing a fusion of all sub-castes around the original theory of *Mulavasi* or broken men, Dravidian or non-Aryan racial theory of cultural identity. Most of the Dalits are prized fighters of the upper castes and have been practising martial arts from time immemorial. It can be revived for the sake of cultural identity. The cultural centre can concentrate on the traditional Dalit art, music and literary activities. Religion and religious identity did not help much in the formation of Dalit identity so far. In fact, it may act as counterproductive as Dalits are spread into several faiths during the last 400 years and this will create intra-religious conflict within the Dalit formation. The Dalits who were converted into different faiths have remained as separate entities, unlike that of the upper castes whose caste identity is always maintained despite their conversion.

### Educational Development

The literacy rate among the Dalits, particularly the female literacy, is very low. The excessive dependence on the government on the educational development of the Dalits resulted in the underdevelopment of many and capturing of all the positions and places by some. The original Phule–Ambedkar project of people's education movement at the grassroots or habitation level needs to be revived. It is also necessary to educate the parents to allow their children to learn and also inform them about the availability of opportunities and government schemes, such as hostels and scholarships, to enable them to continue their studies. Except in one or two states, Dalits in the rural areas in a majority of the states do not have access to this information (see Chapter 9). A majority of the Dalits and Adivasis are opting for liberal arts and science courses which have no job market. Therefore, the Dalit organizations should develop self-help groups at the habitation level to educate the children both in formal and non-formal streams. Education does not mean the three Rs (reading, writing and arithmetic) alone. Computer literacy and technical knowledge are important for survival in the 21st century. The educated Dalits must take the responsibility of transferring their knowledge to rural masses. It is necessary to start technical institutions on a voluntary basis with the support of government, NGO and community support. No Dalit in the rural and semi-urban areas is able to start a workshop or repair shop on his own because of lack of technical skills and other support services. The Muslim and OBC categories are now in a position to give necessary guidance on this as many of them belong to the artisan categories. Some Dalit sub-castes do also come from certain artisan castes, such as weavers and bamboo workers. The skills of these groups need to be strengthened with additional inputs and support. This can be further elaborated.

### Economic Support Programmes

The Protestant ethic in the west resulted in the development of an industrial economy and economic development. But the Dalits who are termed by Ambedkar as Protestant Hindus never concentrated on their economic self-sufficiency. A small section of government employees has emerged in recent years with some economic base. But, majority of them use their unearned incomes in conspicuous consumption, drinking, debauchery and luxurious living. This will not help the Dalits. Majority of the Dalits live in rural areas and depends upon agriculture. Land reforms have become redundant in the mainstream left programmes. Therefore, Dalits need to develop their own strategies for the distribution of surplus land and other common property resources in the rural areas with the support of parties and groups who share their strategy. Here, one must be very cautious to the fact that the income and jobs from agriculture sector are declining, while the service sector is fast expanding. In addition to agriculture, there are several agro-based industries that are coming up in the rural areas. Dalits do not have access to these even as labourers, as they do not have the skills. It is necessary to develop cooperative effort with the support of government and schemes, such as horticulture, fish farming, dairying and hundreds of such schemes to make the Dalits economically self-sufficient. The habit of thrift and savings need to be inculcated by using the schemes, such as DWCRA. Simple and easy to implement entrepreneurial skills are to be inculcated among the Dalits. It is necessary to develop projects for getting financial support from commercial banks and financial institutions rather than from the SC corporations who give petty loans that do not sustain a project. The experiences of Punjabi Dalits in this area can be explored. Some lumpen Dalit youth work as brokers in the slums and rural areas for the upper caste contractors. They need to be liberated and made independent contractors to work with government construction programmes under reservation scheme. The experience of the African Americans in the USA through the provisions of section 8(a) of Small Business Act in getting government contracts needs to be studied. It is estimated that the African Americans with 74 per cent high school degrees are now spread in 5 important industries in the USA. These economic programmes are suggested as a short-term measure to develop certain skills of economic empowerment. This does not mean that the Dalits are interested in privatization. Their emancipation lies with the nationalization of means of production and creation of equality of opportunities. The Dalits have suffered social exclusion for centuries and they should not be subjected to economic alienation in the 21st century.

### Health and Family Welfare

Most of the Dalits suffer from several diseases due to unhygienic living conditions. A band of health workers are to be trained to educate the Dalits on health and family planning.

# Long-term Project of Dalit Emancipation

The long-term project of Dalit emancipation is a serious issue that needs to be examined under a sound theory of liberation. However, we are giving below certain stray ideas that can be examined for a serious discussion.

## Political Power

It is always repeated in Ambedkar meetings that the Dalits must not remain as the ruled forever, and they should emerge as the rulers of the country. The experiences of Ambedkar during his lifetime as a defeated political leader after 1951 and the short-lived Mayavathi government in Uttar Pradesh are two examples available before the group. On the other hand, the Adivasi uprisings and their concerted effort to get a separate identity made them to wield power. They have achieved two independent states for themselves. Dalits as flag bearers in liberation and semi-liberation struggles and the material benefits obtained vis-à-vis the sacrifices made by them need to be assessed by the theoreticians to develop a theory of Dalit empowerment. The emergence of the oligarchy of *Shudra* non-Brahmin castes and *Dvija* castes as the present ruling formation at the centre and in some states show one of the ways through which how minorities can also emerge as rulers. However, the amount of organizational support, the perseverance and the strategic moves these castes have made are to be studied carefully to launch a Dalit empowerment strategy. The ruling castes in power never split, but the Dalits are always willing to fragment and remain as commodities in the political market. How to change this situation? The caste identity needs to be protected and knitted around some kind of a homogeneity and inclusive of all the deprived. This requires continuous presence of political workers with total commitment to the Dalit cause in the Dalit habitations. For this, it is necessary to recruit a band of workers in each tehsil/mandala and at the district headquarters. There are no organizational structures for the Dalits at the district headquarters and at the state level except a few loose formations.

## Economic Independence

The Dalits have been subjected to social and economic oppression. But, the Dalit leadership has given priority to social persecution by neglecting the more important base of this oppression, the economic power. The *Dvijas* have realized this and started entering into economic base after the economic reforms. They are now in commanding heights of the economy by creating few scams and modifications in economic policies and with an understanding with the international capital. The emergence of middle castes, such as Naidu, Reddy, Gowda, Yadav, Kammas, in cornering contracts and public sector sales outlets needs to be carefully studied. If a strategy can provide economic emancipation for the entire community with little bloodshed, why not copy it? This may be difficult, but not impossible. For instance, the emergence of *Kammas* as an organized hard-working community from that of an agrarian labour to that of political and economic power took around 5 decades of hard work and discipline. The economically developed Dalits in different parts of the country can form into a separate group, such as the *Kammas* or *Marwaris* or *Jats*, who help their own community clientele in the economic emancipatory project. This requires a consciously developed Dalit or *bahujan* group. It is possible to identify at least a few dozens of ex-bureaucrats who have resources and access to power to lead the group. There are several schemes that are thrown open for Dalits and Adivasis to achieve economic self-sufficiency. This is necessary because the political power can be sustained only with economic power. Both are mutually interrelated.

The ultimate aim of this formation is to socially and economically empower the Dalits and Adivasis to liberate the castes that are under social enclosure. The social and economic inequalities will disappear once the base of the exploitative MOP is dismounted. It is not automatic. It requires enormous moral courage and ideological commitment to bring all the exploited under a platform with Dalits and Adivasis remaining a vanguard.

## Notes

1. Rodney Hilton, *The Transition from Feudalism to Capitalism* (London: Verso, 1978).
2. David Harvey, *A Companion to Marx's Capital* (London: Verso, 2010).
3. Ibid., 293.
4. Durand, *Fictitious Capital*.
5. Hymer Stephen, 'The Multinational Corporation and the Law of Uneven Development', in *Introduction to the Sociology of Developing Societies*, ed. H. Alavi, T. Shanin and Teodor Shanin (London: Macmillan, 1982).
6. R. Jamil Jonna and John Bellany Foster, 'Marx's Theory of Working Class Precariousness—Its Relevance Today'. *Monthly Review* 1 April 2016.
7. Rajasekhar Vundru, *Ambedkar, Gandhi and Patel: The Making of India's Electrical System* (New Delhi: Bloomsbury, 2018).
8. Perry J. Michael, *The Idea of Human Rights: Four Inquiries* (New York: Oxford University Press, 1998).
9. K. S. Chalam, *Introduction to Human Rights and human Development* (New Delhi: Uday Publication House, 2018).
10. Yengde Suraj, *Caste Matters* (Delhi: Penguin, 2019).

# Select Bibliography

ADRF. *Progress towards Inclusive Sustainable Development in India: A Study of Dalits and Adivasis in 2030 Agenda*. Delhi: Asia Dalit Rights Forum, 2017.
Ahir, D. C. *The Legacy of Dr. Ambedkar*. Delhi: B. R. Publishing Corporation Publication, 1990.
Ahlawat, S. R., ed. *Economic Reforms and Social Transformation*. Jaipur: Rawat, 2008.
Aiyangar, K. V. R. *Aspects of Social and Political System of Manu Smriti*. Lucknow: Lucknow University, 1941.
Alavi, H. *Feudalism and Capitalism in Indian Agriculture*. Mimeo, 1975.
Ali, S. N. *Geography of Puranas*. Delhi: People's Publishing House, 1966.
Altekar, A. S. *State and Government in Ancient India*. Delhi: Motilal Banarsidas, 1949, Reprinted 1977.
Althusser, L. *Reading Capital*. Paris: New left Books, 1965.
Ambedkar, B. R. *Babasaheb Ambedkar Writings and Speeches, 17 Volumes*. New Delhi: Ambedkar Foundation, 2010.
Anderson, Perry. *Arguments within English Marxism*. London: Verso, 1980.
Anna, Arendt. *The Origins of Totalitarianism*. New York: Harcourt Bruce, 1950.
Arjun, Appadurai. *Modernity at Large: Cultural Dimensions of Globalization*. New Delhi: Oxford University Press, 1997.
Bagchi, A. K. *The Political Economy of Underdevelopment*. Cambridge, UK: Cambridge University Press, 1982.

Bailey, Anne M., and J. R. Llobera, ed. *The Asiatic Mode of Production: Science and Politics*. London: Routledge, 1981.
Banaji, Jairus. 'For a Theory of Colonial Mode of Production'. *Economic and Political Weekly* 7, no. 52 (1972): 2498–2502.
———. *Theory as History: Essays on Modes of Production and Exploitation*. Leiden/Boston: Brill, 2010.
Bandyopadhyay, Sekhar. *Decolonization in South Asia: Meanings of Freedom in Post-Independence West Bengal, 1947–1952*. London: Routledge, 2009.
———. *From Plassey to Partition and After*. Delhi: Orient Black Swan, 2014.
Bandyopadhyay, Sekhar, and Anasua Basu Ray Chaudhury. *In Search of Space: The Scheduled Caste Movement in West Bengal after Partition*. Kolkata: Mahanirban Kolkata Research Group, February 2014.
Banerjee, Sumanta. 'Pitfalls of Neo-nationalism'. *Economic and Political Weekly*, 40, no. 33 (2005): 3629–3631.
Baran, P. A. *The Political Economy of Growth*. New York: Monthly Review Press, 1957.
Barua, B. M. *The Ajivakas*. Calcutta: Calcutta University Press, 1920.
———. *Pre-Buddistic Indian Philosophy*. Calcutta: Calcutta University Press, 1921.
Basham, A. L. *The Wonder That Was India*. Delhi: Rupa and Co, 1981.
———. *History and Doctrines of Ajivikas: A Vanished Indian Religion*. London: Luzac & Co., 1951; Delhi: Motilal Banarsidas, 2002.
Basu, K. 'Discrimination as Focal Point: Markets and Group Identity'. *Forum for Social Economics* 46, no. 2 (2017): 128–138.
Baxi, Upendra. *Inhuman Wrongs and Human Rights: Unconventional Essays*. New Delhi: Har Anand, 1994.
———. *The Future of Human Rights*. New Delhi: Oxford University Press, 2010.
Bayly, Susan. *Saints, Goddesses and Kings: Muslims and Christians in South Indian Society, 1700–1900*. New York: Cambridge University Press, 1989.
Bell, D. *The Coming of Post-industrial Society*. New York: Basic Books, 1973.
Béteille, A. *Caste, Class, and Power: Changing Patterns of Stratification in a Tanjore Village*. Berkeley, CA: University of California Press, 1965.

Bhalla, G. S. and G. K. Chadha. *Green Revolution and Small Peasants: A Study of Income Distribution among Punjab Cultivators*. New Delhi: Concept Publishing House, 1983.

Bhattacharya, N. N. *India Religious Historiography*. Delhi: Munshiram Manoharlal Publishers, 1996.

———. *History of the Tantric Religion*. Delhi: Munshiram Manoharlal Publishers, 1999.

Blaug, M. *Economic Theory in Retrospect*. London: Hieman, 1981.

Bob, C. 'Dalit Rights Are Human Rights: Caste Discrimination, International Activism, and the Construction of a New Human Rights Issue'. *Human Rights Quarterly* 29, no. 1 (2007): 167–193.

Buchanan, J. M., and G. Tullock. *The Calculus of Consent: Logical Foundations of Constitutional Democracy*. Ann Arbor, MI: University of Michigan, 1962.

Carswell, G., and G. De Neve, 'Litigation against Political Organization? The Politics of Dalit Mobilization in Tamil Nadu India'. *Development and Change* 46, no. 5 (2015): 1106–1132.

Chacko, M. Priyaram. *Caste, Business and Entrepreneurship in South India*. New Delhi: Kanishka Publishing House, 1991.

Chakrabarti, Anjan, and Stephen Cullenberg. *Transition and Development in India*. London: Routledge, 2013.

Chalam, K. S. *Education and Weaker Sections*. New Delhi: Inter India, 1988.

———. *Readings in Political Economy*. Hyderabad: Orient Longman, 1999.

———. *Caste-based Reservations and Human Development in India*. Delhi: SAGE Publications, 2007.

———. *Economic Reforms and Social Exclusion*. Delhi: SAGE Publications, 2011.

———. *Social Economy of Development in India*. Delhi: SAGE Publications, 2017.

———. *Introduction to Human Rights and Human Development*. New Delhi: Uday Publishing House, 2018.

———, ed. *Relevance of Ambedkarism in India*. Jaipur, Rajasthan: Rawat, 1993, 2nd ed. 2018.

Chalam, K. S., and C. S. Rao. *Science and Civilization*. Andhra Pradesh: Andhra University Press, 1998.

Chattopadhya, K. P. *Ancient Indian Culture Contacts and Migrations*. Calcutta: Sanskrit College, 1970.

Chattopadhyaya, D. P. *Lokayata: A Study in Ancient India Materialism*. Delhi: Peoples Publishing House, 1959.
———. *Indian Atheism*. Delhi: People's Publishing House, 1969.
———. *What Is Living and What Is Dead in India Philosophy*. Delhi: People's Publishing House, 1976.
Childe, Gordon. *The Aryans: A Study of Indo-European Origins*, New York: Alfred Knof, 1926.
Cohen, Gerry. *Karl Marx's Theory of History: A Defence*. Oxford/ Princeton: Clarendon Press, 1978.
Colletti, Lucio. *From Rousseau to Lenin; Studies in Ideology and Society*. Translated by John Merrington and Judith White. New York: Monthly Review Press, 1974.
Corbridge, S., J. Harriss, and C. Jeffrey. *India Today: Economy, Politics and Society*. London: John Wiley & Sons, 2013.
Cunningham, Alexander. *The Ancient Geography of India*. London: Trubner & Co., 1871.
Damodaran, H. *India's New Capitalists: Caste, Business, and Industry in a Modern Nation*. Basingstoke, UK and New York: Palgrave, 2008.
Daron, Acemoglu, and James A. Robinson. *Why Nations Fail: The Origins of Power, Prosperity and Poverty*. London: Profile Books, 2013.
Das, A. C. *Rig Vedic India: Cultural History of India as Depicted in Rig Veda*. New Delhi: Cosmo Publications, 2003.
Das, Kornel, and Giridhar Gamango. *Lost Jain Tribes of Trikalinga* (Koraput & Bastar). Maniguda, Orissa, 2010.
Das, S. K. *The Economic History of Ancient India*. Allahabad: Vohra Publishers, 1980.
Denison, E. F. *The Sources of Economic Growth in the United States and the Alternatives before Us*. New York: Committee for Economic Development, 1962.
Derret, L. D. M. *Religion, Law and State in Ancient India*. London: Faber and Faber, 1968.
Deshpande, A. *The Grammar of Caste: Economic Discrimination in Contemporary India*. Oxford, New York: Oxford University Press, 2017.
Deshpande, A., and T. Weisskopf. 'Does Affirmative Action Reduce Productivity? A Case Study of the Indian Railways'. *World Development*, 64 (2014): 169–180.

DeVries, Willem A. *Hegel's Theory of Mental Activity*. New York: Cornell University Press, 1988.
Dirks, N. B. *Castes of Mind: Colonialism and the Making of Modern India*. Princeton, NJ: Princeton University Press, 2001.
Doniger, Wendy. *The Hindus: An Alternative History*. Penguin: New York, 2009.
———. *On Hinduism*. Aleph Book Company: Delhi, 2013.
Downs, A. *An Economic Theory of Democracy*. New York: Harper, 1957.
Dunn, Joseph P. *The Fall and Rise of Asiatic Mode of Production*. London: Routledge, 1982.
Durant, Will. *The Story of Philosophy*. New York: Washington Square Press, 1953.
Forrester, Duncan B. *Caste and Christianity: Attitudes and Policies on Caste of Anglo-Saxon Protestant Missions in India*. New Jersey: Curzon Press, 1980.
Foucault, Michel. *The Archaeology of Knowledge*. London: Routledge, 1989.
Frank, A. G. *Capitalism and Underdevelopment in Latin America: Historical Studies of Chile and Brazil*. New York: Monthly Review Press, 1967.
Frankel, F., and M. S. A. Rao, eds. *Dominance and State Power in Modern India: Decline of a Social Order*, 2 Vols. Delhi: Oxford University Press, 1990.
Fuller, C. 'Misconceiving the Grain Heap: A Critique of the Concept of the Indian *Jajmani* System'. In Money and the morality of exchange, edited by Parry and M. Bloch, 33–63. Cambridge: Cambridge University Press, 1989.
Fuller, C., and H. Narasimhan. *Tamil Brahmans: The Making of a Middle-class Caste*. Chicago, IL: University of Chicago Press, 2014.
Gadgil, D. R. *Origins of Modern Indian Business Class*. New York: Institute of Pacific Relations, 1959.
Giovanni, Arrighi. *The Long Twentieth Century: Money, Power and the Origins of Our Times*. London: Verso, 1994.
Gowri, Viswanathan. *Outside the Fold: Conversion, Modernity and Elite*. Delhi: Oxford University Press, 1998.
Gramsci, Antonio. *Selections from Prison Note Books*. Hyderabad: Orient Longman, 1996.
Guérin, I., B. D'Espallier, and G. Venkatasubramanian. 'The Social Regulation of Markets: Why Microcredit Fails to Promote Jobs

in Rural South India'. *Development and Change* 46, no. 6 (2015): 1277–1301.

Gunnar, Myrdal. *Asian Drama: An Enquiry into the Poverty of Nations*. New York: Twentieth Century Fund, 1968.

Hardgrave, Robert. *The Nadars of Tamilnad: The Political Culture of a Community in Change*. Berkeley, CA: University of California, 1969.

Harnecker, Marta. *Rebuilding the Left*. Delhi: Danish Books, 2007.

Harriss-White, B. *Dalits and Adivasis in India's Business Economy: Three Essays and an Atlas*. Gurgaon, India: Three Essays Collective, 2014.

Harvey, David. *A Companion to Marx's Capital*. London: Verso, 2010.

Hazlehurst, Leighton W. *Entrepreneurship and the Merchant Caste in a Punjabi City*. Durham, NC: Duke University Press, 1966.

Heinrich, Michale. *An Introduction to the Three Volumes of Karl Marx's Capital*. Delhi: Akaar, 2013.

Hindess, B., and P. Q. Hirst. *Pre-capitalist Modes of Production*. London and Boston: Routledge and Kegan Paul, 1975.

Hobsbawm, E. *The Age of Extremes: The Short Twentieth Century*. London: Michael Joseph, 1994.

Hobson, J. A. *Imperialism: A Study*. Ann Arbor, MI: University of Michigan Press, 1965.

Hoselitz, Bert F. *Sociological Aspects of Economic Growth*. New York: Free Press, 1960.

Human Rights Watch. *Broken People: Caste Violence against India's 'Untouchables'*. New York: Human Rights Watch, 1999.

Hutton, J. H. *Caste in India: Its Nature, Function and Origin*. Bombay: Oxford University Press, 1969.

ICRIER. *FDI in Retail Sector, India (2005–2007)*. New Delhi: Govt. of India Publication, 2008.

Iyer, L., and T. Khanna, A. Varshney. 'Caste and Entrepreneurship in India'. *Economic and Political Weekly* 48, no. 6 (2013): 52–60.

Jaffrelot, C. *India's Silent Revolution: The Rise of the Lower Castes in North India*. London: C. Hurst & Co. Publishers, 2003.

Jha, D. N. *Ancient India: A Historical outline*. Delhi: Manohar Publishers, 2018.

Jodhka, Surinder S., and Katherine Newman. 'In the Name of Globalisation: Meritocracy, Productivity and the Hidden Language of Caste'. *Economic and Political Weekly* 42, no. 41 (13–19 October 2007): 4125–4132.

Jurgen, Habermas. *Between Facts and Norms: Contributions towards a Discourse Theory of Ethics*. Cambridge, MA: MIT Press, 1996.

Kahn, J. S., and J. R. Llobera, eds. *The Anthropology of Pre-capitalist Societies*. London and Basingstoke: The Macmillan Press: 1981.

Kain, P. 'Marx's Dialectic Method'. *History and Theory* 19, no. 3 (1980): v294–312.

Kane, P. V. *History of Dharmasastra*, Vol I 1930, Vol II 1941. Pune: Bhandarkar Oriental Research Institute.

Keane, D. *Caste-based Discrimination in International Human Rights Law*. Aldershot, UK: Ashgate, 2007.

Khilnani, Sunil. *The Idea of India*. New Delhi: Penguin Books, 2004.

Kosambi, D. D. *An Introduction to the Study of Indian History*. Bombay: Popular Prakashan, 1956.

———. *Myth and Reality*. Bombay: Popular, 1962.

———. *The Culture and Civilization of India*. Delhi: Vikas Publishing House, 1997.

Kulke, Herman, and Dieter Rothurmund. *A History of India*. Delhi: Rupa and Co., 1991.

Kuppuswami, Alladi. *The Constitution What It Means to the People*. Hyderabad: Gogia Law Pub., 1996.

Laclau, E. 'Feudalism and Capitalism in Latin America'. *New Left Review*, no. 67 (May–June 1971): 19–38.

Lenin, V. I. *Development of Capitalism in Russia*. Moscow: Lenin's Collected Works.

Lipton, M. *Why Poor People Stay Poor: Urban Bias in World Development*. London: Temple Smith, 1976.

Little, I. M. D. *Boom, Crisis and Adjustment: The Macroeconomic Experience of Developing Countries*. New York, NY: Oxford University Press, 1993.

Lohia, Ram Manohar. *Collected Writings of Ram Manohar Lohia*, 9 vol., edited by Mastram Kapoor. New Delhi: Anamika Publishers, 2011.

Ludowyk, E. F. C. *The Footprint of the Buddha*. London: George Allen & Unwin, 1958.

Lutz, Mark A. *Economics for the Common Good*. London: Routledge, 1999.

Mandel, Ernest. *An Introduction to Marxist Economic Theory*. New York: Young Socialist Alliance, 1967.

———. *Late Capitalism*. New York: Humanities Press, 1975.

Marx, Karl. *Capital: A Critique of Political Economy Vols. I–III*. Internet Archive.

Mehta, P. L., and Neena Verma. *Human Rights under the Indian Constitution*. New Delhi: Deep & Deep Pub, 2000.
Mishra, Chandra Vinay. *Reservation Crisis in India*. Delhi: The Bar Council of India Trust Publication, 1991.
Misra, H. *Apasthamba: Grhya Sutra*. Varanasi: Chowkhmba, 1971.
Mosse, D. *The Saint in the Banyan Tree: Christianity and Caste Society in India*. Berkeley, CA: University of California Press, 2012.
Muir, J. *Original Sanskrit Texts on the Origin and History of the People of India*. Trübner: London, 1868–1871.
Munshi, K., and M. Rosenzweig. 'Traditional Institutions Meet the Modern World: Caste, Gender, and Schooling Choice in a Globalizing Economy'. *American Economic Review* 96, no. 4 (2006): 1225–1252.
Narsu, P. Laxmi. *A Study of Caste*. New Delhi: Samyak Prakashan, 1922.
———. *The Essence of Buddhism*. New Delhi: Samyak Prakashan, 1993.
Naval, Viyogi. *The Founders of Indus Valley Civilization and Their Later History*. New Delhi: Blumoon Books, 2006.
Nayyar, Deepak. *Trade and Globalization*. Delhi: Oxford University Press, 2008.
North, D. C. *Institutions, Institutional Change and Economic Performance*. Cambridge, MA: Cambridge University Press, 1990.
Nove, Alec, and D. M. Nuti. *Socialist Economics*. Baltimore, MD: Penguin, 1972.
Omvedt, Gail. 'Capitalism and Globalization Dalits and *Adivasis*'. *Economic and Political Weekly* XL, no. 47 (2005): 4881–4885.
———. *Seeking Begumpura: The Social Vision of Anticaste Intellectuals*. New Delhi: Navayana, 2008.
Panikkar, K. M. *Geographical Factor in Indian History*. Bombay: Bharatiya Vidya Bhavan, 1959.
Parvathamma, C. *Scheduled Castes and Tribes*. New Delhi: Ashish Publication, 1984.
———. *Reservation: A Pie in the Sky*. Hunsur: Deed Publication, 1999.
Patil, Sharad. *Dasa-Sudra Slavery P-II*. Pune: Sugawa Prakashan, 1991.
Patnaik, Utsa, ed. *Agrarian Relations and Accumulation: The Mode of Production Debate in India*. Delhi: Oxford University Press, 1990.
Posner, R. A. *The Economics of Justice*. Cambridge, MA: Harvard University Press, 1981.

Poulantzas, Nicos. *Classes in Contemporary Capitalism*. London: New Left Books, 2000.
Prakash, A. *Dalit Capital: State, Markets and Civil Society in Urban India*. New Delhi: Routledge India, 2015.
Radhakrishnan, S. *Indian Philosophy*, 2nd ed. Oxford: University of Oxford, 2009.
———. *The Philosophy of Hinduism*. Delhi, 2016.
Rao, V. Lakshman. *Industrial Entrepreneurship in India*. Allahabad: Chug Publishers, 1986.
Richard, Garbe. *Philosophy of Ancient India*. Chicago, IL: Open Court, 1899.
Saiyadain, M. S. and A. Monappa. *Profile of Indian Managers*. New Delhi: Vidya Vahini, 1977.
Sankalia, H. D. *Pre-history and Proto-history of India and Pakistan*. Bombay: University of Bombay, 1962
Saraswati, Swami Dayanand. *The Light of Truth or An English Translation of Satyarth Prakash*, trans. Thompson, E. P. *The Poverty of Theory and Other Essays*. London: Merlin Press, 1978.
Sayana, Madhava. *Sarva Darsana Sangraha*, ed. V. S. Abhayanakar. Poona: Bhandarkar Oriental Research Institute, 1924.
Schumpeter, Joseph. *Capitalism, Socialism and Democracy*. New York: Harper, 1942; London: Routledge, 2013.
———. *History of Economic Analysis*. New York: Oxford University Press, 1954.
Sekher, Bandopadhyay. *Caste, Protest and Identity in Colonial India: The Nama Sundras of Bengal*. London: Routledge, 1997.
Sen, Amartya. *Inequality Reexamined*. Cambridge: Harvard University Press, 1995.
———. *Development as Freedom*. Delhi: Oxford University Press, 1999.
———. *The Idea of Justice*. New Delhi: Oxford University Press, 2011.
Shah, A., J. Lerche, R. Axelby, D. Benbabaali, B. Donegan, J. Raj, and V. Thakur, *Ground Down by Growth: Tribe, Caste, Class and Inequality in Twenty-first-century India*. London: Pluto Press, 2018.
Shamasastry, R., ed. *Kautilya's Arthasastra*. Mysore: Mysore Printing and Publishing House, 1924.
Sicklígar, P. C. *Atrocities on Scheduled Castes and Scheduled Tribes: Prevention and Implementation*. Jaipur: Mangal Deep Pub., 2002.

Singh, K. B. *Scheduled Caste Welfare: Myth or Reality*. New Delhi: A. P. H. Publication, 2003.
Singh, S. K., and A. K. Singh. *OBC Women Status and Educational Empowerment*. Lucknow: New Royal Book Co., Pub., 2004.
Singh, Subhash Chandra. *Social Justice and Human Rights in India*. New Delhi: Serials Pub., 2006.
Srivastava, Deepak. *Globalization, Privatization and WTO with Reference to India*. New Delhi: Sarup & Sons Pub., 2003.
Stein, M. A., ed. *Kalhaṇa's Rājataraṅgiṇī*. (Bombay, 1892), Cambridge, UK: Cambridge University Press.
Stiglitz, J. E. *Globalization and Its Discontents*. New York: Norton, 2002.
Sundar, N., and T. Madan, eds. *The Scheduled Tribes and Their India: Politics, Identities, Policies and Work*. New Delhi: Oxford University Press, 2016.
Taylor, John. *From Modernization to Modes of Production*. London and Basingstoke: Macmillan Press, 1979.
Teertha, Swamy Dharma. *The Menace of Hindu Imperialism*. Lahore: Harbhagwan, Happy Home Publications, 1942.
Teltumbde, Anand. *B. R. Ambedkar: India and Communism*. Delhi: Left Word, 2017.
Thapar, Romila. *The Past and Prejudice*. New Delhi: National Book Trust, 1979.
———. *Early India: From the Origins to AD 1300*. Delhi: Penguin, 2002.
Timberg, Thomas A. *The Marwaris: From Traders to Industrialists*. New Delhi: Vikas, 1978.
Trautmann, T. R. *Aryans and British India*. Delhi: Yoda Press, 2004.
Tucker, Robert C. *Philosophy and Myth in Karl Marx*. Cambridge, NY: Cambridge University Press, 1961.
Upadhya, C. 'Employment, Exclusion and "Merit" in the Indian IT Industry'. *Economic and Political Weekly* 42, no. 20 (2007): 1863–1868.
van der Veer, Peter. *Imperial Encounters: Religion and Modernity in India and Britain*. New Jersey: Princeton University Press, 2001; New Delhi: Permanent Black, 2001.
Ward, Rev W. *A View of the History, Literature, and Religion of the Hindoos: Including a Minute Description of Their Manners and Customs, and Translations from Their Principal Works*, Vol. I, 3rd ed. London: Black, Parbury, and Allen, 1817.

Wheeler, Mortimer. *Early India and Pakistan*. London: Thames and Hudson, 1959.
Williamson, J. G. 'Democracy and the Washington Consensus'. *The World Development*, 21 August 1999.
Witsoe, J. *Democracy against Development: Lower-caste Politics and Political Modernity in Postcolonial India*. Chicago, IL: University of Chicago Press, 2013.
Wittfogel, K. A. *Oriental Despotism: A Comparative Study of Total Power*. New Haven, CT: Yale University, 1957.
Wood, Allen W. *Karl Marx*. New York: Rutledge, 2004.
Yujiro, Hayami, and Yoshika Godo. *Development Economics*. New Delhi: Oxford University Press, 2005.

# About the Author

**K. S. Chalam** is a well-known political economist and educationist, and a former member of the Union Public Service Commission, New Delhi. He has been the Vice Chancellor of the Dravidian University, Kuppam, Andhra Pradesh. From 1976 to 2005, he taught in the Department of Economics, Andhra University, Visakhapatnam, Andhra Pradesh. He is known as the founder of the Academic Staff College Scheme in the country and was its first director. He was on the Planning Board of the Madhya Pradesh government from 2002 to 2004. He was the recipient of the UGC Young Social Scientist Award in Economics in 1984.

Dr Chalam has authored *Caste-based Reservations and Human Development in India* (2007, SAGE Publications) *Economic Reforms and Social Exclusion: Impact of Liberalization on Marginalized Groups in India* (2011, SAGE Publications), *Social Economy of Development in India* (2017, SAGE Publications) and around 20 other publications in English. He has also edited *Governance in South Asia: State of the Civil Services* (2014, SAGE Publications). He has travelled widely and has participated in and chaired sessions at various national and international conferences. He was associated with the National Human Rights Commission, New Delhi, as a Special Rapporteur.

# Index

Adivasis
 future, 229–33
agenda, 247
Ambedkar movement, 223
Andhra Pradesh, 178
 caste discrimination
  most affected districts, 188–92
 crimes against Dalits, 178–81
 offences
  atrocities committed against Scheduled Castes, 181–86
Anglo-Saxon legal system, 139
apex court
 elusive social justice, 149–54
 flaw in legal process, 151
Aryans, 34
 Aryanization, explained by D. R. Bhandarkar, 45
Asiatic mode of production (AMP), 3
 caste, 4
 concept of Feudalism, 2
 edited by Anne Bailey, 11
 issues raised by K. S. Chalam, 5
 Marxian concept, 3
 queer concept, 2
 spirit, 5

bank Brahminization, 53
bank nationalization, 227
Bank Nationalization Act 1969, 144
belief system
 analysis, 36
 lower castes, 35
 native Indians (NI), 35
Bengal Bonded Warehouse Association Act 1838, 23
Bhopal Conference, 220
Brahmin
 Brahminization, explained by D. R. Bhandarkar, 45
*Dvija*, 109

hegemony of pundits, 37
Hinduism, 37

Cambridge project
  Caste and Indian Economy, 113
capital, 16
*Capital in the Twenty-first Century*, 60
capital
  patrimonial, 133
  social, 62
capitalism, 124
  development and resilience in the 21st century, 125
  economists regarded, 124
  notion entered India, 124
capitalist ideology, 79
case
  Criminal Appeal No. 416 of 2018 delivered on 20 March 2018, 155
  marine fisher folk, 104
caste, 4, 49
caste mode of production (CMOP), 4
  assumes, 21
  caste and class, 21–25
  characteristics, 16–20
  features, 9–16
    unchangeable, 10
  *Jajmani* system, 15
  nature, 5
  operation, 124
caste
  Ambedkar's narration, 12
  Anand Teltumbde raised the dichotomous, 25
  argument on race, 28

discrimination, composite index, 186–88
*Dvija*, 109
economic asset, 52
economic power in India, 55–57
India, 79
Indian Economy,
  Cambridge project, 113
Indian subcontinent, 108
Marxian political economy and, 20–21
MOP, 80
non-*Dvija*, 109
oppressive force, 55
politicization, 24
question, 5
race, 25–29
socio-economic and cultural ethos, 206
source of deprivation, 80–81
source of economic power, 56–57
source of exploitation, 80
system, MCCs, 229
treatment as property, 108–10
ubiquitous, 19
colonial inquiry, 43
colonial mode of production
  concept, 7
colonialism, 210
communication
  channels, 163, 168
  decision-making process, 163
  Indo-European language speakers, 38
  Sanskrit language, 41

composite index
  caste discrimination,
    186–88
Congress Socialist Party (CSP),
  2
corruption and rent seeking,
  123
crony capitalism, 125
  advantage, 128
  analysed by experts under
    neoclassical framework,
    128
  caste
    based, 127–29
  essential conditions to sustain, 126
  India and capitalist class,
    136
  inequality widened through
    trade, 129–31
  Lenin's explanation of
    imperialism, 126
cultural nationalism, 42
culture of poverty, 244–45

Dalit movement
  agenda and programme of
    action, 247
  long-term agenda and programme of action
    economic independence,
      252–53
    political power, 251–52
  short-term agenda and programme of action, 247
    concentrate on Dalit formation, 247–48
    economic support programmes, 249–50

educational development,
  248–49
health and family welfare, 250
Dalits, 15
  concentrated mostly in agriculture sector, 228
  deficiencies in emergence of
    formation with *bahujans*, 205–8
  entry in civil service and
    modern occupations,
    24
  future, 229–33
  not homogeneous community, 222
  process of production, 13
  productive forces, 14
  strong and weak aspects of
    movement, 242–44
  weaknesses of movement,
    223
democracy
  explained by Ambedkar, 237
  transitional phase, 237
deprivation, 81
  economic, 81–82
  economic exploitation, 84
  fisher folk, 98–100
  indicators for fisher folk,
    83–84
  isolated villages, 101–4
  multiple indices, 105
  Peter Townsend's approach,
    82
  social exclusion, 100–1
dharmashastras and caste
  codes, 139
discrimination
  ICERD's definition, 26

division of society
  based on one's Karma and
    guna, 194
Dravidian movement, 225
  erosion, 225
  Mandal Commission, 226
Durban Conference, 220
Dvija castes, 109, 173
  benefitted by state policies,
    72
  Brahmin, 52
  economic power of domi-
    nant, 109
  emergence of oligarchy, 251
  operators in stock market,
    119
  opportunities, 56
  social capital, 62
Dvija project, 79, 110–14
  development of elite class,
    227
  manifestation in stock
    market, 118–21
  New Economic Policy,
    114–21

economic deprivation, 81–82
  defined, 81
economic exploitation
  deprivation, 84
economic power, 51
  caste as source, 56–57
  defined by J. Pen, 51
education, 59
  component of concept of
    human capital, 59
  concepts of merit and effi-
    ciency, 71
  decline of educational dif-
    ferences, 71

democratization and deri-
  sion of knowledge,
  73–74
development in India
  association with structure
    of society, 70
  disparities and divides,
    70–73
  national policy, 67–69
  training, 72
  Westernization of higher
    level, 69–70
educational backwardness
  reasons, 163
  communication channels,
    166–68
  decision-makers in
    family, 169–70
  incentives known to
    Dalits, 163–66
  role perception of
    respondents about
    VEC, 168–69
educational policy
  East India Company, 66
  history, 65–67

feminism
  link with Marxism, 29
  subsumed under MOP, 29
fisher folk
  average monthly per capita
    income, 84–85
  average savings and income,
    87–88
  economic status and social
    resilience, 104
  healthcare, 84
  highly indebted, 88–91
  income dependency, 83

Index   269

income from non-fishing
  activities, 85–87
indicators of deprivation,
  83–84
main source of living, 83
marine, multiple deprivations of, 98–100
marketing of fish by fisherwomen, 91–92
poverty among marine,
  92–94

globalization, 209
  attention to developed
    metropolis, 217
  competitive edge of developing countries, 216
  future of Dalits and
    Adivasis, 229–32
  network age promoted, 219
  political and social fallout,
    215
  situation in Brazil, 218
Gramscian category of
  intellectuals, 221

Hinduism
  Brahmins, 37
  colonial rulers, 40
  K. B. Krishna's dissertations
    on materialism, 46
  Sanskritized, 39
  Vedic, 40
Hindutva
  colonial approach and
    Marxist writing,
    41–46
  Savarkar, 42
human capital, 62
  categories, 62

development and inequities
  in India, 59–74
  formation, 62–64
  measures, 63–64
  stock in India, 64–78
human development
  alternative measure of GDP,
    62
  definition, 62
  evolution, 62
human rights
  concept, 238–39
  Dalits rights, 245–47
Hunter Commission, 66

imperialism
  conquest of the Americas in
    framework of mercantilist system of Atlantic
    Europe, 210
  devastation of world, 211
  industrial revolution, 210
  monopolies, 214
  tools, 213
incentives
  known to Dalits, 163–66
  respondents' knowledge,
    164
Indian Constitution
  124th amendment, 154
  amendments, 142
  fourth part, 49
  principle, 155
  social justice, 146–49
  under Article 17, 175
Indian economy
  role of agriculture sector,
    236
Indian history
  category of caste, 9

Indian Marxists, 33
Indian Penal Code (IPC) categories of crime against Scheduled Castes, 176
Indian Slavery Act 1843, 23
Indianization
　explained by D. R. Bhandarkar, 45
Indira Sawhney case, 151
Indo-European
　language speakers, 38
　project, 37
Indus and Harappan civilizations, 39
industrial policy, 124
insider trading, 113
intra-caste differentiation, 204

*Jajmani* system, 15, 108
judiciary
　deprivation of social justice, 139–61
　formulated by Marxist scholars, 139
　modern, 139
justice
　principles, 148
　social, principles enunciated by Rawls, 148

Kautilya
　Arthashastra, 110
Kothari Commission (1964–1966), 67

laissez-faire system, 125
Land Acquisition Act 1894, 144
liberal licensing policy, 114
liberty

　economic reforms, Government of India in 1991, 114

Manu ideology, 79
Maratha pride, 38
Marxian political economy and caste, 20–21
Marxism
　influence on Indian scholars, 46
　link with feminism, 29
　means of production, 7
　mode of production (MOP), 6
　　colonial, 6
　　concept, 7
　　concept by Karl Marx, 1
　　feminism subsumed under, 29
　　productive forces, 14
　　types, 7
　modern judiciary, 139
multi-caste corporations (MCCs), 229

National Commission for SCs and STs in its fifth report, 179
native Indians (NI), 34
　belief systems, 35
neoclassical economic model of equilibrium, 17
New Economic Policy, 111, 114–16
　*Dvija* project, 118–21
　economic reforms of the Government of India in 1991, 114
liberty, 114
　prescriptions, 115

*Index* 271

non-Brahmin
  castes emergence of oligarchy, 251
  movement, 22
non-*Dvija* castes, 109
  fundamentalist ideas, 42
notion of Hindutva or Hinduism, 35

patrimonial capital, 133
Payment of Wages Act 1936, 23
per capita income, 84
  average monthly, 84–85
political economy, 194
poverty
  India, studies, 94–98
  lines, 92
  marine fisher folk, 92–94
power, 50, 52
  categories of non-economic version, 50
  categories on the basis of big business houses, 52
  defined by R. K. Hazari as concentration of economic resources by R. K. Hazari, 52
  economic, 53–54
  Galbraith's theory, 50
pre-capitalist socio-economic formations, 11
private property concept, 142–46
  contradictions, 143
  limitations of constitutional provisions, 143
  role of Ambedkar, 143

Protection of Civil Rights (PCR), 175
  defined atrocity, 176
pseudo religious secularists, 54

race
  argument on caste, 28
  caste as an oppressive force, 55
  invention, 26
racial discrimination, 25
  argument, 26
  related intolerances, 26
  superiority, 25
  tenets of Hindu caste system, 27
reservations
  public sector employment, 221
Right to Fair Compensation and Transparency in Land Acquisition and Rehabilitation Act 2013, 145

Sanatana, 36
Sanskrit language, 41
  code language, 41
  higher education, 69
  Indo-European project, 37
  Indo-European term by Thomas Young, 38
  origin of Hindi, 37
  symbol of hegemony, 38
Scheduled Castes, 152, 173
  crimes categories, 176
  dominant castes among, 199–3

implementation of reservations, 224
increase in population, 196–99
Indira Sawhney case, 151
offences
  atrocities committed against in Andhra Pradesh, 181
  committed against in India, 179
  versus atrocities, 175–78
post-metric scholarship for the SCs during 1993–1994, 205
term coined, 195
Scheduled Tribes, 141, 152
  implementation of reservations, 224
  Indira Sawhney case, 151
  PCR Act, 175
  Traditional Forest Dwellers (Recognition of Forest Rights) Act 2006, 145
schooling, 59
Secondary Education Commission (1952–1953), 67
social barriers
  impediments of information flow, 162–70
social capital, 62
social exclusion
  accumulation, 235, 237
  deprivations, 100–1
  forms, 101

social justice
  elusive in apex court, 149–54
  Indian Constitution, 146–49
  principles enunciated by Rawls, 148
stabilization policy, 114
*stare decisis*, 159
status anxiety, 203

Technology Achievement Index (TAI), 217
The Idea of Justice
  components of theory of justice, 147
The Structure of Scientific Revolutions, 1
theory of Coase, 145
Theory of Justice by John Rawls, 148
transnational corporation
  emergence, 212

unchangeableness
  CMOP, 10
  importance, 10
  socio-economic character of labour, 10
University Education Commission (1948–1949), 67
untouchableness
  occupational mobility, 11
  occupations categories, 15
Upanishads, 41

*varnas*, 107

Village Education Committee
(VEC), 168
 role perception of respondents, 168
Village Gods of South India
 belief systems of lower castes, 35
Viswa Brahmin, 15

Watandari Abolition Act, 23
Wealth of Nations, 59
Weberian class, 5
Westernization of higher education in India
 role of M. N. Srinivas, 69
 number of courses included, 69
 Sanskritization, 69